TESLA
GUIDE
MISSING USER MANUAL

Introduction

There's no experience quite like driving a Tesla. When compared to a traditional internal combustion engine, the instant acceleration comes as a shock, while regenerative braking feels unnatural. But then something clicks at the back of your brain. The acceleration feels natural -- like you're connected directly with the car -- and the ability to start and stop with a single pedal makes total sense. You'll begin to enjoy driving, even in stop-start traffic. All of a sudden, you wonder why cars haven't driven this way for the last 100 years.

Since the first customer deliveries of the Model S in 2013, Tesla has transformed how we drive our cars. It has rolled out a worldwide charging network, introduced over-the-air software updates, and proved that electric vehicles can be faster, more fun, and more advanced than any traditional car.

This book is a guide to everything Tesla forgot to include in the manual. You'll find an overview of the Tesla line-up, detailed information on Autopilot, the Supercharging network, in-car entertainment, the touchscreen and much more.

Just before I go, if there's anything you would like to know that isn't covered in this book, send me an email at tom@tapguides.co.uk, and I'll be happy to help :)

Tom Rudderham, Author

Printed on 100% recycled paper
The interior of this book is free from glossy coating, and is printed using 100% recycled paper.

Copyright © 2019 by Tap Guides Ltd
All rights reserved. No part of this publication may be reproduced, stored or transmitted in any form or by any means, electronic, mechanical, photocopying, recording, scanning, or otherwise without written permission from the publisher. It is illegal to copy this book, post it to a website, or distribute it by any other means without permission.

Get yourself 1,000 free Supercharging miles

Thinking of buying a Tesla? Use the following web URL to place your order, and you'll receive 1,000 free miles of Supercharging after delivery:

https://ts.la/thomas85324

About the author

Tom joined the EV revolution early. His first electric car was a BMW i3, followed by a Tesla Model S, X, & 3.

Tom kicked off his writing career at Future Publishing, working for magazines including MacFormat, Computer Arts, Imagine FX, and the Official Windows Magazine.

Since 2012, he has written a large range of best-selling technology books and manuals, covering every major Apple product since the launch of the iPhone 5, alongside a number of best-selling games.

Published by:

Tap Guides Ltd. Exeter
www.tapguides.co.uk

ISBN:
9781698485966

Contents

A Brief Introduction

EV Terminology	6
What's it Like to Drive an Electric Vehicle	8
What's it Like to Live With a Tesla	10

Autopilot

An Overview of Autopilot	50
Autopilot Features	52
Autopilot 1, 2, 2.5 and 3	56
Driving with Autopilot	58
Do's and Don'ts of Using Autopilot	60
Autopilot Hardware 3 Upgrade	62

The Tesla Family

Model S	16
Model X	18
Model 3	20
Model Y	22
Roadster (coming 2020)	24
Cybertruck (coming 2022)	26
Model S vs X vs 3 vs Y	28
The Realistic Range of Each Vehicle	36
How the Model S has Evolved	38
How the Model Y compares with the 3	42
The Model 3/Y Battery	44
Model 3/Y HVAC system	46

Charging Your Car

A Guide To The Supercharger Network	66
Charging Speeds	70
Charging at Public Networks	72

The Touchscreen Explained

An Overview of Navigation	76
An Overview of the Driver's Display	77
Quick Controls	78
Suspension (Model S & X)	79
Lights	80
Locks (Model 3 & Y)	81
Display	82
Driving	84
Autopilot	85
Navigation	86
Safety & Security	87
Service	88
Software	89

Caring For Your Vehicle

Paint Protection	116
Cleaning Your Tesla	118
CCS Combo 2 Upgrade	120
What To Do If There's A Problem	122

In-Car Tech

Voice Commands	92
The Toybox	94
Video Entertainment	96
Games	98
Dashcam	100
Sentry Mode & PIN to Drive	102
Go Camping in your Tesla	104

Energy & Efficiency

Consumption and Energy Graphs	108
Tips For Maximizing Range	110
What To Expect In Winter	112

The Tesla Community

Bjørn Nyland	126
Olly Ryan	127
YouTube channels to follow...	128
Social Media Groups and Websites	129

A Brief Introduction

EV Terminology

Wondering what all those words and phrases mean?

Every Tesla vehicle is a state of the art piece of equipment, so perhaps it's inevitable that talking about them involves using a wide-ranging assortment of words, phrases, and terminology. In this book, you're going to hear a lot about the Tesla hardware, software, and features. Don't worry, each one of them will be explained as we go along, so you'll never feel confused or become lost halfway through a paragraph; but to get you started, here are a few of the words you'll see and hear when learning about electric vehicles...

"kW"

This is a kilowatt, which is equal to one thousand watts. To put that into perspective, the typical iPhone battery stores around 10 watts, which means a Tesla Model S 100D could charge an iPhone 10,000 times.

"kWh"

This is short for kilowatts per hour. It refers to the total number of kilowatts transferred in or out of the battery during an hour.

"Regenerative breaking"

When you take your foot off the accelerator pedal, the car uses its motor to capture the momentum of the vehicle and slow it down. Which means whenever a Tesla decelerates or goes down a hill, it's re-capturing energy and putting it back into the battery.

"MCU"

Short for the Media Control Unit, this is the main display in your Tesla. Vehicles manufactured between 2013 and 2018 come with the original MCU, often referred to as MCU1. Later cars and both the Model 3 and Y come with the MCU2, which supports video playback and faster processing for things like software updates and navigation routing.

Chapter 1

"Type 2"

A blue type 2 cable comes equipped with every Tesla vehicle, and allows to the car to be charged at the majority of public networks and at home. All Teslas within the US come with a Type 2 port for charging.

"BEV"

A term used to describe a battery electric vehicle, such as a Tesla.

"PHEV"

A plug-in hybrid electric vehicle. These combine a traditional engine with a small battery that can power the vehicle for a (relatively) short distance.

"ICE'd" or "ICEing"

A term used when an internal combustion engine vehicle is blocking a charging station.

"Frunk"

Also known as a front-trunk, every Tesla vehicle has a frunk under the hood which can be used to store everyday items or charging equipment.

"CCS"

This is the name of the charge port/cable found at most rapid chargers. It can transfer/accept up to 350 Kw of energy. You'll find a CSS port on all Model 3's sold in the EU. It's possible to buy a CCS adaptor for the Model S & X.

"CHAdeMO"

A Japanese-developed standard for fast charging BEV's, you might see CHAdeMO charging cables at third-party charging networks. A CHAdeMO adapter is available for Tesla vehicles via the Tesla Store.

"ICE vehicle"

This refers to a traditional internal combustion engine vehicle.

"60 / 70 / 75 / 85 / 100 / P"

Look on the back of a Model S or X, and you might see the above numbers. They represent the size of the battery pack in kWh. If you see a "P" before the number, then this represents the Performance model.

A Brief Introduction

What's it Like to Drive an Electric Vehicle

If you've never driven an electric vehicle, here's how it compares to a traditional gasoline car...

Before Tesla was king of the electric car world, there was a general consensus that electric vehicles were slow and cumbersome. "Milk float" was a term often used to describe early electric cars, referring to the electric vans that delivered milk to school children in the 1970s and 80s. They were slow, ugly, and produced an irritable electric whine. In order for Tesla to be a success, it had to prove to everyone that electric vehicles could be faster, simpler, and more attractive than traditional cars, and that's exactly what the company did when it unveiled the Roadster, then later the Model S.

The first impression anyone has when stepping on the pedal of an electric car is that it's fast. That's all thanks to the instant torque of an electric motor, which provides 100% of its power from a standstill.

That's the first thing you'll need to get used to when swapping from a traditional vehicle to a Tesla. That all the power you could possibly need is available at any time, and that you're able to outrun nearly any other car on the road -- especially at traffic lights.

The next thing you'll need to get used to is regenerative braking. In short, whenever you lift your foot off the pedal, the car will immediately start to slow down, until eventually it comes to a stop and applies the brake. This enables the vehicle to use the momentum of the car to generate electricity and put it back into the car's battery. You'll soon learn how to predict traffic up ahead, then use regenerative breaking to gather as much energy as possible. You'll also see downhill slopes as your friend, because the steeper a hill, the more energy you'll recover.

Chapter 1

With all this acceleration available, and the ability to drive with just a single pedal, you'll soon begin to learn that electric vehicles are easier to drive than any other type of vehicle on the road. There are no gears to worry about, and your foot doesn't need to swap pedals, which means you have more time to focus on the road ahead and your speed. With the safety features of Autopilot included with every Tesla, your car will also break for you in emergencies, and even steer around potential collisions with other vehicles or pedestrians.

The range of an electric vehicle is often a common worry with most drivers. Tesla has worked around this problem by optimizing every component of its cars, and by including massive batteries that can provide hundreds of miles of range. It's also possible to quickly charge a Tesla at any Supercharger station, of which there are tens of thousands around the world. Set a destination in your Tesla, and it will automatically calculate a route which includes stops at Superchargers along the way. It will even suggest how long you need to charge the car before continuing.

With time you'll learn how to drive more efficiently to maximize the amount of range available. This book includes a few helpful tips in this regard, such as using neutral mode to coast along the road, driving behind large vehicles, minimizing acceleration, and lowering the AC power. Check out pages 102 for more on that.

In short, driving an electric car is so much easier than a regular gasoline vehicle. It's also faster and more fun. Once you go electric, there's no looking back.

9

A Brief Introduction

What's it Like to Live With a Tesla

It's nothing like living with a traditional car...

I've been fortunate enough to drive all three Tesla vehicles to date. The Model S was my first Tesla, with a 75 kW battery, white interior, opening sunroof, carbon fibre decor and Full Self Driving. Later I swapped it for a Long Range Model 3, and while it spent a few weeks in the Service Center I was loaned a 100D Model X. Needless to say, I've spent a long time driving Tesla vehicles. I've also lived both with and without a home charger, so I've experienced regular trips to public charging points and Superchargers.

If you've ever had doubts or concerns about living with a Tesla, then I'm here to put them to rest. Tesla vehicles are faster than their gasoline competitors, more comfortable to drive, have more storage, and if you have a charging point at home, then they're more convenient too. Let's go over some of the key points of what it's like to live with a Tesla...

Range

Visit the configuration page for your Tesla, and you'll see some promising range figures. In real life, you can expect to see lower numbers unless you drive with a very steady foot on a warm, windless day. That's because the range of any vehicle (not just electric cars) is affected by driving speed, acceleration, rain, and low temperatures.

Managing battery health

Batteries lose their total energy capacity over time, but not as much as you'd think. After one year of ownership, a typical Tesla has lost between 2 and 5% of its original charge capacity. To maintain the health of your car's battery, it's not a good idea to repeatedly charge it to 100%, so you'll soon learn to keep it anywhere between 30 and 80%. That being said, all Tesla's come with an eight-year, 100,000-mile warranty, so you really shouldn't worry.

Acceleration

Tesla vehicles are blazing fast. It's easy to become a bully on the road, beating everyone at the lights and overtaking those who aren't in a rush. You'll soon learn that a) it's a waste of energy, and b) there's no need to rush - that will mean less time spent enjoying the car.

Charging at home

The ideal scenario. With a home charger, you can return from a trip or a day at the office, plug the car in overnight, then return to it in the morning to find a full charge. You'll never worry about range, and never need to visit a public charging point unless you're traveling a long distance.

Living without a charger at home

This is where I am right now, but it's never been a problem. With time I've figured out where all the local charging points are. Most of my charging is done at the gym where there are free 7 kW charging points, and when I need a quick top-up, I can visit the local Supercharger. Local shopping malls also provide free charging points. In short, if you don't have a charging point at home, then you'll quickly learn where the most convenient charging spots are.

How long it takes to charge

A common worry, and a reasonable one too. Using a plug outlet at home, it would take a day or more to fully charge a Model 3 or Y. At a 7 kW charger, that would take around 10 hours. At a Tesla Supercharger, around 30-45 minutes. Planning your schedule and life around charging your car is a real thing. I spend a lot more time at the gym because I know the car is charging outside, and when I travel long distance, I make sure there's a Supercharger along the way.

Autopilot

Every Tesla comes with Autopilot included, and it's a life-changer. Long journeys are easier because the car is actively steering and changing lanes, and it's genuinely fun to watch vehicles, lane lines and objects appear on the Autopilot display. It also amazes anyone who gets into the car and experiences it for the first time.

Public perception

As you begin to drive your Tesla around public spaces, you'll quickly notice the looks it gets from fellow drivers and pedestrians. Some will be admiring, other's inquisitive, a very few disapproving. Kids, however, love Teslas vehicles. Especially younger children, who often point and cheer at the car while their parents wonder what all the fuss is about.

Repairs and maintenance

Here's where things can be hit or miss. Right now, Tesla is a growing company, and with it comes a few teething pains; primarily with repairs and maintenance. In the ideal scenario, you'll be able to report an issue using the Tesla app, book a mobile Service Technician, then get your vehicle repaired a few days later. Realistically, appointments might be weeks or months away, and the nearest Service Center might be hundreds of miles away. You might also become frustrated when text messages are ignored, and appointments are cancelled.

Continued across the page...

Comfort

You can't beat an electric car when it comes to ride quality, noise and vibration. It doesn't matter how quiet your old petrol car was, because in a Tesla, there's no engine to make noise and vibration, and no gears to cause jerkiness as the car accelerates. Opt for a Model S or X with air suspension, and you'll find the ride unbelievably smooth as the car gently glides over subtle bumps in the road. Overall, the experience of driving a Tesla (with a steady foot) is calm and collected, which means you'll usually arrive at your destination feeling more relaxed than in a traditional car.

Audio quality is better

Because there's no engine in a Tesla, the only noise you're going to hear when driving is wind noise and the sound of the tires rolling along the road. At low speeds on a freshly tarmacked road, music playback quality is amazing in any Tesla. You'll hear every note, beat and backing instrument.

One pedal driving is much easier

Whenever you take your foot off the accelerator, an electric car will automatically slow down so it can recoup excess energy from the vehicle's momentum. It takes a few hours of driving to get used to this, but once you do your foot will really appreciate not having to swap pedals all the time. Eventually, you'll wonder why cars haven't always driven this way.

Chapter 1

There's no creep
Because Tesla vehicles don't have a motor ticking away under the hood, the car never rolls when you put it into Drive mode. Instead, it stays perfectly stationary until you press the accelerator pedal. This totally makes sense, but if you've been driving a regular car for a number of years, it might take you by surprise the first few times you turn on the vehicle.

You'll spend a lot of time looking at your phone
Not while driving of course, but when you're outside of the car. Using the Tesla app it's possible to monitor the car's charge level, toggle the air conditioning, honk the horn, activate Sentry mode, and even open the trunk/frunk. The Tesla app will quickly become one of the most used apps on your phone, so put it on the homepage where it's easy to access.

The unexpected things about owning a Tesla
You'll be approached by strangers who want to ask about the car. You'll spend silly amounts of time researching charge points in the area. You'll become obsessed over efficiency on long drives. You'll be able to go camping in the car and use the touchscreen to watch Netflix movies before falling asleep. Overall, your life is going to change a lot, and for the better.

The Tesla Family

With the world's fastest saloon, the best family-sized SUV, and the safest mid-size vehicle in its lineup, Tesla is already covering most the bases. They're selling like hotcakes too. At the time of writing (January 2020), Tesla has sold more than 900,000 cars and is fast reaching its one-millionth sale.

Over the next few years, the company promises to release even more best-in-its-class vehicles; with the all-new Roadster, the larger than life Model Y, and the incredibly powerful Cybertruck.

All of these vehicles appeal to different aspects of the electric automobile market. This chapter will take an overall look at each, compare the S, X, 3, and Y, then take a deep dive into the changes made to the Model S since its release in 2013.

Model S	**16**
Model X	**18**
Model 3	**20**
Model Y	**22**
Roadster (coming 2020)	**24**
Cybertruck (coming 2022)	**26**
Model S vs X vs 3 vs Y	**28**
The Realistic Range of Each Vehicle	**36**
How the Model S has Evolved	**38**
How the Model Y compares with the 3	**42**
The Model 3/Y Battery	**44**
Model 3/Y HVAC system	**46**

The Tesla Family

Model S

The ultimate sedan, with gut-punching speed...

It cannot be understated how important the Model S was to the transformation, development and acceptance of electric vehicles. Before the first prototype Model S was introduced to the world on April 2009, EV's were widely considered to be slow, impractical and have a short-range. The Model S proved everyone to be wrong. When deliveries to customers started in June 2012, the top-spec Signature Performance model included an 85-kWh battery, a range of 300 miles, and could propel itself from 0 to 60 mph in just 3.9 seconds. Perhaps more important than its specifications was the introduction of free, over-the-air software updates, which continuously updated the car with new features, improved range and better performance. No manufacturer before (or since) has continued to tweak and improve its vehicles with such regularity.

The Model S was also a staggeringly beautiful car. With its low stance and wide body, it has a road presence like no other. Since its introduction, the appearance of the vehicle has only changed in subtle ways, with the nose cone being the only significant revision. The same can be said for the interior, with tweaks to the chairs, materials and a reorganization of the center console being the biggest changes. Flick over to page 40 to learn more about the evolution of the Model S.

More than eight years after its introduction, the Model S is still winning awards, it's still the fastest production car, and it still has the longest range of any EV.

Model S Specifications

Width
77.3 in (1,964 mm)

Length
195.9 in (4,980 mm)

Height
56.5 in

Seating
5 Adults

Storage
28 cubic feet

Supercharging
Free Unlimited Supercharging

Long Range

Battery
100 kWh

Acceleration
3.7 seconds 0-60 mph

Range
390 miles (WLTP)

Drive
All-Wheel Drive

Wheels
19" or 21"

Weight
2,214 kg

Displays
Driver Display + 17" Touchscreen

Air filters
HEPA air filtration system

Doors
Auto-presenting door handles

Tailgate
Automatic powered tailgate

Warranty
8 years, or 150,000 miles, whichever comes first. 70% battery retention included during warranty period.

Performance

Battery
100 kWh

Acceleration
2.4 seconds 0-60 mph

Range
348 miles (WLTP)

Drive
All-Wheel Drive

Wheels
20" or 22"

Weight
2,241 kg

Displays
Driver Display + 17" Touchscreen

Air filters
HEPA air filtration system

Doors
Auto-presenting door handles

Tailgate
Automatic powered tailgate

Warranty
8 years, or 150,000 miles, whichever comes first. 70% battery retention included during warranty period.

The Tesla Family

Model X

The best SUV in its class…

If there was ever a show-stopping car, then this is it. Heads are turned every time the Falcon Wing doors are opened in public, and it has a road presence like no other SUV. Of the entire Tesla family, the Model X has the most cargo space, the most seating, the biggest windscreen, a 5-star safety rating, the most advanced doors, and the best party trick: "Holiday Show", which performs a light show while flapping the doors to the tune of Wizards in Winter.

If you have a large family, need lots of storage, and regularly make long trips, then the Model X really is the only choice of Tesla. It doesn't come cheap, however. The base Long Range model starts at $84,990, while the Performance model comes to $104,990. That hefty price gets you the best SUV in the world, however; plus the promise of full autonomy, insane acceleration, and more gadgets than you could ever wish for.

Model X Specifications

Width
78.7 in (1,999 mm)

Length
198.3 in (5,036 mm)

Height
66.3 in (1,684 mm)

Seating
Up to 7 Adults

Storage
88 cubic feet

Supercharging
Free Unlimited Supercharging

Long Range

Battery
100 kWh

Acceleration
4.4s 0-60 mph

Range
351 miles (WLTP)

Drive
All-Wheel Drive

Wheels
20" or 22"

Weight
2,533 kg

Displays
Driver Display + 17" Touchscreen

Air filters
HEPA air filtration system

Doors
Self-presenting front door
Falcon Wing rear doors

Tailgate
Automatic powered tailgate

Warranty
8 years, or 150,000 miles, whichever comes first. 70% battery retention included during warranty period.

Performance

Battery
100 kWh

Acceleration
2.7s 0-60 mph

Range
305 miles (WLTP)

Drive
All-Wheel Drive

Wheels
20" or 22"

Weight
2,572 kg

Displays
Driver Display + 17" Touchscreen

Air filters
HEPA air filtration system

Doors
Self-presenting front door
Falcon Wing rear doors

Tailgate
Automatic powered tailgate

Warranty
8 years, or 150,000 miles, whichever comes first. 70% battery retention included during warranty period.

The Tesla Family

Model 3

The best car in the world...

There has never been a more hyped car than the Model 3. Before it was officially unveiled, Tesla had already received more than 150,000 preorders. Just days later, after the car had been revealed, that number increased dramatically to 325,000 preorders.

There's a good reason for this: no EV vehicle before has promised to bring affordable, long-distance autonomous driving to the world. Two years later, when the Model 3 was finally delivered to customers, it met those expectations... and more.

It's difficult to understate how great the Model 3 is. It takes the best technology from Tesla, then improves it even further, with more advanced battery chemistry for faster charging and longevity, a better-built cabin, and improved efficiency. Sure, it's not as luxurious as it's larger S and X siblings, it has less storage, and it doesn't have air suspension, but at half the price it's an incredible car. It also promises to hold its value thanks to regular software updates that have (to date) improved range, acceleration, security, autonomy, and even added a wide number of entertainment options.

Chapter 2

Model 3 Specifications

Width
72.8 in (1,850 mm)

Length
184.8 in (4,690 mm)

Height
56.8 in (1,440 mm)

Seating
5 Adults

Storage
15 cubic feet

Supercharging
Pay Per Use

Standard Plus	Long Range AWD	Performance
Battery 54 kWh	**Battery** 75 kWh	**Battery** 75 kWh
Acceleration 5.3s 0-60 mph	**Acceleration** 4.4s 0-60 mph	**Acceleration** 3.2s 0-60 mph
Range (WLTP) 254 mi	**Range (WLTP)** 348 mi	**Range (WLTP)** 329 mi
Drive Rear-Wheel Drive	**Drive** Dual Motor All-Wheel Drive	**Drive** Dual Motor All-Wheel Drive
Wheels 18" Aero Wheels	**Wheels** 18" Aero Wheels	**Wheels** 20" Performance Wheels
Weight 1,611 kg	**Weight** 1,847 kg	**Weight** 1,847 kg
Displays 15" Centre Touchscreen	**Displays** 15" Centre Touchscreen	**Displays** 15" Centre Touchscreen
Speakers Standard audio	**Speakers** 14 speakers, 1 subwoofer, 2 amps and immersive sound	**Speakers** 14 speakers, 1 subwoofer, 2 amps and immersive sound
Maps B&W maps, no traffic	**Maps** Satellite-view maps & live traffic	**Maps** Satellite-view maps & live traffic
Streaming Audio Not included	**Streaming Audio** Streaming music & media	**Streaming Audio** Streaming music & media
Floor Mats Not included	**Floor Mats** Included	**Floor Mats** Included
Warranty 8 years, or 100,000 miles, whichever comes first. 70% battery retention included during warranty period.	**Warranty** 8 years, or 100,000 miles, whichever comes first. 70% battery retention included during warranty period.	**Warranty** 8 years, or 100,000 miles, whichever comes first. 70% battery retention included during warranty period.

The Tesla Family

Model Y

The best SUV in the world

At its unveiling in March 2019, the Model Y didn't exactly set the world on fire. That's because we'd seen most of the car before, in its smaller sibling: the Model 3.

Looks aside, however, and it's difficult to understate the importance of the Model Y. It takes the best parts of the Model 3, such as incredible efficiency, a modern cabin, and support for 250kW Supercharging, then adds additional storage, a higher driving position, and SUV-styling. It's the ultimate electric vehicle for anyone that needs practicality and speed in an affordable package.

At the time of writing only the Long Range and Performance versions of the Model Y are available to order. The specifications for both are across the page. The Standard Range (coming 2021) promises to match most requirements, but lower costs by featuring a smaller and lighter battery, shorter range (230 miles), and lower quality audio system.

Chapter 2

Model Y Specifications

Width
83.8 in (2,129 mm)

Length
187 in (4,751 mm)

Height
63.9 in (1,624 mm)

Seating
7 Adults

Storage
68 cubic feet

Supercharging
Pay Per Use

Long Range AWD

Battery
77.5 kWh

Acceleration
4.8s 0-60 mph

Range (WLTP)
316 mi

Drive
Dual Motor All-Wheel Drive

Wheels
19" Gemini Wheels

Weight
2,003 kg

Displays
15" Centre Touchscreen

Speakers
14 speakers, 1 subwoofer, 2 amps and immersive sound

Maps
Satellite-view maps & live traffic

Streaming Audio
Streaming music & media

Floor Mats
Included

Warranty
8 years, or 100,000 miles, whichever comes first. 70% battery retention included during warranty period.

Performance

Battery
77.5 kWh

Acceleration
3.5s 0-60 mph

Range (WLTP)
315 mi

Drive
Dual Motor All-Wheel Drive

Wheels
20" Performance Wheels

Weight
2,003 kg

Displays
15" Centre Touchscreen

Speakers
14 speakers, 1 subwoofer, 2 amps and immersive sound

Maps
Satellite-view maps & live traffic

Streaming Audio
Streaming music & media

Floor Mats
Included

Warranty
8 years, or 100,000 miles, whichever comes first. 70% battery retention included during warranty period.

Roadster (coming 2020)

The ultimate driving machine...

If you care less about practicality and more about raw statistics, then the Roadster is the ultimate car. Literately. When it launches in 2020, the Roadster will be the faster production car ever produced, and it'll have the longest range of any supercar - not just electric cars.

At its unveiling event, Elon Musk referred to the Roadster as "the desert". That's a good way to think about it because right now the company is focusing all of its resources on producing as many affordable mass-market EV's as possible. Think Model 3 and Model Y. When the next-generation Roadster does launch in 2020, it's going to be a true smackdown to the world of supercars, because Tesla is aiming to smash as many world records as possible with one vehicle. Think fastest acceleration, fastest quarter-mile record, most cargo capacity, and furthest range. It's also trying to make the world's sexiest car, and to that extent, they've already achieved it.

To date, very few facts about the Roadster have actually been confirmed. We haven't seen the finished steering wheel, central touchscreen interface, or even the production seating; but there are a few things that have been confirmed. The base price of the Roadster is expected to be around $200,000. It will include seating for four passengers, a 0-60 time of 2.1 seconds, and storage both in the trunk and in the frunk. Those with a little more cash will be able to order a "Space X" package, with an expected price starting at $250,000. It will offer seating for only two people, replacing the back seats with a composite-pressure vessel that will hold compressed air. Surrounding the car will be ten small rocket thrusters, which will release the compressed air to maximize acceleration and braking, enabling the Space X Roadster to achieve a 0-60 time of *at least* 1.9 seconds. Powering either spec of the Roadster will be a double-stacked 200 kWh battery pack, with a range of approximately 1,000 kilometers/620 miles. That's twice as much energy as you'll find in a Long Range Model S or X.

Roadster Specifications

Acceleration 0-100 km/h	1.9 sec
Acceleration 1/4 mile	8.8 sec
Top Speed	Over 400 km/h
Wheel Torque	10,000 Nm
Kilometer Range	1000 kilometers
Seating	4
Drive	All-Wheel Drive

Acceleration

The Roadster 's 0-60 time promises to be a world-record 1.9 seconds. Accelerating at that speeds will be the equivalent G-Force of 1.45. That's more than a Buggati Veyron (1.2 Gs) and almost half the G-Force experienced by astronauts curing the Space Shuttle launch (3 Gs).

Range

With an estimated range of 1,000 km (or just over 600 miles), the Roadster promises to have the furthest range of any Tesla vehicle to date. That's all thanks to a massive 200 kWh battery under the floor.

Interior

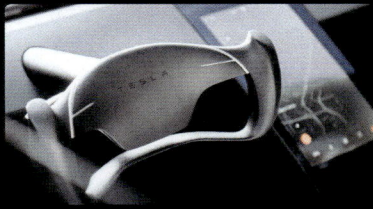

The final design of the interior has yet to be unveiled, but we can expect to see a butterfly steering wheel (pictured above), alongside a single, curved, 17-inch touchscreen.

Cybertruck (coming 2022)

Turning conventions inside out...

No vehicle before or since has caused such a visceral reaction on people viewing it for the first time. You'll either love the Cybertruck or hate it, but give it time to sink in, because once you learn about its features and manufacturing process, then you'll start to understand why the Cybertruck looks the way it does.

The appearance of the Cybertruck is almost an inevitable consequence of its manufacturing process. Its outer shell is made from folded Cold-Rolled stainless-steel. Think of an origami puzzle, and you'll get the idea. This means there's no paint shop required, and no expensive tooling machines are needed for production. It also means the Cybertruck is strong. You can take a sledgehammer to it and not leave a mark.

With such thick stainless steel comes a cost: weight. To keep the vehicle balanced, designer Franz von Holzhausen turned to another inevitable choice that gives the Cybertruck its distinctive appearance: a triangle set on its hypotenuse. On one side is the cabin, with room for six adults. At the other is a tapered sail-sided bed with 100 cubic feet of exterior, lockable storage.

Powering the Cybertruck are two inductive rear motors, with the Model 3's permanent-magnet motor repurposed upfront. Together they have a total towing capability of over 14,000 pounds and a 0-60 time of less than three seconds. Double-stacked battery boxes also give the Cybertruck a potential range of 500 miles. That's further than any Tesla vehicle to date.

	Single Motor RWD	Dual Motor AWD	Tri Motor AWD
Acceleration 0-100 km/h	<6.5 sec	1.9 sec	1.9 sec
Range	250+ Miles	300+ miles	500+ miles
Storage	100 FT3	100 FT3	100 FT3
Vault Length	6.5 FT	6.5 FT	6.5 FT
Towing Capacity	7,500+ LBS	10,000+ LBS	14,000+ LBS
Adaptive Air Suspension	Standard	Standard	Standard
Ground Clearance	UP TO 16"	UP TO 16"	UP TO 16"

Acceleration

Thanks to its tri-motor all-wheel-drive, the Cybertruck promises to accelerate from 0 to 60 miles an hour in less than 2.9 seconds. It can also reach 1/4 of a mile in 10.8 seconds.

Practicality

Tesla ticked all the boxes when designing the Cybertruck. There's up to 3,500 pounds of payload capacity in the 6.5 foot bed, 110/240V outlets, and a slide-down tonneau which can be locked in place. Air suspension can be lowered (or raised) by four inches, and even used as a compressor.

Interior

The interior of the Cybertruck is just as radical as its exterior. There are no curves to find, not even on the back of the seats. Upfront is a massive 17-inch horizontal touchscreen, with a huge windshield above to rival even the Model X.

Model S vs X vs 3 vs Y

It's showdown time. Let's take a look at all three vehicles and compare range, practicality, looks and more...

So you've decided to buy a Tesla, but you're not quite sure which one is right for you. Each model is surprisingly different. There's the Model S, with its classic design, spacious interior and blisteringly fast speed; there's the Model X, with its showpiece Falcon Wing doors and cavernous interior; there's the Model 3, representing the most affordable Tesla to date; then finally there's the Model Y, which takes the best from every Tesla vehicle to date and combines them into an incredibly practical package.

With three cars to choose from, you've probably got a lot of questions. What are the ins and outs, the ups and the downs, the best to drive and the most practical? Let's take a deep-dive and compare all three...

Model S

It makes the most sense to start with the Model S. It's the vehicle that proved to the world that electric cars are the future, that electric cars can be powerful, practical and fun; and that you don't need to compromise on range. Seven years later, and the Model S is still the fastest Tesla available with the most range.

Model S: Looks

It's been around since 2013, but it has a classically beautiful design that still turns heads to this day. Out of all the Tesla's available, the Model S still has the most road presence, thanks in part to its low profile, wide stance and perfect proportions.

Model S: Drive

If you were to compare driving a Model S with a Model 3 then you'd describe it as "luxurious". The adaptive air suspension is silky soft - even over large bumps, and the cabin has a lower, wider feel to it. There's more to play with too, such as the physical air vents and (in older models) opening sunroof. Is it as fun as a Model 3? No. The steering isn't as direct, and the windscreen is shallower, making the cabin feel more cocooned, rather than open.

Model S: Range

Since its launch in 2013, the Model S has been king of range in the electric car market; and it still stands on top of the pack seven years later. The latest Long Range Model S has an EPA rating of 373 miles. In real terms that's around 336 miles, which is comparable to most ICE cars on the roads today.

Model S: Interior

The interior of the Model S has barely changed since its launch in 2013. The most notable tweaks being extra storage in the center console, vegan-leather seats, brushed metal around the touchscreen (rather than silver metal), and revised control stalks. Nevertheless, the 17-inch touchscreen is still the largest screen of any car in the world, while the instrument panel behind the wheel is greatly appreciated.

Model S: Tech

The Model S is packed with technology that you won't find in a Model 3 or Y, including adaptive air suspension, an instrument display behind the steering wheel, a medical-grade HEPA air filter, and a powered lift-gate. However, there are a few areas where it falls behind. For example, if you want to use public CCS charge points, then you'll need to buy a CCS adaptor (see page 112); the batteries are 18650 cylindrical cells, rather than the denser and more efficient 2170 cylindrical cells found in the Model 3 and Y, and the Model S still uses Mercedes parts for the control stalks and windows controls, unlike the Model 3 and Y which include custom-built parts.

Model S: Value for money

The Model S isn't exactly value for money. Its double the price of a Model 3, but it has similar range and older battery technology. If value for money is a concern, then the Model 3 SR+ is a heck of a bargain.

Model S: Practicality

There's a lot to like about the Model S when it comes to practicality. It all starts with the handles, which automatically present themselves when you approach the vehicle. It's followed by the powered liftgate boot door, which you can open and close by double-pressing the back of the key.

Where the Model S falls down (and only slightly) is its size. This is a wide car designed for American roads. If you're driving it in the States then you'll appreciate its size, because the Model S stands up admirably against towering SUVs and muscle cars; but in Europe, the Far East and Australia, the Model S barely fits into parking spaces and takes up the width of most road lanes. Try to drive it along country lanes in the U.K., and you're likely to brush up against hedges and walls.

Model X

The ultimate family cruiser, the Model X owns the road with its powerful presence. It's falcon wings are show stoppers everytime they're opened in public, and the large cabin makes longer road trips a comfortable breeze. Of all the Tesla vehicles to date, the Model X is the choice to go for if you have a large family and regularly undertake long journeys.

Model X: Looks

The Model X can be pretty subjective when it comes to looks. Some absolutely adore it, while others don't like its egg-like shape. Personally, I believe the Model X looks downright awesome in real-life. It has a real presence to it, thanks in part to its height. Stand next to a Model X and you can't help but feel a little intimidated. Similarly, it looks imposing when viewed in the rear mirror. When parked, with its Falcon Wing doors opened, there's nothing else on the market like a Model X. If you're undecided, take a trip to your local Tesla store or Supercharger where you're bound to see an X in person.

Chapter 2

Model X: Drive

It's similar to the Model S, but you sit much higher, which offers a better view of the road. There's a little body roll on sharp corners, but the air suspension is well suited for the size of the vehicle, so long trips are comfortable. The Model X doesn't offer the same punchy acceleration as you get on the Model S, and doesn't feel anywhere near as sprightly as the Model 3 or Y, but still feels commanding on the road.

Model X: Range

The Model X has the lowest range of all the Teslas. Configure the Long Range version and you'll see an EPA rating of 328 miles, so that's around 298 miles in the real world when you factor in real life driving conditions. However, when you consider that the Model X is nearly 800 kg heavier than the Model 3, the range of the X is actually rather impressive.

Model X: Interior

The Model X takes what's best about the Model S interior and ramps it up. Alongside the same 17-inch touchscreen and instrument panel, the Model X gains an even bigger windscreen - one that almost stretches to the B-pillars, giving an incredible view out of the front. It's also more practical than the Model S, with additional seating, space, and even pockets on the back of the front seats.

Model X: Tech

The Model X is the most tech-heavy Tesla available. Not only does it get everything offered on the Model S (such as dual displays, air suspension, and a powered lift-gate), but you also get the incredible Falcon Wing passengers doors. The front doors can also self-present themselves when you walk up the vehicle, and it's possible to automatically close them by pressing the brake pedal.

Model X: Value for money

It might be more than double the money of a Model 3, but there's nothing in its class to match the Model X. This is the only SUV you can buy with Falcon Wing doors and it has the largest windscreen of any production car. Range is also pretty good when compared to other EV SUV's such as the Audi e-tron and Jaguar I-PACE.

Model X: Practicality

It's the clear winner. In total you'll find 88 cubic feet of storage available when the rear seats are down (compared to 68 cubic feet in the Model Y, 28 cubic feet in the Model S, and 15 in the Model 3). The Falcon Wing doors make climbing into the back incredibly easy, even in a tight parking sport, and it's possible to carry up to seven adults when configured with the third row of seats.

If the Model X falls down anywhere in practicality terms it's because of it's sheer width. The X is nearly two meters wide (1,999 mm to be exact), so for anyone who regularly drives down narrow country lanes, or lives in a city that pre-dates the modern car (most of Europe for example), the Model X can be cumbersome to drive. Small car parks can also be a problem.

Model S vs X vs 3 vs Y

Model 3

Since its introduction in April 2016, the Model 3 has turned the automobile industry on its head, outselling its closest traditional rivals in nearly every market where it has been available. It takes the best of it predecessors -- namely long-range, fast performance, and a massive touchscreen -- then adds even more advanced battery technology, more direct steering, faster Supercharging rates and a more polished interior. For those who don't need a luxurious ride or hundreds of liters of storage, it's the best Tesla to date.

Model 3: Looks

The Model 3 has a subjective look. Some people love it, while others are put off by its tall stance and mouthless nose. From an off-set angle, it has a timeless appearance, with strong shoulders and sharp creases along its body; but when viewed directly front-on (as most other drivers will see in their wing mirror), the Model 3 can look a little plump and shapeless. Whatever paint color it comes in, the Model 3 looks attractive, but the red or blue options particularly suit the car.

Model 3: Drive

The Model 3 feels completely different to drive than it's bigger siblings. The steering is more direct, the car is more agile, and the ride is more firm because of the coil suspension. Think of the Model S and X as luxurious cruising vehicles, while the Model 3 as a more sprightly and fun to drive go-kart.

Model 3: Range

Opt for the Standard Range Model 3, and you can expect a realistic range of about 230 miles in the summer and 190 in the winter. Go the for Long Range, and that jumps up to 310 miles in the summer and 260 in the winter. The Performance model (with its larger wheels) will realistically see 280 miles in summer and 230 in winter.

Model 3: Interior

The Model 3's interior is all about the touchscreen display. Everything from the speedometer to the glovebox button is located on the screen. The rest of the cabin is surprisingly sparse but well built and sturdy. You'll also find back-seat storage, coat hooks and door bins -- all of which are missing from the Model S.

Model 3: Tech

Given its lower price-point and physical size, it's no surprise to learn that the Model 3 is less technologically advanced than it's two larger siblings. You won't find air suspension, a powered lift-gate, medical-grade air filter, or a second driver's display.

However, the Model 3 is more advanced in other areas. It can charge faster than any other Tesla (up to 250 kW at a V3 Supercharger), and it's batteries are predicted to last longer. Purchase the vehicle outside of the U.S, and you'll get a CCS charge port, rather than Tesla's own proprietary connector; which means you can charge the car at third-party charging networks without the use of an adaptor. The touchscreen has deeper blacks, more vivid colors and less ghosting. The cabin airflow is managed through a single air vent. It has an interior camera for future use as a robo-taxi (yes, really), and if you're really into your in-car entertainment, the Model 3 has a horizontal display (rather than vertical) for better visual

Model 3: Value for money

The Model 3 is hands-down the best value for money Tesla. Perhaps even the best value vehicle you can buy. It has supercar performance, incredible range, and shares the same self-driving technology as seen in the Model S and X. Factor in its go-kart-like handling, all-glass roof, over-the-air updates and in-car entertainment options, and you'll struggle to find another car that offers the same things for a similar price.

Model 3: Practicality

Yep, you guessed it: the Model 3 is the least practical of all the Tesla vehicles. Unlike the Model S and X, the Model 3 doesn't have a powered lift-gate. It's smaller too, opening to reveal a space just about large enough to crawl into (helpful to know if you're planning to camp in your car). Space in both the front and back is smaller than the S and X, primarily because the vehicle is thinner than its siblings, leaving less room for the center console. Headroom is more than adequate, however, with plenty for both the driver and passengers.

On the plus side, the smaller size of the Model 3 means it's more practical for city driving. It's also much easier to squeeze into small parking spaces or drive down narrow country lanes.

Model Y

The Model Y slots nicely between the Model X and 3. It offers seating for seven adults, a powered liftgate, masses of storage, a modern design, landscape-orientated touchscreen, and affordable price point. In many ways, it takes the best that Tesla offers and wraps it into an SUV-style body that's all the craze right now. It has the potential to be Tesla's best-selling vehicle, ever... but time will tell at the time of writing, as the third row of seats has yet to become available, while the Standard Range model is still not in production.

Model Y: Looks

In-person the Model Y looks like a more aggressive, bulked-up Model 3. That's a good thing, as many consider the Model 3 to look squat and featureless when viewed directly face-on. With its taller roofline and tweaked front-end, the Model Y sits better in a rear-view mirror. It also has more attractive wheels across the board and comes straight out of the factory with "de-chromed" windows and door handles.

Model Y: Drive

It feels like a Model 3, so the steering is direct, and the ride is firm, but you sit much higher, offering a more commanding view of the road ahead.

Model Y: Range

The Standard Range Model Y promises to deliver 230 miles of range when it hits the road in 2021. In the meantime, both the Long Range and Performance models offer 316 miles of range when specced with the 19" Gemini wheels. That falls to 280 miles when the vehicle is specced with the 21" Überturbine Wheels.

Model Y: Interior

Just like the Model 3, the Y's interior is focused completely around the landscape-orientated touchscreen. It's a modern, clean interior all-round, and easy to keep clean thanks to the vegan leather. In the back, you'll find a few extra inches of leg and headroom, plus a more spacious feel thanks to the lack of a support beam across the center of the glass roof.

Model Y: Tech

The Model Y is packed with the latest technology from Tesla. It can charge up to 250 kW at a V3 Supercharger, has a pin-sharp display, an interior camera for future use as a robo-taxi, and a horizontal display (rather than vertical) for better visual experiences. It's basically a Model 3, but with a few additions. The first is a powered liftgate, which can be opened remotely using the Tesla app or by pressing the rear-hatch button. The second is a heat pump for better efficiency in winter. Heat pumps are three times more efficient than resistance heaters, so you can expect to see higher ranges in cold temperatures when compared to a Model 3.

Model Y: Value for money

If space and practicality is your number one requirement, then the Model Y represents the best value Tesla vehicle you can buy. It has nearly as much storage as a Model X (68 cubic feet compared to the Model X's 88 cubic feet) but costs roughly half the price. It also offers a similar driving position and range.

Model Y: Practicality

For its price-point, this is the most practical Tesla vehicle available. It offers a massive amount of storage - 68 cubic feet in total when you factor in the trunk, frunk, and cabin. It has an automatic tailgate, plus two switches in the trunk which automatically drop the back seats. In the cabin, you'll find front and rear door pockets, three separate storage areas in the center console, lit vanity mirrors, and plenty of headroom. Consider all of this is squeezed into a vehicle only a few inches longer and wider than the Model 3, and you'll come to the conclusion that the Model Y is an incredibly practical car.

The Tesla Family

The Realistic Range of Each Vehicle

Discover the true range of each Tesla...

Website URL: Visit **https://teslike.com/range/** to find the original source of the data shown across the page.

Ask the average Tesla owner to think of one thing they'd like to change about their car, and they'll probably say "nothing". Ask them again, however, and then they might admit that more range would be nice. Especially if they believed the estimated range Tesla advertised on its website before buying the car.

Here's a small nugget of information for you: the official range of each Tesla vehicle isn't particularly accurate. Tesla isn't going out of its way to deceive people, but instead relies on test data from the United States Environmental Protection Agency (EPA). The test involved placing the car on a dyno then simulating both city and highway driving. However, the city driving test is performed at an average speed of 21 mph, while the highway test is done at 48 mph, resulting in unrealistically high range figures. In the real world, most Tesla drivers will see lower range estimates unless they're driving steady and slow on a warm day.

Another little nugget: the range difference between each Tesla vehicle can vary massively. On the bottom end, a Model X 60D (manufactured up until 2017) had a realistic range of 194 miles; while at the top end, the Long Range Model S has a realistic range of 336 miles. There are myriad reasons for this, such as:
- Car size and weight
- Vehicle design (a Model X has a lower co drag coefficient than a Model S or 3).
- Battery size
- Wheel size
- Current temperature

Perhaps the best source of information about real-world range is the Teslike website. It's run by Troy Teslike, who continuously maintains a number of helpful spreadsheets about real-world range, battery specs, gross margins and delivery estimates. If you're interested in comparing the range between each Tesla vehicle, then it's a treasure-trove of information. Not only does Troy compare the basic specification of each car, but also how the wheel size and speed can dramatically lower range and efficiency.

Across the page is the latest version of the Teslike range chart (as of January 2020). You can use it to accurately compare the Model S, X, and 3 (accurate data for the Model Y is still being collected), with separate rows for each battery size and wheel configuration. To find the very latest version of the chart with even more information, open your browser and go to **teslike.com**.

Chapter 2

Production end date	Model 3	Advertised EPA range	Real-world range	55 mph	60 mph	65 mph	70 mph	75 mph	80 mph
2019	Model 3 MR 18" Aero wheels	264 mi	261 mi	329	304	279	256	236	215
2019	Model 3 MR 18"	264 mi	251 mi	316	292	268	246	227	207
2019	Model 3 MR 19"	264 mi	246 mi	309	285	262	240	221	203
2019	Model 3 LR 18" Aero wheels	325 mi	331 mi	417	385	354	324	298	273
2019	Model 3 LR 18"	325 mi	318 mi	401	370	340	312	287	262
2019	Model 3 LR 19"	325 mi	311 mi	392	361	332	305	281	257
2019	Model 3 SR 18" Aero wheels	220 mi	215 mi	270	249	229	210	193	177
2019	Model 3 SR 18"	220 mi	206 mi	260	240	220	202	186	170
2019	Model 3 SR 19"	220 mi	202 mi	254	234	215	197	182	166
Current	Model 3 SR+ 18" Aero wheels	338 mi	237 mi	298	275	253	232	213	195
Current	Model 3 SR+ 18"	325 mi	228 mi	287	264	243	223	205	188
Current	Model 3 SR+ 19"	318 mi	222 mi	280	258	238	218	201	183
Current	Model 3 LR AWD 18" Aero wheels	440 mi	308 mi	387	357	329	301	277	254
Current	Model 3 LR AWD 18"	423 mi	296 mi	373	344	316	290	267	244
Current	Model 3 LR AWD 19"	413 mi	289 mi	364	336	309	283	261	238
Current	Model 3 P 18" Aero wheels	440 mi	308 mi	387	357	329	301	277	254
Current	Model 3 P 18"	423 mi	296 mi	373	344	316	290	267	244
Current	Model 3 P 20"	400 mi	280 mi	353	325	299	274	252	231

	Roadster & Model S			55 mph	60 mph	65 mph	70 mph	75 mph	80 mph
2010	Roadster	244	162	202	186	171	157	145	132
2014	Model S 60 19"	208	193	240	221	204	187	172	157
2016	Model S 60 19"	210	204	254	234	215	197	182	166
2017	Model S 60D 19"	218	215	268	247	227	208	192	176
2016	Model S 70 19"	234	206	257	237	218	199	184	168
2016	Model S 70D 19"	240	229	285	263	242	221	204	187
2016	Model S 75 19"	249	240	298	275	253	232	214	195
2019	Model S 75D 19"	259	251	312	288	265	243	224	205
2014	Model S 85/P85 19"	265	244	304	280	258	236	218	199
2014	Model S 85/P85 21"	265	227	283	261	240	220	202	185
2015	Model S 85D 19"	270	265	330	304	280	256	236	216
2015	Model S P85D 21"	253	252	314	289	266	244	225	205
2015	Model S P85D 19"	242	242	302	279	256	235	216	198
2016	Model S 90D 19"	294	284	353	326	300	275	253	231
2016	Model S P90D 19"	270	272	339	312	287	263	242	222
2016	Model S P90D 21"	270	253	315	291	267	245	226	206
2019	Model S 100D 19"	335	319	397	366	337	309	284	260
2019	Model S P100 21"	335	296	369	341	313	287	264	242
2019	Model S P100D 19"	315	303	377	348	320	293	270	247
2019	Model S P100D 21"	315	282	351	324	298	273	251	230
2019	Model S Standard Range 19"	285	257	320	295	272	249	229	210
Current	Model S Long Range 19"	370	336	418	386	355	325	299	274
Current	Model S Long Range 21"	370	312	389	359	330	302	278	255
Current	Model S Performance 19"	345	322	400	369	340	311	287	265
Current	Model S Performance 21"	325	298	371	343	315	289	266	243

	Model X			55 mph	60 mph	65 mph	70 mph	75 mph	80 mph
2017	Model X 60D 20"	200	194	237	219	201	184	170	155
2019	Model X 75D 20"	238	231	283	261	240	220	202	185
2019	Model X 75D 22"	238	196	240	222	204	187	172	157
2017	Model X 90D 20"	257	251	307	283	260	238	220	201
2017	Model X P90D 20"	250	241	295	272	250	229	211	193
2017	Model X P90D 22"	250	205	251	231	213	195	179	164
2019	Model X 100D 20"	295	291	356	328	302	277	255	233
2019	Model X 100D 22"	295	247	302	279	256	235	217	198
2019	Model X P100D 20"	289	287	351	324	298	273	251	230
2019	Model X P100D 22"	289	244	298	275	253	232	214	195
Current	Model X Long Range 20"	325	298	364	336	309	283	261	238
Current	Model X Long Performance 20"	305	292	357	330	303	278	256	234
Current	Model X Long Performance 22"	270	250	305	282	259	237	219	200

The Tesla Family

How the Model S has Evolved

The exterior might look familiar, but nearly every component of the car has changed over the years...

When buying a car, it's often a good to idea to wait for the latest design refresh to ensure you're getting the very latest technology, style, and to avoid significant depreciation as the car ages. That's not how Tesla works. It doesn't release yearly refreshes to its vehicle line-up. Instead, the company continually tweaks, iterates, and improves every component of each car, month-by-month, sometimes even week-by-week. This means you can purchase a Tesla at any point and know that you're getting the very best tech Tesla can offer, but for those looking to upgrade from an older car to the latest, knowing what has changed and what has stayed the same can be tricky.

There have been some exceptions to the rules, and they were all related to the Model S...

In 2014, Tesla introduced the first generation of Autopilot. You'll know if a Model S supports this first generation of self-driving because it has a single camera above the windscreen. Later that year the company also introduced the first dual-motor Model S at the end of 2014: the P85D.

2016 was the year of atheistic changes, most prominent being the removal of the faux-front grille on the nose of the car, replacing it instead with a much cleaner look. An optional solid glass roof was introduced that year, alongside a painted roof or an active panoramic sunroof. Autopilot version 2 was also introduced at the end of 2016. It added a total of eight cameras to the car — three above the windscreen, two cameras above the front wheels, two cameras on the door pillars, and a reverse camera.

In 2018, the company simplified the options available for the Model S. It removed the black textile interior, active sunroof, rear-facing child seats, and 21-inch Black Arachnid wheels.

2019 was a pretty big year for the Model S. It received a new, more efficient electric motor, increasing the total range of the Model S to 370 miles; while an improved adaptive air suspension meant the ride was smoother.

Those are just the big changes made to the Model S over the years. Flick over the page and you'll find a plethora of minor changes that most people won't have noticed...

Chapter 2

How the Model S has Evolved

	2013-2014	2014-2015	2016-Present
Headlights	The original HID headlights are easy to spot on older cars - just look for the round bulbs. The turn signal bulb is also inset into the headlight.	The HID headlights are still present.	Now fully LED, with better vision at night, and a sleeker look on the front of the car. The turn signals now run on the outer-edge of the headlight.
Rear diffuser	The original design of the Model S included an obvious rear diffuser, with a silver trim running along the top edge.	It's more subtle now, with no silver edge.	The same minimized design.
Body skirts	Running along the side of the car, below the doors, is a charcoal grey body skirt.	The body skirt is now painted the same color as the car.	Still the same color as the car.
Roof rack	There are four manual ports for attaching roof racks onto the car.	The same manual ports are still present.	The four ports are smaller and slightly inset into the roof.
Front-facing radar	Complete missing. Instead, the 2013 Model S only included parking sensors.	Now included, to aide the first generation of Autopilot to stay a safe distance from the car in front. You can spot the radar sitting below the nose cone on the front of the car.	It's no longer visible at the front of the car, but it's still there.
Frunk	It's completely massive on the original car, with extra space going back towards the dash of the car. The frunk hood is also insulated and includes a double-latch mechanism.	Same big trunk area and double-latch mechanism.	The hood is no longer insulated, and the storage area is significantly smaller to accommodate the HEPA filter and front motor. It also has a single-latch closing mechanism.
Charge port	A manual port with a magnetic latch, located on the rear-left brake light.	Still a manual port, located on the rear-left brake light.	It's now fully mechanical, so you can open the charge port from inside the car or with the mobile app.
Steering wheel	The original Model S had a leather steering wheel. It's slightly thicker than later cars and becomes shiny with age.	A newer steering wheel was introduced with the 2014 cars. It's slightly thinner and came in an optional vegan leather cover.	The same, newer steering wheel is included. It now only comes in vegan leather.

Chapter 2

2013-2014	2014-2015	2016-Present
Upper dash		
You'll find either suede or leather covering the top of the dash in the original Model S. There's also an obvious vent beneath the windscreen.	The same leather or suede is present up to 2015, with the same venting below the windscreen.	A smoother vegan leather covers the top of the dash from 2016 onwards, and the obvious air vents at the bottom of the windscreen have been moved below a subtle grill.
Front door handle pockets		
You'll find a plastic surface lining the inside of the door handle pockets.	They're still lined with plastic.	The door handle pockets are now lined with suede, making them feel softer to the touch.
Dome lights		
The original Model S has cool, white, LED dome lights in the ceiling.	The same white LEDs are present in these cars.	The dome lights inside the car now have a yellow tint. It's less futuristic but easier on the eyes.
Indicator stalks		
A thinner cruise control stalk was present on the top left-side of the steering wheel, with a short gear selector on the right. The indicator was located underneath the cruise control stalk.	Newer stalks were included from 2015 onwards. The Autopilot stalk was moved down, and the turn signal stalk up. The gear stalk was also made slightly longer.	The same stalks were included - and are still included to this day.
Front seats		
The 2013 Model S came with all-leather seats. A performance version was available, which included red stitching along the edges of the seating, and suede fabric on the lumbar supports. There's also a pocket on the very front of the driver seat for storing small objects or paperwork.	The second generation seats still included a pocket on the front of the driver's chair. The headrests were also thickened.	From 2015 onwards, the Next Generation seats became available. They were initially available in both real leather and vegan leather. However, later cars were only available in vegan leather. There's no secret pocket on the driver's chair, but for longer journeys, these seats were much more comfortable.
Back seats		
Initially, the Model S back seats had smaller headrests. These offered better visibility for the driver, but less support for back passengers.	The same, smaller headrests, can still be found.	Much bigger headrests come with the latest Model S cars. They almost reach the roof of the car, so offer better support for passengers, but limit the view out of the back.
Center well		
The original Model S came with a "yacht floor" in the center well. It was great for quickly placing items and had plenty of storage, but items would move around during fast acceleration or braking.	The yacht floor still remained, but now came in a choice of materials such as rubber carbon fibre.	Completely redesigned from 2016 onwards. It's now split into a center console with cup holders and a smaller area for storing small items and charging mobile devices.

The Tesla Family

How the Model Y compares with the Model 3

The two vehicles might look similar, but they have some remarkable differences

Trunk

Probably the most significant difference between the Model Y and Model 3 is the trunk opening. It's a powered lift-gate on the Model Y, which means you don't have to physically haul it upwards and over your head, then pull it back down to close it. Instead, all you need to do is pull on the trunk hatch button and watch it slowly rise, then press the close button when you're done and watch the trunk close itself. The actual trunk opening is much larger on the Model Y, offering both additional width and height for storing items. Once you look inside, you'll notice that the trunk has extra storage for items on both the left and right sides (behind the tail lights), plus an additional shallow storage area just behind the passenger seats. Interestingly there's no cargo shelf as found in the Model 3. This has the benefit of offering more space for physical items, but can potentially let people see what you're carrying in the trunk (if they have a torch to shine through the tinted rear window).

Look to the left side of the trunk, and you'll see two switches. Pull these, and the two passenger seats will fall downwards automatically. These are not included with the Model 3, meaning owners need to physically pull the seats down. One interesting note is that these switches will not bring the passenger seats back up; you still need to do this manually in the Model Y.

Chapter 2

The Model Y is a much larger vehicle than the Model 3, intended more for family use rather than day-to-day commuting. Sit in the back of a Model Y, and you'll find more legroom than the Model 3. Headroom is also better, thanks to the higher roofline of the Model Y. Look up, and you'll notice there's no crossbeam separating the front and back cabins, which gives a far more roomy and spacious feeling for passengers in the back of a Model Y. Look down, and you'll see the Model Y has two USB-C ports for charging electrical devices, rather than two USC-A ports (AKA regular USB).

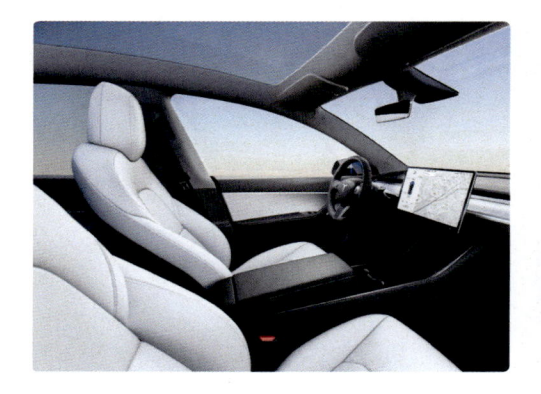

Heat Pump

Unlike the Model 3, which uses a resistance heater for warming the cabin in cold weather, the Model Y includes a heat pump beneath the front bonnet. Heat pumps are three times more efficient than resistance heaters, which means less energy is used when the weather is cold during winter months.

Windows

The Model Y has tinted rear windows as standard from the factory, unlike the Model 3, which has clear glass. This offers additional privacy for rear passengers while making it difficult for vehicles in traffic behind the Model Y being able to see into the cabin.

Chrome

The Model Y comes de-chromed straight from the factory, so instead of silver door handles, badges and window trim, it's a smokey black color instead. This gives the Model Y a "meaner" appearance than the Model 3.

Seating

The Model Y rides higher than the Model 3, offering better visibility on the road. The front seats are also mounted higher than in Model 3, which means your legs rest in a more downward position.

Wheels

Both the base Model Y and the Performance edition come with entirely different wheels than the Model 3. The general consensus is these new wheels look more attractive than the standard Model 3 Aero wheels.

Wireless charging

The Model Y includes dual wireless chargers in the upper front center console. With Model 3 there's only a holder for your mobile phones.

Radar heater

To prevent ice and snow from accumulating on the front radar, the Model Y includes a radar heater. On the Model 3, you need to clear any weather-related debris manually.

The Tesla Family

The Model 3/Y Battery

Containing the most power-dense and efficient battery cell Tesla has ever created

While the automotive industry comes to terms with moving to a fully electric future, Tesla continually pushes the very fringes of battery technology forward, with surprising breakthroughs that result in incredible efficiency.

There are two sizes of battery, depending on the configuration chosen. Both the Standard Range Model 3 and Y include a 50 kWh battery, while the Long Range and Performance vehicles include a 75 kWh battery. To put that into perspective, the average cellphone has a battery size of 2,500mAh. Perform some complicated mathematics, and you'll discover that a Long Range Model 3 with a full battery could charge that cellphone 6,000 times. Or to put it into another perspective, the Model 3 uses the equivalent energy of 6,000 cellphone batteries to haul itself (and passengers) along the road for more than 300 miles.

When initially designing the Model 3, Tesla didn't just take the Model S battery and place it below the floor. Because of its shorter wheelbase, that would have resulted in a taller vehicle than we see today. Instead, Tesla designed an entirely new battery cell. It's called the 2170 cell. That's because each cylindrical call is 21mm wide and 70mm high. When compared to the previous generation cell in the Model S and X (18650), each one contains 30 - 33% more energy.

In total, there are 4,416 cylinder cells in the Long Range Model 3 battery. These are divided into four rectangular models which sit alongside each other. The outer two models are 67.5" (1715 mm) in length, and weigh 191 lbs (86.6 kg), while the two center modules are longer, both being 73" (1854 mm) in length and 207 lbs (98.9 kg) in weight.

Tesla didn't just make the battery cells within the Model 3 smaller; it also reduced the wiring harness used to connect the drive units, charge port, air-conditioner and heaters to just 1,500 meters. That's half the length used within the Model 3, leading to energy efficiency and a less complicated manufacturing process. Key to this reduction was an integrated hub of multiple battery management systems, alongside a high-voltage controller.

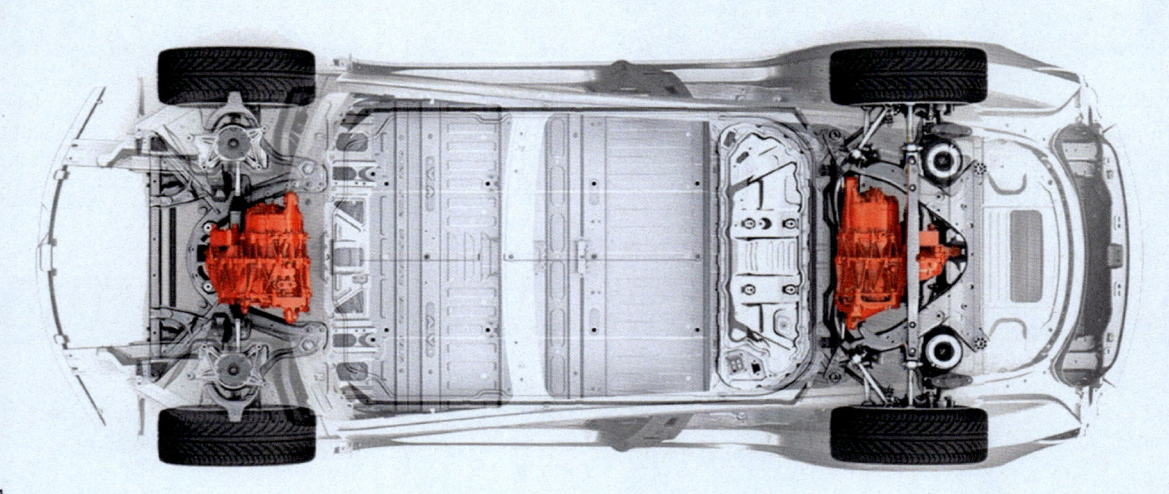

As energy flows in and out of a Model 3/Y battery pack, a significant amount of heat is generated by the cells. To keep temperatures under control, Tesla has run a layer of aluminum-extruded channels along the length of the battery pack. The aluminum is then curved around each cell to ensure heat is quickly dissipated away from it and out from the battery pack. Basically, Tesla has built an internal cooling system into the Model 3/Y battery pack, rather than relying on an external cooling system as seen in earlier battery designs.

Tesla's Battery patent

If you want to learn more about how the Model 3/Y battery pack was developed, visit the link below to explore Tesla's patent, which explains the system in detail:

https://patentscope.wipo.int/search/en/detail.jsf?docId=US254721855&tab=DRAWINGS

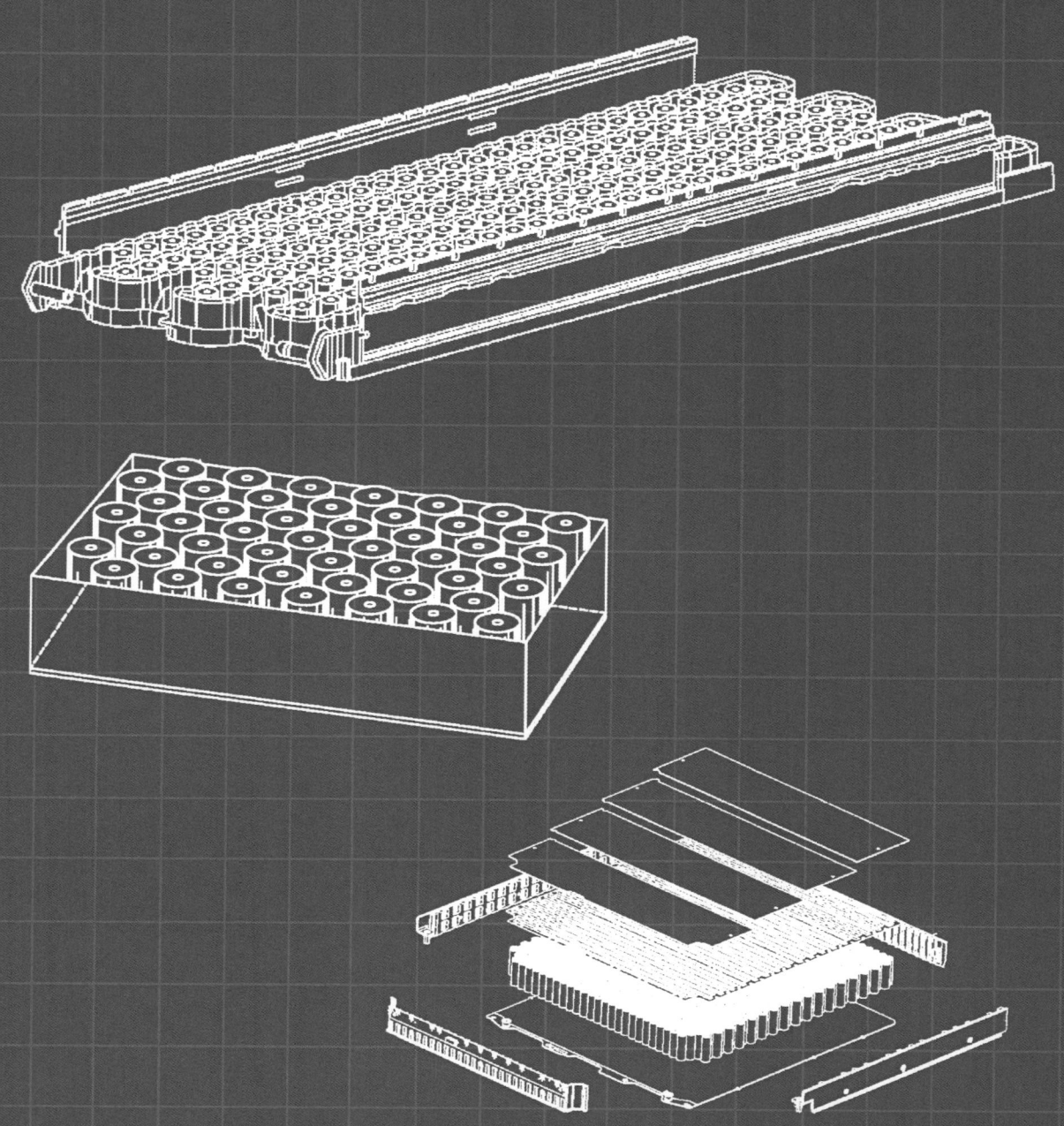

The Tesla Family

Model 3/Y HVAC system

To create a clean-looking dash, Tesla went back to the drawing board

Hop into a Model 3 or Y for the very first time, and one of the first things to catch your attention might be the lack of air vents. Instead, you'll see just a long, clean dash that stretches from A-pillar to A-pillar. This fresh, minimalistic look is an intentional design choice, and it helps to make both the Model 3 and Y calming environment to occupy.

You might have noticed that traditional automotive vents vent to be circular or rectangular. They're also placed flush to the surface of the instrument panel. There's no sensible reason for this. It's just how things have been for as long as anyone remembers — even the Model S and X share this traditional design language. There's one common downside to this arrangement: multiple point-like outlets are not optimized for distributing air over a large area, so you end up with multiple vents scattered throughout the cabin.

To enable such a clean dash for the Model 3 and Y, Tesla had to go back to the drawing board and completely redesign the heating, ventilation, and air conditioning (HVAC) system, resulting a delightfully simple system that uses just two vents to distribute jets of air. Best of all, it's possible to control the flow of air using the touchscreen using your fingers. With just a swipe of a finger, you can move the air over the steering wheel (helpful for keeping it warm during the winter), point it upwards, or direct it around your face.

Here's how the patent describes airflow is controlled using the two vents:
"The system can provide good control of the vertical position of the planar jet of air also when the vent is mounted in a non-flush position with regard to an instrument panel or other structure. This can be accomplished by a secondary outlet downstream of the main vent. For example, the secondary outlet can control the main air jet by feeding a low pressure zone that would otherwise keep the main jet attached to the instrument panel. As another example, the secondary outlet can push the main jet away from the structure, thereby adding momentum to it, in analogy with free air jets colliding."

Tesla's HVAC patent

If you want to learn more about how the HVAC system works, visit the link below to explore Tesla's patent, which explains the system in detail:
https://www.scribd.com/doc/359220547

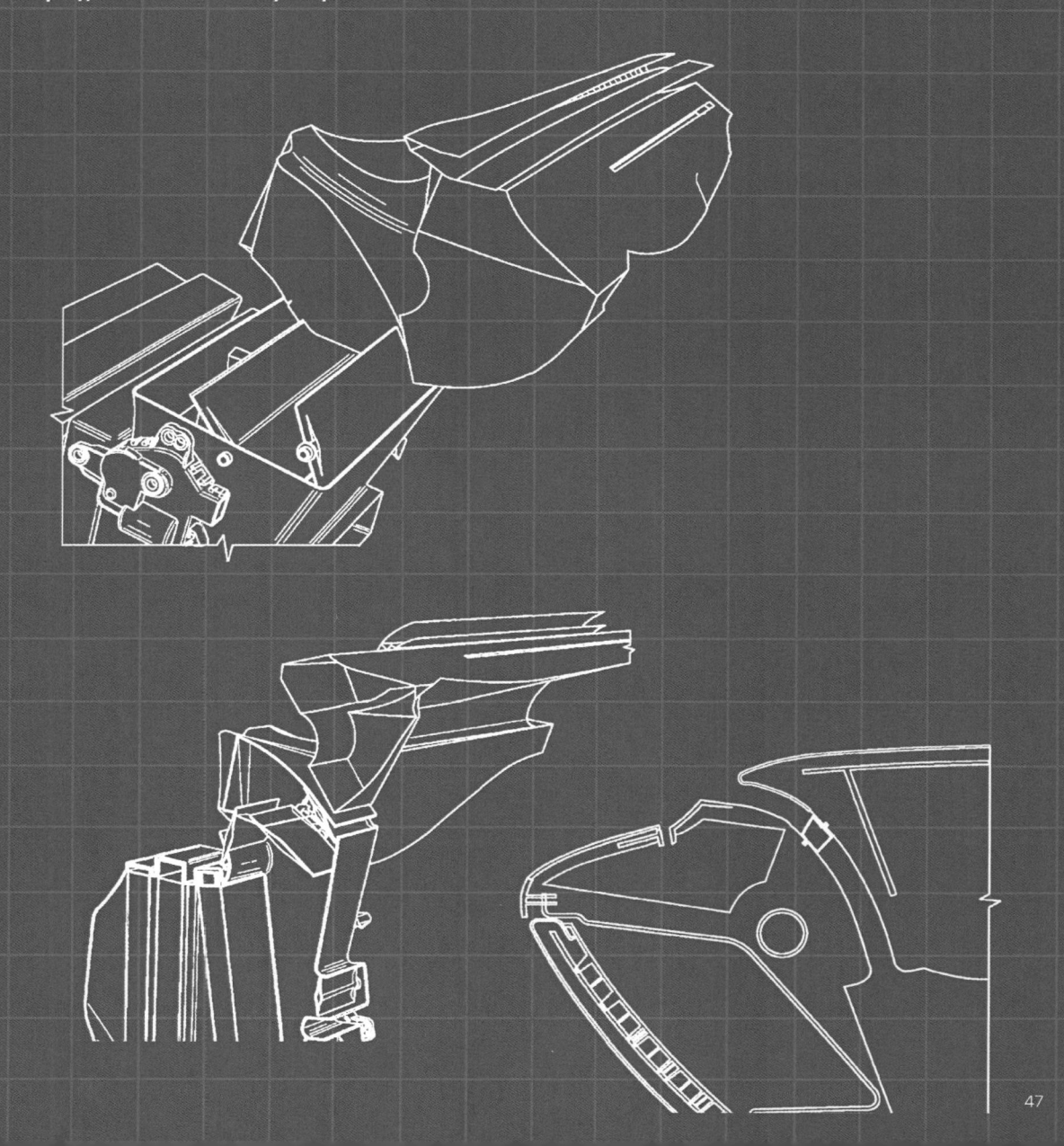

Autopilot

One day, many years from now, most cars will drive themselves. It's a dream of most car manufacturers, taxi companies and ride-sharing services, and it will mean a complete overhaul in not just how we travel, but also how we perceive car ownership.

Tesla is at the forefront of this self-driving revolution. Every single one of its cars includes the hardware necessary for full autonomy, including eight cameras and a suite of twelve ultrasonic sensors; while beneath the bonnet is a supercomputer that's continually analyzing the world around it.

We're still a long way from being able to get from A to B without any driver intervention. At the time of writing, it's still necessary (and required by law) to hold onto the steering wheel when Autopilot is activated. Still, with each software update, Tesla's fleet of cars become more intelligent and adept at navigating the world's roads.

This chapter will take a broad look at Autopilot, explaining the basics of how it works, what it's like to use, plus some dos and don'ts.

An Overview of Autopilot	50
Autopilot Features	52
Autopilot 1, 2, 2.5 and 3	56
Driving with Autopilot	58
Do's and Don'ts of Using Autopilot	60
Autopilot Hardware 3 Upgrade	62

49

An Overview of Autopilot

The self-driving technology inside your Tesla is its secret weapon. Sure, other car manufacturers have similar features for keeping within a lane and recognizing road signs, but no one's doing it quite like Tesla.

Achieving full autonomy — where the car drives itself from A to B — isn't going to happen overnight, but as a Tesla driver, you're fortunate enough to witness it happen, step-by-step, over time.

Breaking down full autonomy into manageable pieces is part of Tesla's battle-plan. Think of it like a jigsaw puzzle, where each piece represents a complex challenge such as following a lane, recognizing vehicles, looking for a parking spot, or speed limit recognition. The list is nearly endless, but as each piece of the puzzle is worked on, Tesla is fortunate enough to have people sitting in cars, using the system and actively watching in real-time. If something goes wrong, Tesla can look for Autopilot disengagements and try to work out how to fix the problem; and as disengagements reduce to the point where they're nearly non-existent, then the piece of the puzzle has been solved.

Theoretically, once all the pieces of the puzzle are complete, Tesla will achieve full autonomy — with the approval of regulators across the world — and it can only improve over time.

Chapter 3

The cameras and sensors powering Autopilot

Just like a human driver, a Tesla drives with its eyes. But unlike a human driver, your Tesla has eight eyes (or rather, cameras), dotted around the vehicle. They provide a 360-degree view around the car with a range of up to 250 meters of range. Essentially, your Tesla is constantly watching traffic behind, in front, and at the sides at all times to enable Autopilot, and to keep you safe.

Front-facing cameras

Above the windscreen and just behind the rear-view mirror are three cameras. They provide a 3D-view of the world ahead.

Side cameras

You'll find a forward-facing camera on each door pillar, plus a back-facing camera above each front wheel.

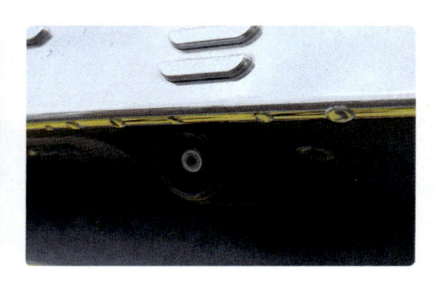

Back camera

The back camera is tucked next to the registration plate.

Complimenting those eight cameras are a suite of twelve ultrasonic sensors. They can detect both hard and soft surfaces, and enable Autopilot to recognize curb edges, walls, bushes, barriers and much more. A forward-facing radar provides data about the world on a redundant wavelength that can see through rain, fog, and dust. It also detects cars ahead, enabling Autopilot to keep a safe distance from the vehicle in front when visibility is limited.

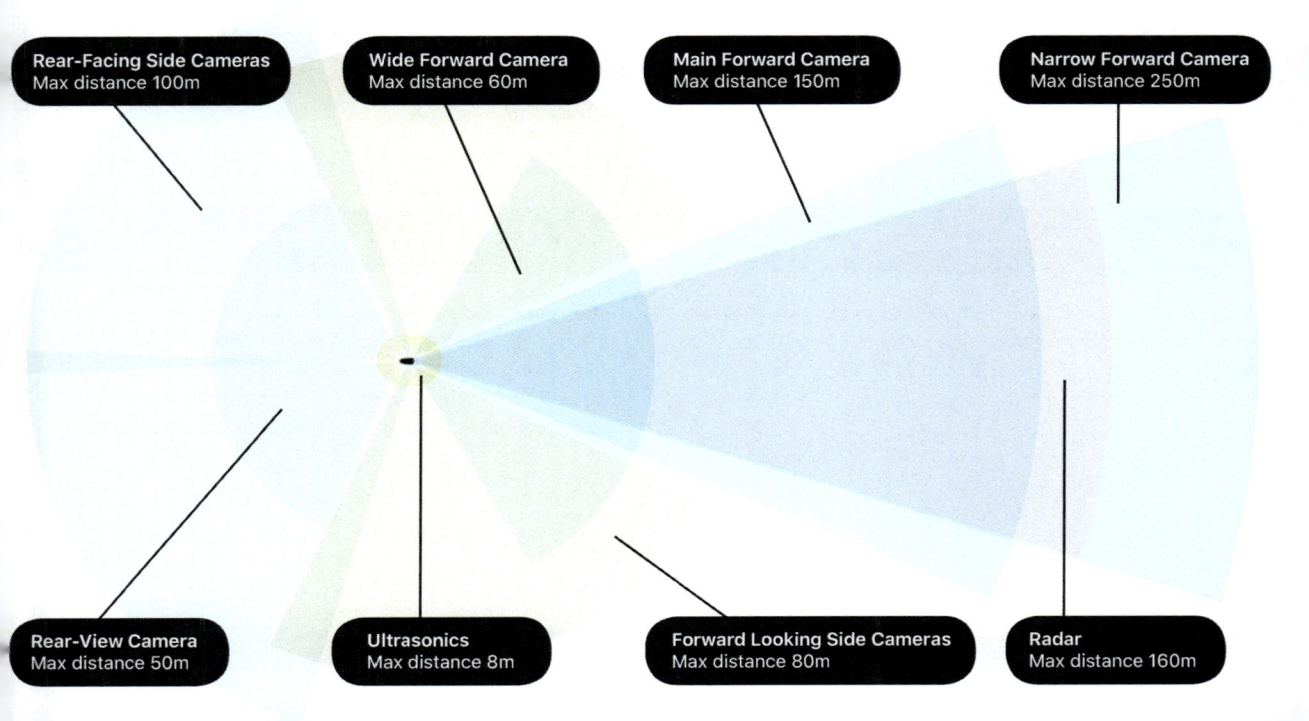

Rear-Facing Side Cameras
Max distance 100m

Wide Forward Camera
Max distance 60m

Main Forward Camera
Max distance 150m

Narrow Forward Camera
Max distance 250m

Rear-View Camera
Max distance 50m

Ultrasonics
Max distance 8m

Forward Looking Side Cameras
Max distance 80m

Radar
Max distance 160m

Autopilot Features

Discover what each version of Autopilot includes...

Every Tesla vehicle comes with the hardware necessary for full self-driving on Autopilot, but there are two distinct versions available: Standard Autopilot and Full Self Driving. Standard Autopilot is free and comes pre-built into every car that leaves the factory. In contrast, Full Self Driving is an optional extra, and can be purchased either at the time of configuration or at a later date via the Tesla Account page at www.tesla.com. Here's what is in included in either version:

Standard Autopilot

Adaptive cruise control

The vehicle will take control of the accelerator and brake pedals. It will automatically follow a set speed limit, slow down to match vehicles ahead, and even follow bumper-to-bumper traffic.

Autosteer

The car will automatically follow the road ahead, steering around corners and navigating around objects.

Object recognition

To help understand the world around it, the car will recognize other vehicles - including the type of vehicle - plus roadside objects such as traffic cones, bollards, trash cans, and disabled parking bays. These are displayed appropriately on the Autopilot display.

Safety features

Autopilot can detect a potential front or side collision with another vehicle, bicycle or pedestrian within a distance of 525 feet (160 m). If one is found it sounds a warning. If a collision is imminent, the car can automatically break or swerve out of the way.

Stop sign recognition

The car will automatically recognize stop sign warnings. It may warn you in some cases if it detects that you are about to run a stop sign, in addition to stop lights, while Autosteer is in use.

Adjacent lane speed adjustments

When the vehicle detects that adjacent lane traffic is significantly slower, Autopilot will automatically reduce your driving speed. It will also highlight the adjacent lane with arrows. The automatic speed adjustment can be temporarily overridden by pressing the accelerator pedal.

Full Self Driving

Automatic lane changing

The car can automatically change lanes when the indicator stalk is pressed. To do this, the car is constantly scanning traffic around, in front and behind. When it's time to change lanes, the car can alter its speed to match traffic.

Navigate on Autopilot

The vehicle will automatically change lanes to overtake slow traffic, exit the freeway, and navigate freeway interchanges. Outside of the US this feature will only suggest lane changes.

Summon

Using the Tesla app, it's possible to move the car forwards or backwards. This is helpful for when the car is parked in a small space.

Enhanced Summon

With this feature it's possible to summon the vehicle across a parking lot. It will automatically pull out, navigate the parking lot and find your location. Great for when it's heavily raining and you don't want to get soaked.

Autopark

When driving below 10 mph, the car will actively scan for parking spaces using its radar, ultrasonic sensors and cameras. When it sees one, it will display a "P" symbol on the instrument panel alongside a "Park" button. When the park button is pressed, the car will automatically park itself in the suggested space.

Machine Learning

Understanding machine learning is key to knowing what your Tesla is doing when it's driving along the road. You will have experienced machine learning many times without even knowing it. Machine learning is used by Google to crawl the web and present results, it's used by Apple to work out your daily schedule, and it's used by common photo apps to recognize people and objects in the photos you take. Tesla does something similar for Autopilot. It's teaching the computer to identify other vehicles, objects and scenery using the cameras around the vehicle.

Take trucks, for example. Your Tesla knows what a truck looks like because it has been fed tens of thousands of photos of trucks at different angles and in different lighting conditions. When your car comes across a truck in real life, it compares the video feed from its cameras with the thousands of images it has seen of trucks, then it gives a false or positive result. If it's positive, then you'll see a truck on the AP display in the correct orientation, and the car will react appropriately (for example if you're overtaking a truck the car will "lean" away from it to give extra room). All of this happens 30 times a second, with the feeds from all eight cameras.

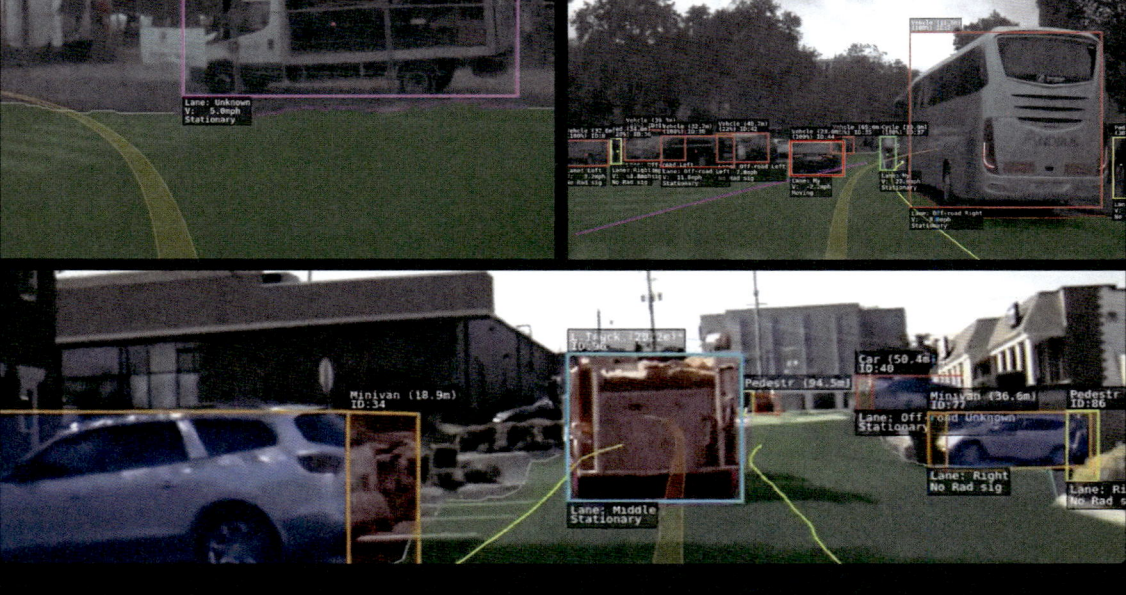

Here's what Autopilot sees as you drive along the road. Notice how vehicles are recogized and labelled, with tags including Minivan, Truck, Car and Moto. The system is also actively recognizing the road, lane markings, and pedestrians. You can see this in action via: **https://bit.ly/2ouOFyd**

Chapter 3

The future of Autopilot

If Tesla's plan for Autopilot comes to fruition, one day you'll be able to climb into your vehicle and tell it where to go. If you don't say anything, it will take a look at your calendar and take you to your next appointment. If there's nothing there, then it will either take you home or to work (depending on your current location). Along the way, your Tesla will take the optimal route, navigate urban streets (even without any markings), work its way through complex intersections, stop at red lights, and react appropriately to other vehicles and pedestrians. It will even drop you off then go to find a parking space.

Smart Summon

With Smart Summon, your car will come to collect you when it's time to go. It'll navigate parking garages, car parks, and maneuver around objects along the way.

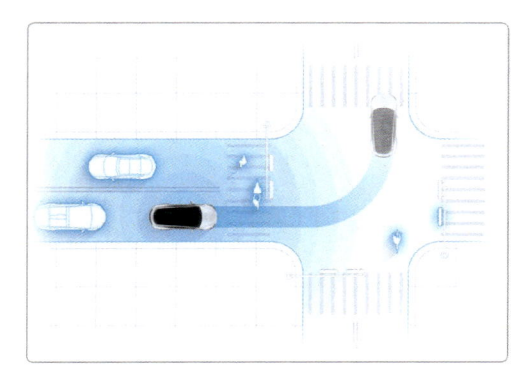

On the road

Your vehicle will automatically stop at red lights, wait for passing traffic, and pull out safely. It will also be able to navigate complex junctions.

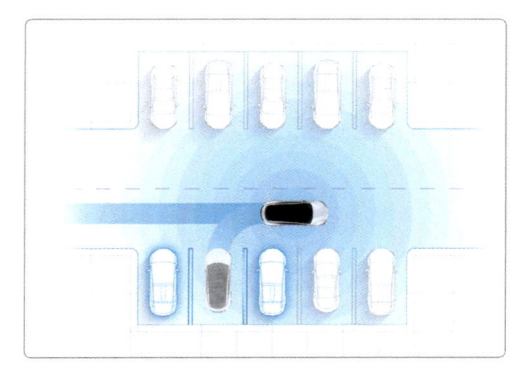

At the end of the ride

When you're at your destination, just climb out of the car and it will go to find a parking space. In time, Tesla plans to introduce a robotaxi service, where the car will spend the day (or night) collecting passengers while you work or sleep. The company even revealed pricing:

- <$0.18 per mile.
- $0.65 gross profit per mile)
- 90,000 annual mileage
- ~$30,000 total gross profit per car, per year.

Before you get too excited, keep in mind that nothing on this page is guaranteed to happen. Hardware, software, and government regulations could all get in the way.

Autopilot

Autopilot 1, 2, 2.5 and 3

As technology progresses, so does the hardware inside each Tesla...

As Tesla continuously pushes the limits of self-driving technology, it has introduced a number of hardware changes to its Autopilot system over the years. Here's a roundup of each version, the capabilities introduced and how to work out which version of Autopilot your car has...

Autopilot 1 (Model S)

2014-2016

The original iteration of Autopilot. It was powered by a single camera mounted to the top of the windshield, along with a computer manufactured by Mobileye EyeQ3. Autopilot 1 is capable of:

- Lane keep with centering
- TACC (Traffic Aware Cruise Control)
- Emergency collision avoidance
- Can tell the difference between a lorry, car, motorbike and person
- Lane change with indicator signal
- AutoPark with self-parallel parking
- Automatic high/low beam headlights
- Vehicle Lane avoidance

Chapter 3

Autopilot 2 (Model S & X)
October 2016-2017

Tesla dramatically overhauled Autopilot in 2016. The new system was powered by eight cameras around the vehicle, ultrasonic sensors, and an Nvidia Drive PX 2 GPU for CUDA based GPGPU computation. It has all the AP1 features plus:

- Eight 360° surround cameras (60M-250M range)
- Twelve updated ultrasonic sensors (8M range)
- Detection of both hard and soft objects at nearly twice the distance of the prior system
- Improved forward-facing radar (160M range)
- Capable of 200 frames per second of data
- Recognition of vehicles in opposite lanes
- Automatically change lanes
- without requiring driver input
- Automatic onramp and offramp
- Ability to steer tighter bends
- Sentry Mode
- Enhanced Summon

Autopilot 2.5 (Model S, X & 3)
August 2017-2019

Perhaps realizing that Autopilot 2 wasn't quite fast enough for what they had planned, Tesla made some minor additions to the Autopilot hardware around the time the Model 3 was released:

- A new secondary custom-built GPU for more additional power and redundancy
- 3 GPU's instead of 2
- 8GB GDDR5 SDRAM, instead of 6GB
- Dash camera recording

Autopilot 3 (Model S, X & 3)
April 2019 to current

Designed in-house at Tesla, this custom chip is built for one purpose: enable full self-driving across Tesla's fleet of vehicles. The company claims this chip is 21 times faster in frame-per-second processing, versus the previous generation of hardware.

- Custom-built AI Chip
- Capable of 2,300 frames per second of data, with redundancy
- Additional object rendering
- Promise of full self-driving

How do I know which version of Autopilot I have?

You can easily recognize the differences between an Autopilot 1 and 2 Model S by looking for the external cameras on the door pillars and side signals.

The difference between 2 and 2.5 are more tricky. You can tell if a Model S or X has 2.5 by looking for the dashcam icon on the central touchscreen. If it's there, then the vehicle has Autopilot 2.5 hardware.

Similarly, working out if a car has Autopilot 3 hardware requires you to look for something on the screen: objects rendered in the Autopilot visualization. That's right, at the time of writing, only Autopilot 3 hardware can render traffic cones, traffic lights, bollards and trash cans in realtime.

Driving with Autopilot

What's it really like to experience Autopilot?

It takes trust to hand over the controls of a vehicle to someone else, let alone a machine, so the first time you ever engage Autopilot is a disconcerting experience. You'll likely hover your hands over the wheel, rest your foot tentatively on the accelerator, and lean forward with tense round shoulders. Then, as the car begins to follow the lane and slow down with traffic ahead, you'll lean back and begin to relax. It won't be long before you've learned to rest one hand on the wheel and to trust the car to drive itself along the highway. You might even activate Autopilot on a country road or city street, then quickly learn that the software powering Autopilot is far from being ready when it comes to unpredictable situations or 90-degree bends.

That's right; Autopilot is far from perfect. There's still a long way to go before it can be trusted to navigate city streets and narrow roads. At the time of writing, Autopilot cannot be activated without clear lines to follow, it won't stop at red lights, it can't navigate complex junctions, it doesn't recognize emergency vehicles, won't give way to other vehicles, and will often pull up behind a vehicle parked at the side of the road, rather than steer around it.

That will change with time, as the software powering Autopilot begins to learn how to react to situations appropriately. At the time of writing, Autopilot can already recognize traffic lights and knows it should stop, but this feature is unreleased, in a state called "ghost mode". It's basically guessing what to do when it sees a red light, makes a mental note, then watches to see what the driver does. It then marks the situation as a positive or negative, and sends a message back to Tesla headquarters. When all the millions of Tesla vehicles around the world are successfully guessing how to react to a red light, the feature will be rolled out via a free software update, enabling drivers to sit back and let the car slow itself down at red lights.

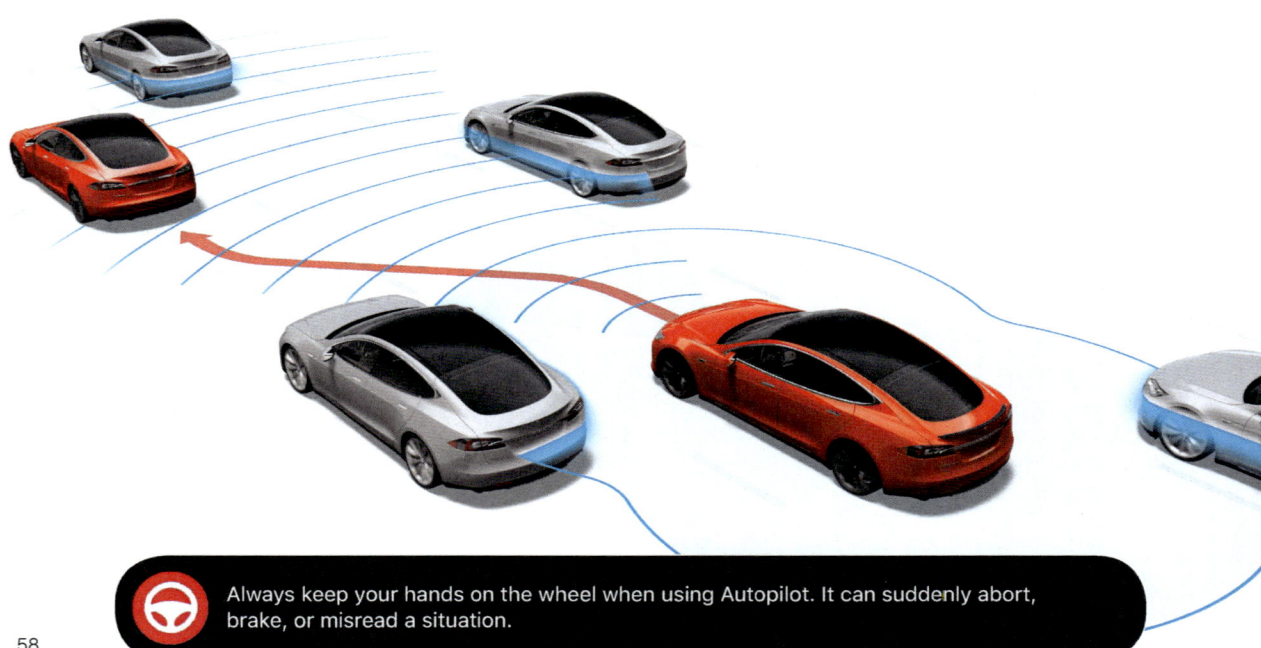

> Always keep your hands on the wheel when using Autopilot. It can suddenly abort, brake, or misread a situation.

Chapter 3

The subtle Autopilot differences between Model 3, S and X.

Drivers going from one Tesla to another might be surprised to learn that Autopilot works slightly differently depending on the type of vehicle...

Model 3 & Y

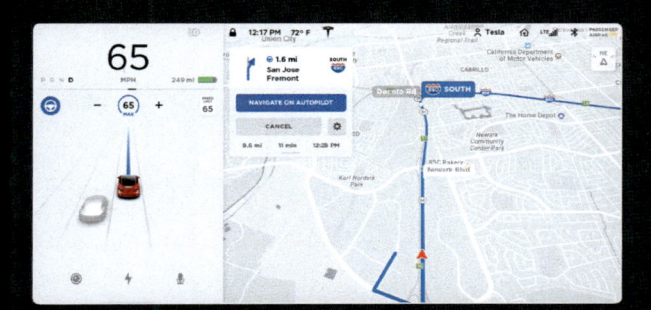

Model 3 & Y Autopilot Display
You'll find the AP display on the driver's side of the central touchscreen.

Activating Autopilot
On a Model 3 and Y, you pull the gear stalk to the bottom twice.

Changing lanes (FSD only)
On a Model 3, or Y you flick the indicator stalk all the way to change lanes.

Changing speed
On a Model 3 and Y, you can adjust the speed by rolling the right scroll wheel up or down. Roll it slowly to change the speed by 1 mph, or quickly to change it by 5 mph.

Match the current speed limit
On a Model 3 and Y, tap the current speed limit symbol, and the car will adjust its speed to match.

Rotate and zoom the top-down AP view
On a Model 3 or Y, you can pan, rotate, and zoom in and out of the Autopilot view by using your fingers. It's great for seeing traffic behind you or far ahead.

Model S & X

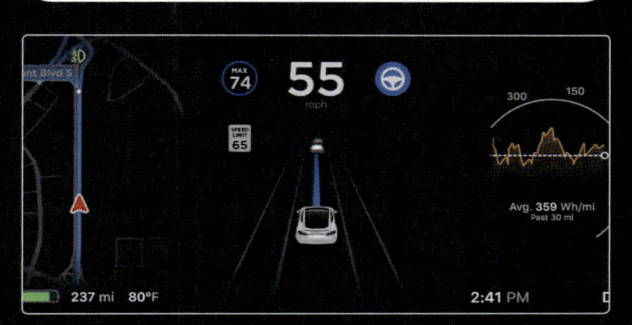

Model S & X Autopilot Display
It's located in the very center of the instrument panel.

Activating Autopilot
On a Model S or X, you flick the Autopilot stalk towards you twice.

Changing lanes (FSD only)
On a Model S or X, you half-pull the indicator stalk.

Changing speed
On a Model S or X, you can adjust the speed by pulling the AP stalk up or down. Pull it lightly to adjust the speed by 1 mpg, or pull it all the way up to change the speed by 5 mph.

Match the current speed limit
On a Model S or X, you need to set the speed manually.

Rotate and zoom the top-down AP view
On a Model S or X, there's no way to do this.

59

Do's and Don'ts of Using Autopilot

Autopilot is an incredible piece of technology that is changing the way we drive, but it's not perfect, so here are some crucial do's and don'ts for when you're using Autopilot...

DO:

✔ Use it on the highway

Steady curves and traffic are the perfect environment for Autopilot.

✔ Watch the road at all times

When traveling at high speeds, Autopilot won't recognize stationary objects in the road.

✔ Use it in stop-and-go traffic

Autopilot is great at following stop-and-go traffic, meaning all you have to do is hold the wheel.

✔ Keep your hands on the wheel

You need to be prepared to take control at any time, and without warning.

✔ Use it on long journeys

Your feet will appreciate the rest, plus it's far easier to monitor a car rather than fully control it.

✔ Keep an eye on the AP display

You'll start to notice lane lines, traffic cones, traffic lights and more - all of which help to understand what Autopilot is seeing and build trust.

DON'T:

✖ Use Autopilot on single-track roads
It doesn't know how to react to parked vehicles or oncoming traffic when there are no dividing lines.

✖ Take it for granted
It could suddenly take a exit without warning, or brake unexpectedly.

✖ Use it in construction areas
Autopilot doesn't always recognize merging lanes with no clear lines.

✖ Use it on city streets
Autopilot struggles with complex junctions, navigating around parked vehicles, 90-degree corners, and traffic lights.

✖ Use it with sleeping passengers
Sudden braking will definitely wake them up!

✖ Use it in parking lots
That's what Enhanced Summon is for. A feature that will bring the car to you.

Autopilot

Autopilot Hardware 3 Upgrade

Find out if you're vehicle is eligible for the latest Autopilot hardware...

Since the introduction of Full Self Driving (AKA Enhanced Autopilot), Tesla has promised to upgrade every vehicle with the FSD package to Autopilot Hardware 3.0. At the time of writing (January 2020), a small number of upgrades have already been performed, but it's not certain whether every single vehicle will be eligible for the upgrade. It's all dependent on two things: the age of the MCU and the Autopilot hardware...

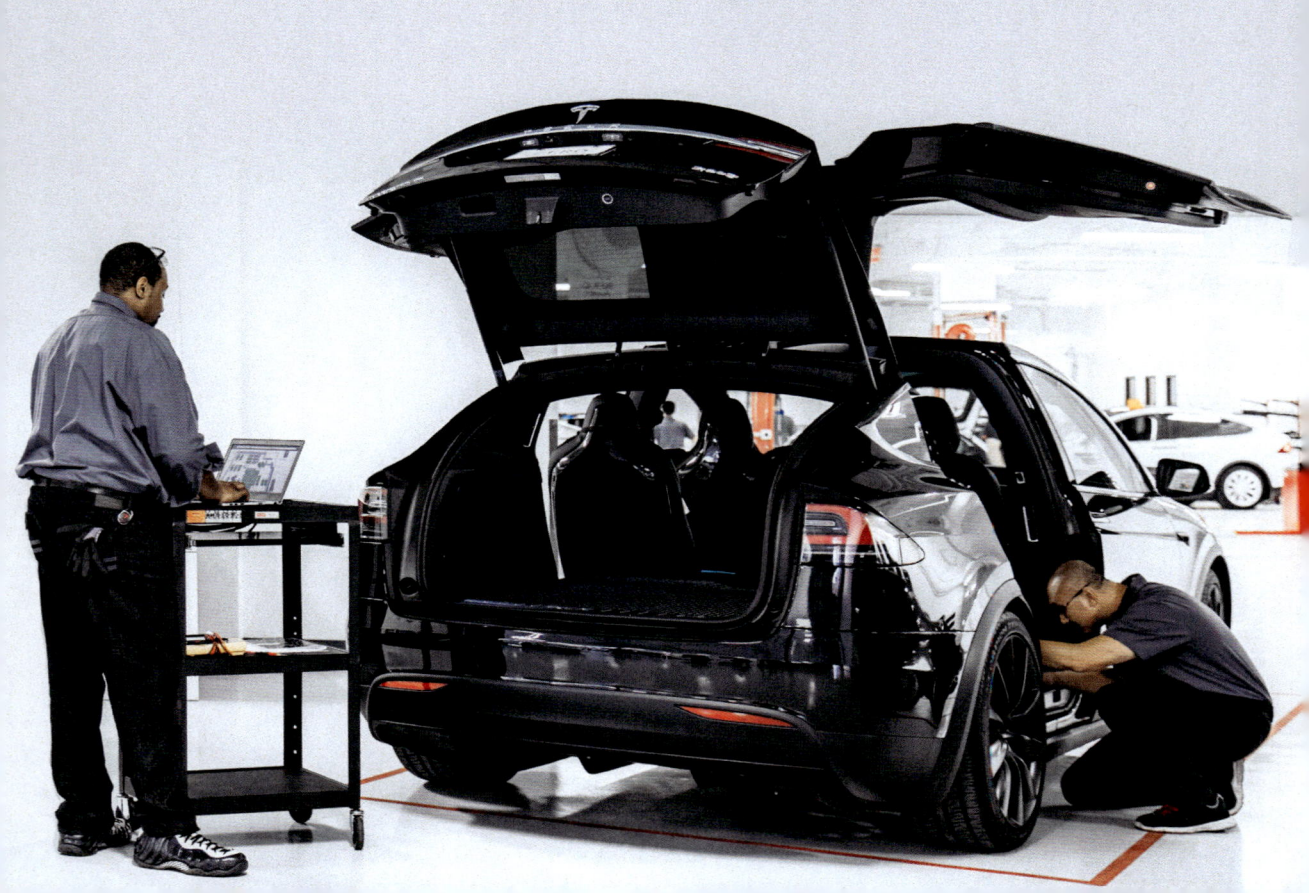

MCU

The MCU is the "Media Control Unit". It powers everything you see and interact with on the central touchscreen, and there are two variants:

- MCU 1: Found in cars manufactured between 2012 and February 2018.
- MCU 2: Included with cars manufactured after February 2018. Plus every Model 3 and Y.

It's easy to work out whether your car has an MCU 1 or 2 unit: the original MCU is slower to respond, takes longer to calculate routes, and doesn't support video-based features such as Tesla Cam, YouTube and Netflix. It's also not fast enough to render 3D games, so the selection of titles in the Tesla Arcade is smaller.

The second-generation MCU was introduced alongside the Model 3, then integrated into the Model S and X from February 2018 onwards. It's considerably faster, enabling smoother touchscreen interactions and video-based functions.

Autopilot hardware

Also known as the "Electronic Control Unit", or ECU for short. It's the computer responsible for powering Autopilot, and there are four variants as we learned on the previous page:

- ECU 1: September 2014 - October 2016
- ECU 2: October 2016 - August 2017
- ECU 2.5: August 2017 - April 2019
- ECU 3.0: April 2019 - Present

The ECU is the component which powers Autopilot. The version in your vehicle can heavily influence the capabilities of Autopilot. For example, ECU 1 vehicles do not support Full Self Driving, Enhanced Summon or traffic light recognition; while ECU 2 and 2.5 vehicles support a limited Full Self Driving feature-set, with reduced rendering of objects on the AP display (for example, they cannot display traffic cones in real-time).

Upgrade Compatibility

At the time of writing, Autopilot 3 is only compatible with MCU 2 hardware. If you have an MCU 1 unit in your vehicle, then you're currently out of luck. Tesla is looking into the possibility of an MCU 1 to MCU 2 upgrade, but early reports say the upgrade would require a completely new MCU module, re-wiring of the APE — including to the backup camera — and a new instrument panel on the Model S and X. How Tesla plans to resolve this problem is yet to be confirmed.

How to get the upgrade

Tesla is slowly rolling out its Hardware 3.0 upgrade to those who have purchased the full Self-Driving Autopilot package. To ease the rollout it's grouping cars by hardware configuration, VIN, and location, with Model S and X cars that include both MCU 2 and ECU 2.5 hardware coming first, followed by Model 3's later in 2020. If you want to skip the queue, then you can request an upgrade to Autopilot 3 through the Tesla app on your phone. With luck, your request will be approved, and the hardware will be retrofitted by either a mobile service technician or at a Tesla Service Center.

Charging Your Car

The Tesla Supercharger network turns long-distance driving into an enjoyable experience, thanks to two things: charging speed and reliability.

My first electric car was a BMW i3. It had a cripplingly short range of only 80 miles (on a warm summers day), so long-distance trips involved stopping every hour at a 50 kW rapid charger. Those chargers often didn't work or were occupied when I arrived, leading to stressful, lengthy trips.

The Supercharger network solves all of those problems. They line the major routes through America, Europe, China, and the East coast of Australia. They're blazing fast, topping out at 250 kW, they often have dozens of charging units, and they're carefully placed to ensure amenities such as food and restrooms are available.

Supercharging is also pretty easy. You roll up, plug in, then wait a short while. Nevertheless, not everyone knows how to find a Supercharger, park the correct way, and connect properly. They might also have questions about pricing, charging speeds and etiquette. There's what this chapter is all about, plus we'll take a look at how to find and charge at public networks.

A Guide To The Supercharger Network	**66**
Charging Speeds	**70**
Charging at Public Networks	**72**

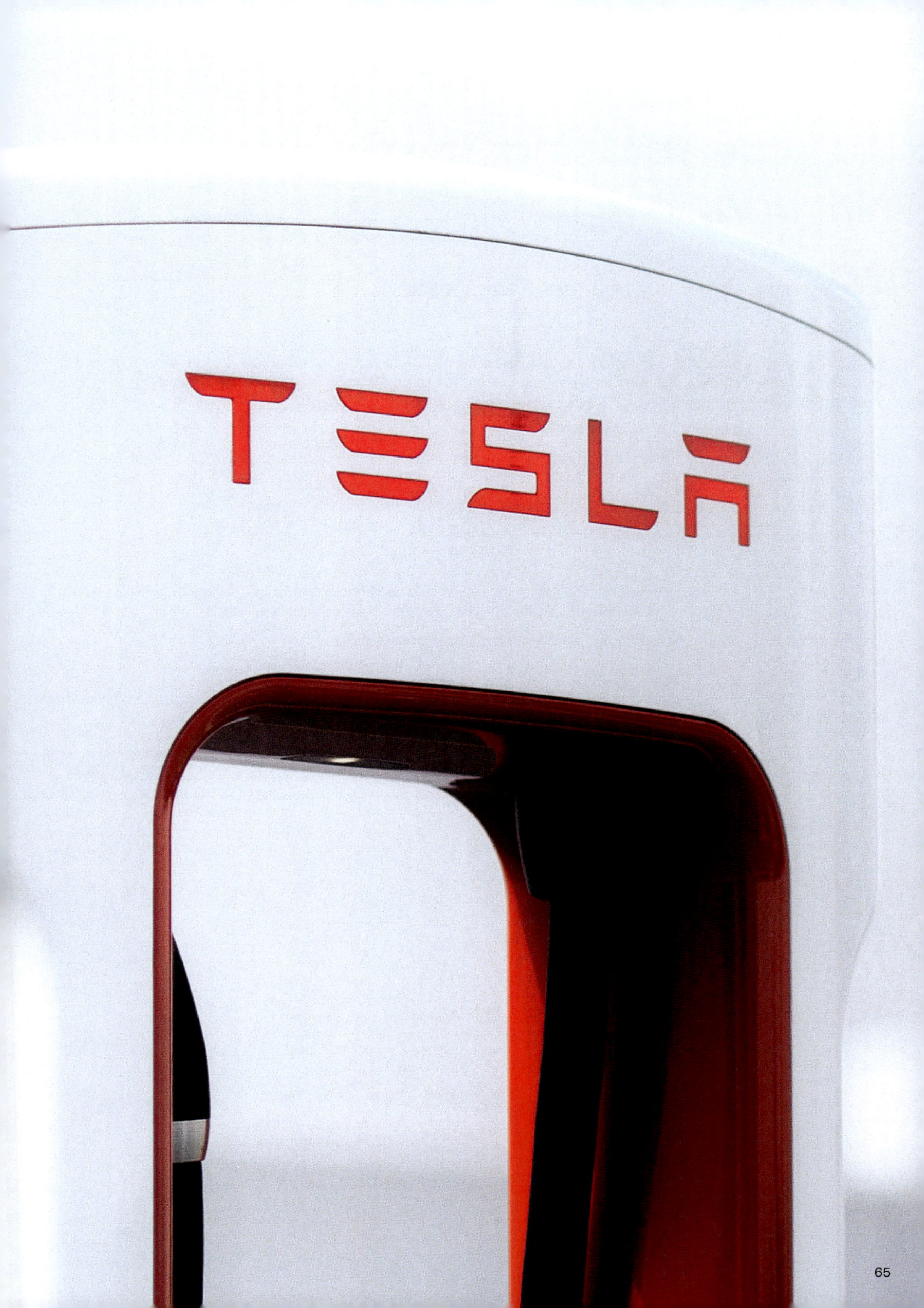
TESLA

Charging Your Car

A Guide To Using The Supercharger Network

Never worry about long distance trips again...

The Supercharger network is quite possibly the best part of being a Tesla owner. Not because it's the fastest network available, or because it's exclusive to Tesla cars -- or because it's so darn reliable -- but because it's so delightfully simple to use. All you do is turn up, plug in, and wait a short while.

That's how it's supposed to work. In reality, those encountering a Supercharger for the first time might fall into one of the following traps:

- They might plug a Type 2 cable into their EU Model 3.
- They'll try to force open the charge port with their fingers.
- They might park the wrong way around.
- They might park adjacent to another car. Parallel supercharger bays (for example 1A and 1B) share the same power source. By sharing power with another car, you're likely to see slower supercharging speeds.
- They'll turn up with a cold battery then wonder why charge speeds are slow.

How to find a Supercharger:

If you're wondering where the nearest Supercharger is then here's a helpful tip: zoom out using the touchscreen map until you see a red pin. This represents a Supercharger. Tap on it, and you'll see how many bays are available, any amenities, and a shortcut for automatically setting the navigation. Alternatively, you can open the Tesla app, tap the Charging option, then see a list of the nearest Superchargers based on your location.

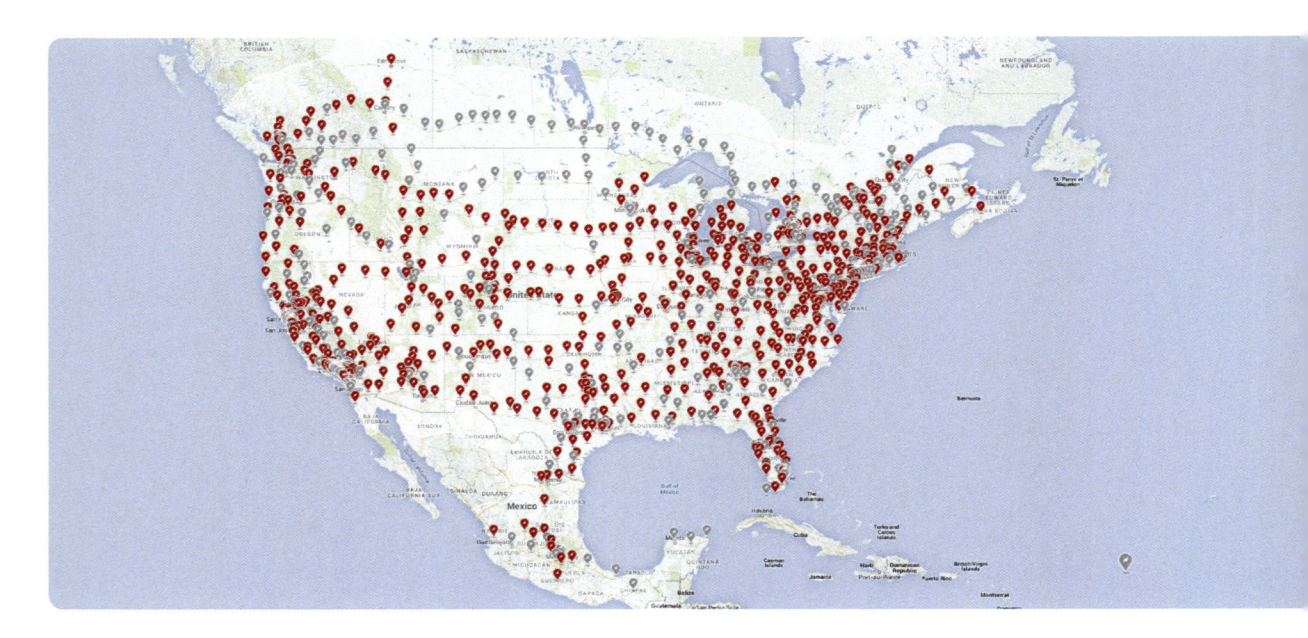

Chapter 4

Before you charge:

Set the Supercharger as a destination using the touchscreen map. Not only will this give you directions, but it'll also pre-heat the car's batteries during the drive, so when you arrive, you'll get the fastest charging speeds possible.

Don't bother using the Supercharger if your car's batteries are more than 80% full. Past that point, the vehicle will charge no quicker than most public rapid chargers. You might also be hogging a Supercharger bay which someone else desperately needs to use.

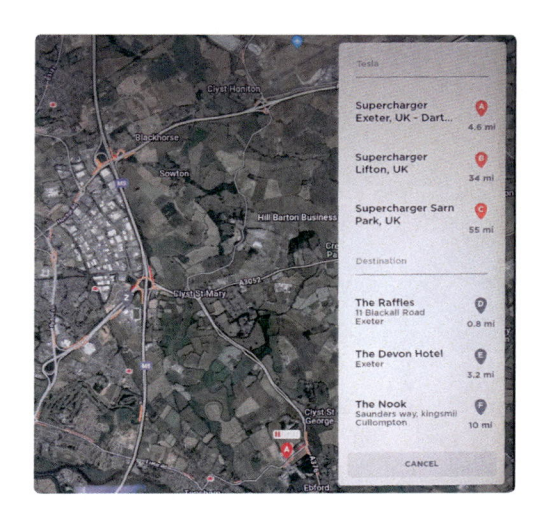

Arriving at a Supercharger:

Most Supercharger bays require you to reverse into the bay. It's fairly simple, just slowly back in while using both the reversing camera and your mirrors to line up nicely with the bay. Some Supercharger bays require to drive inwards, however. You'll usually know because the bay's parking space will be on the right-side of the charging unit (remember, the charge port is on the left side of the car). You might also notice that other cars have driven in nose-first.

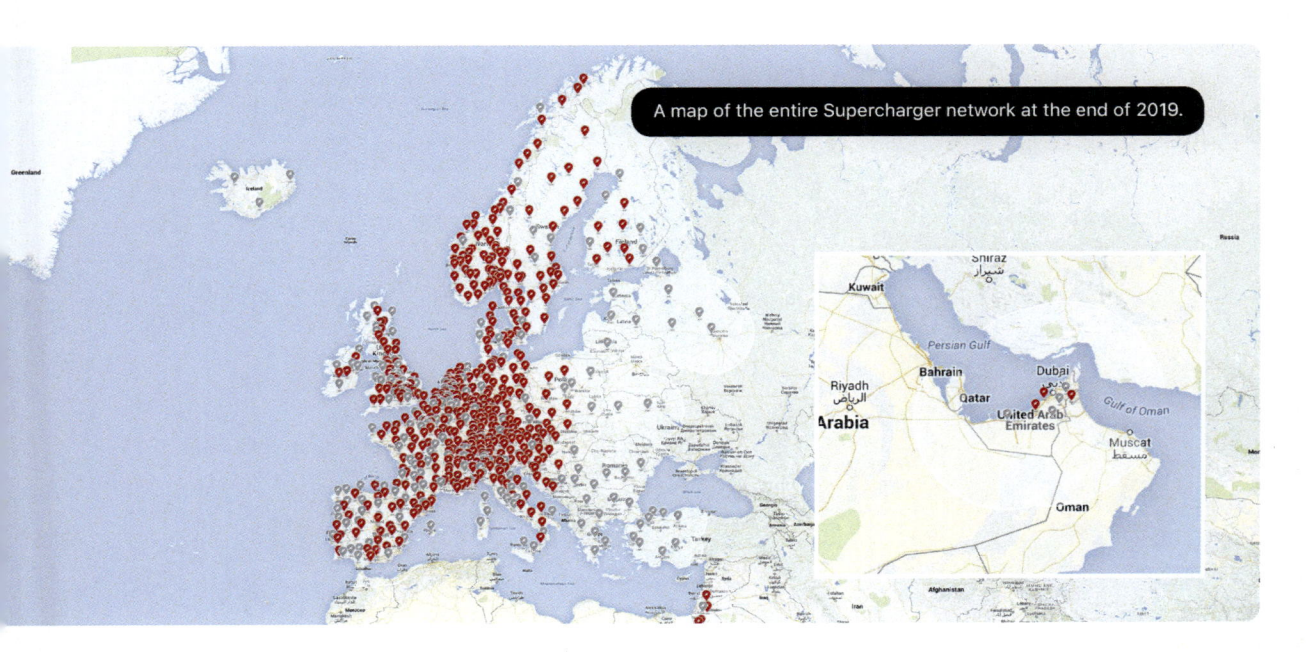

A map of the entire Supercharger network at the end of 2019.

A Guide To Using The Supercharging Network

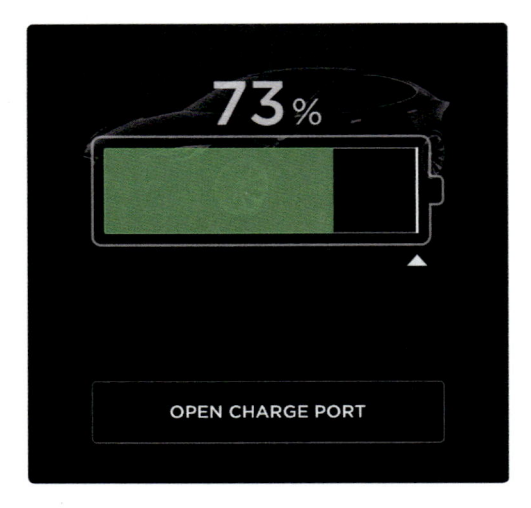

Opening the charge port:

1. Tap the charge icon in the top corner of the vehicle's touchscreen, then tap Open Charge Port.
2. Press the charge port inwards and it'll pop open.
3. Use the Tesla app to open the charge port.
4. Hold the charger cable near the charge port, then press the small dot on the handle.

How to use a Supercharger:

It's easy, just plug the cable into the charge port, and your vehicle will automatically start charging. You can check to see what speeds your car is charging at by looking at the touchscreen, or by using the Tesla app.

If you're driving a Model S or X, then use the smaller Type 2 plug. If you're a Model 3 or Y owner outside of the US, make sure to use the CCS cable to charge your car. It's the larger plug, sitting above the Type 2 plug.

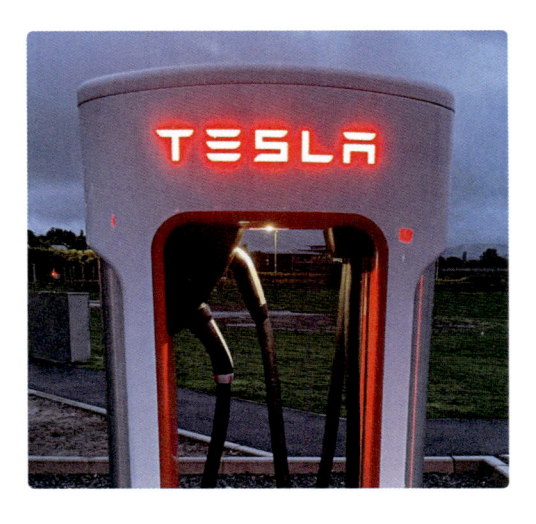

Press the dot to finish the charging session.

How to finish charging:

When the car's batteries are approximately 80% charged, or if you're ready to leave, there are a few ways to stop the Supercharger.

1. Press the small button on the charger handle to stop the charging and release the lock.
2. Tap Stop Charging on the central touchscreen.
3. Use the Tesla app to stop the charging.

Supercharging costs

For the first few years of the Model S and Model X program, Supercharging was completely free for all owners. This was ended in 2017, before being re-instated July 2019. As for Model 3 and Y owners, it's never been free. To find out if free supercharging is enabled on your car:

1. Visit www.tesla.com, then sign in.
2. Select the Manage button by your car.
3. Select View Details.
4. Look for "Supercharging Status". It'll either say "Free" or "Pay Per Use Supercharging".

If you don't have free Supercharging, then prices are $0.26 / £0.24 / €0.25 per kW. That means a full charge from 0% to 100% would cost you approximately $15 / £15 / €15, depending on battery size.

How to pay for Supercharging

Any Supercharging fees will be automatically deducted from the payment card saved to your Tesla account. You can see a history of your charges by going to tesla.com, logging in, then selecting the History option.

Supercharging etiquette

- Don't leave your car plugged in when it has finished charging. You'll be fined $0.50 per minute, or $1.00 per minute if all the Supercharger bays are occupied. You might also be preventing someone else from charging.
- Never park in a charging bay. Again, you might be blocking someone else from charging.
- Don't charge above 80% unless you *really* need to.
- Help other owners if they're struggling. Not everyone knows which cable to use, how to end the charge, etc.
- Always unwind the cable and put it back when you're finished.
- Make sure the car is actually charging if you leave it unattended.
- If the Supercharger unit is damaged or charging unusually slowly, then you'll find a support number on the side of the charger.

Charging Your Car

Charging Speeds

Don't worry if you plug into a supercharger and see slow charging speeds. There's nothing wrong with the car or the supercharger. Instead, it's likely being affected by a range of physical and environmental factors…

The car's battery is cold

The colder the battery, the slower it will charge. This means you'll tend to see slower charging speeds when you've only driven a few miles to the Supercharger, as the car's batteries won't have had time to warm up. In sub-minus temperatures, the car's battery may never warm enough before reaching a Supercharger.

You're sharing the power

Try not to supercharge in a bay adjacent to another Tesla. That's because parallel supercharger bays (for example, 1A and 1B) share the same power source. By sharing power with another car, you're likely to see slower supercharging speeds. If you're using a V3 Supercharger this doesn't count - each stall has it's own power source.

How to achieve quicker charging speeds:

Warm the car's battery before arriving. You can do this in a number of ways:

- Set the Supercharger as a destination on the car's touchscreen. This will tell the vehicle to warm the batteries up as you drive to the Supercharger, AKA preconditioning.
- Use the mobile app to preheat the cabin. This will also warm the batteries.
- Turn off Range Mode in a Model S or X. This will let the car use more energy to warm the batteries.
- Charge during or after a long drive, as the batteries will be heated from dispensing electrons along the way.

> **Supercharger speeds based on temperature:**
>
> These are the charging speeds you can expect to receive based on the temperature of the battery cells in your Tesla:
> - 19c or lower: 60kW
> - 23c or lower: 95kW
> - 40c or higher is required for maximum charging speeds.

Charging Your Car

Charging at Public Networks

Learn how to find the nearest public chargers...

The sheer number of charging networks around the world is pretty staggering. As the EV market continues to grow, a number of companies are starting to realize that providing electricity for drivers is a potential gold mine of revenue. Alas, there are pros and cons to the current situation...

A massive number of charging networks have sprung up over the last few years, each trying to carve out a niche for themselves. To give a few examples:

Ultra rapid networks (100 Kw+)
- Tesla Supercharger
- Electrify America
- Fastned
- Ionity
- Instavolt
- Volta

Rapid charging networks (≤50 Kw)
- Tesla Destination Chargers
- ChargePoint
- Chargemaster
- EVgo
- Shell Recharge
- Ecotricity (UK)

Slow chargers (6 Kw+)
- Pod Point (UK)
- Polar (UK)

Every charging network has its own method of making a payment and starting a charge. Some require you to use a mobile app, a few need an RFID card, while others accept contactless payments. Google each network, check them out and sign up for an account/RFID card if required.

> Public charging tip: If you're planning to charge at a public network, keep your Type 2 cable stored somewhere in the car (the frunk is usually a good place), as you'll need it to charge at Type 2 points.

Chapter 4

Finding a public charger

If you're traveling to somewhere you've never visited before, then it's not a good idea to just turn up and hope that you'll find a public charge point. That's because charge points are rarely signposted, and your car doesn't know how to find them (it can only find Tesla Superchargers). Instead, plan ahead by either using an app on your phone or one of a number of websites that list public charging networks. Here are a few:

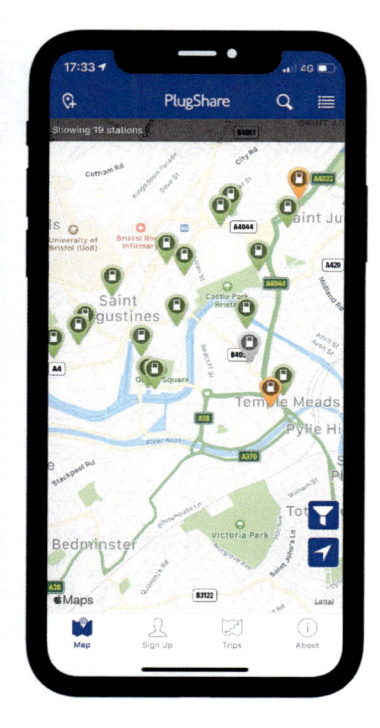

PlugShare
www.plugshare.com

Nearly every public charge point is listed on a map view, with filters for choosing plug type, network, and even amenities.

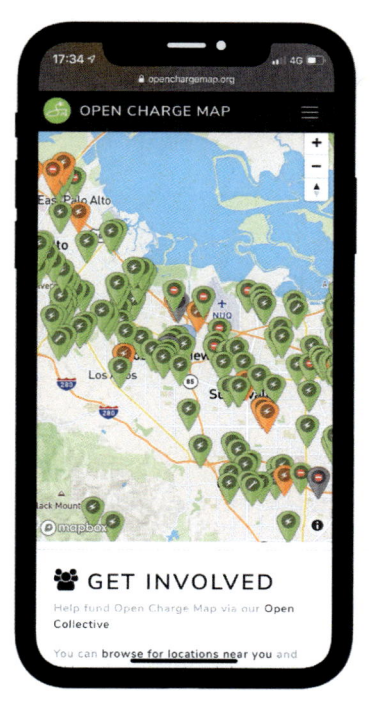

Open Charge Map
www.openchargemap.org

Think of it like Wikipedia, but for charging networks. You'll find a filterable map of public networks and charge points for the entire globe.

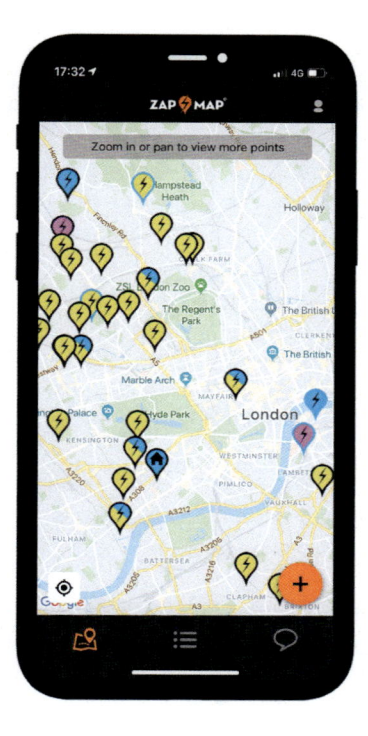

Zap-Map
www.zap-map.com

The best website for finding charge points in the United Kingdom, with filters for searching specific networks and socket types.

Unlike traditional gas stations, where there might be dozens of pumps available at any one time, public charge points are often limited to just one or two sockets. If you're lucky, then you'll arrive to find one free (and working), but if you're unlucky, then you might find the socket already in use or blocked by a traditional gas-guzzling vehicle.

Finding a free charge point doesn't necessarily mean driving from one to another. Instead, you can nearly always get a live status of the charge points in your area by using the respective apps for each network. To give an example, I live in a city called Exeter. Nearly all of the parking lots in the area have charge points that are free to use, and they're all run by a network called Pod Point. If I'm planning to visit the city center I usually open the Pod Point app, go to the map view, and see which charge points are available. I can always find a free charger at at least one of the parking lots, which means I don't have to try my luck as I travel from one to another. You can do the same thing with all the major charging networks around the world — they all have apps which provide a live status of every charge point. Follow this procedure before you head out and you'll nearly always find a free socket to plug into.

73

The Touchscreen Explained

The touchscreen within every Tesla is one of its most essential components. Not only does it provide critical driving information on the Model 3 and Y, but it also enables the driver to set a destination, monitor Autopilot, play media, and configure the car in a massive number of ways.

This chapter is here to explain how the map works, how to read the Autopilot display, and what all those unexplained toggle buttons and settings are for...

An Overview of Navigation	76
An Overview of the Driver's Display	77
Quick Controls	78
Suspension (Model S & X)	79
Lights	80
Locks (Model 3 & Y)	81
Display	82
Driving	84
Autopilot	85
Navigation	86
Safety & Security	87
Service	88
Software	89

75

The Touchscreen Explained

An Overview of Navigation

Get to grips with all the buttons and shortcuts on the navigation view...

If you've ever used Google Maps to explore the world then you'll feel right at home in your Tesla, because it uses the same system to render the world, display live traffic and find information. Whichever Tesla you have, the mapping system is fairly intuitive and easy to use. Nevertheless, here are a few of its features explained...

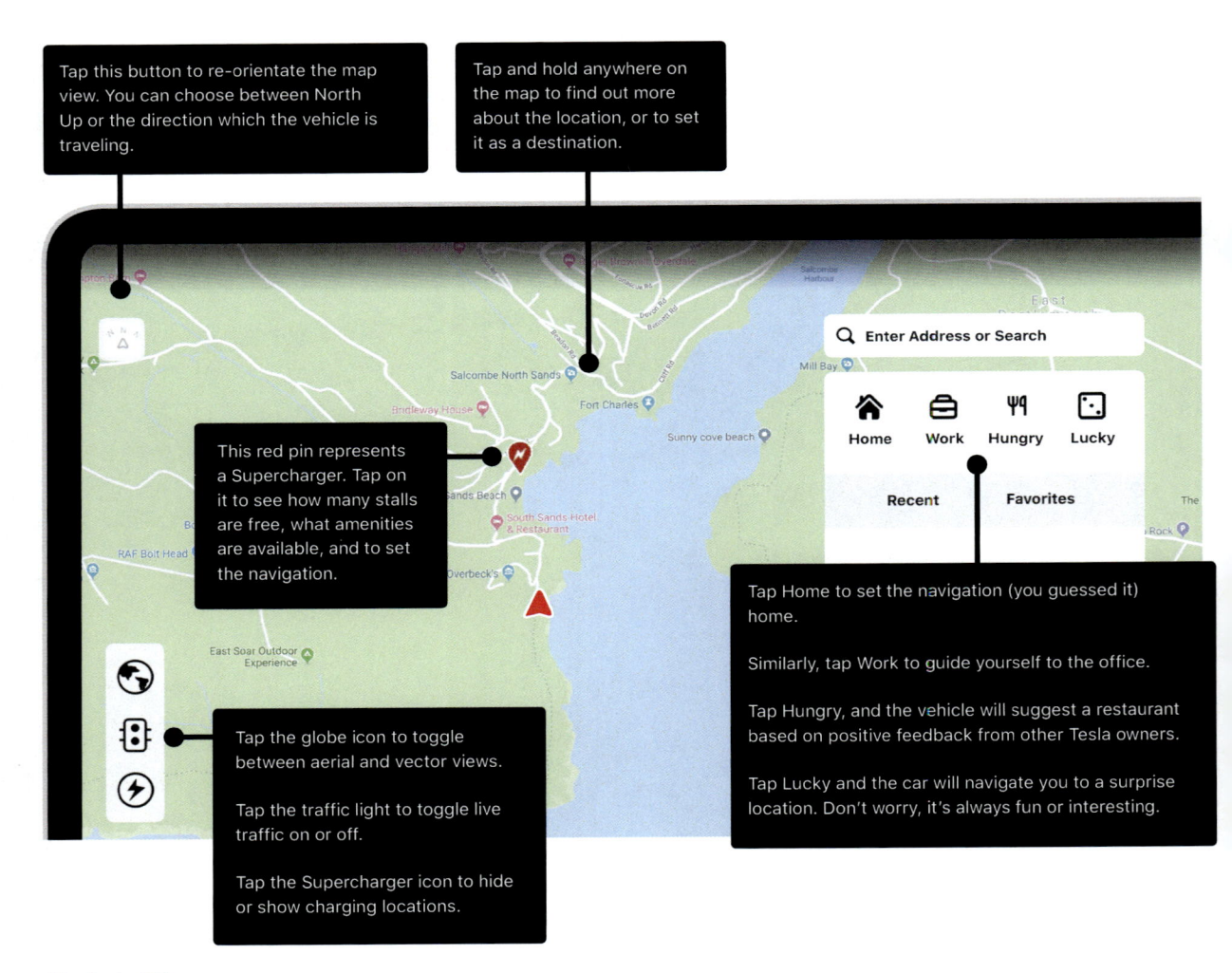

Tap this button to re-orientate the map view. You can choose between North Up or the direction which the vehicle is traveling.

Tap and hold anywhere on the map to find out more about the location, or to set it as a destination.

This red pin represents a Supercharger. Tap on it to see how many stalls are free, what amenities are available, and to set the navigation.

Tap the globe icon to toggle between aerial and vector views.

Tap the traffic light to toggle live traffic on or off.

Tap the Supercharger icon to hide or show charging locations.

Tap Home to set the navigation (you guessed it) home.

Similarly, tap Work to guide yourself to the office.

Tap Hungry, and the vehicle will suggest a restaurant based on positive feedback from other Tesla owners.

Tap Lucky and the car will navigate you to a surprise location. Don't worry, it's always fun or interesting.

Quick Tips:

- When you're ready to go home, just drag the Navigate bar downwards with your finger and the system will automatically calculate a route. If you're already at home, then the system will navigate you to work.

- If you regularly visit a location, search for it then tap the star icon to save it as a Favorite.

Chapter 5

An Overview of the Driver's Display

How to read and interact with the Autopilot view of the road ahead...

One of the most interesting parts of the touchscreen is the Driver's Display view. It shows key information about speed, energy, and a rendering of the world around your vehicle. Not everything is shown, just the most important parts such as lane lines, other vehicles, traffic lights, stop signs and traffic cones.

Here's an overview of the Driver's Display on the Model 3 and Y. On S and X, you'll find the same information in a slightly different configuration in the center of the instrument panel...

A dotted line here means the battery is still cold, which limits the strength of regenerative breaking.

Tap on the speed limit and the vehicle will match its speed.

You can move the Autopilot view around the car by using your fingers.

Swipe across the bottom of the panel to see current energy usage or tire pressure.

77

The Touchscreen Explained

Quick Controls

Quickly access the most commonly used controls in your car...

Tap the menu button, and the Quick Controls panel is the first thing to appear. It's packed with settings and toggle switches, especially on the Model 3 and Model Y which have less physical controls for things such as the windscreen wiper and high beams. Here are the less apparent settings and controls explained...

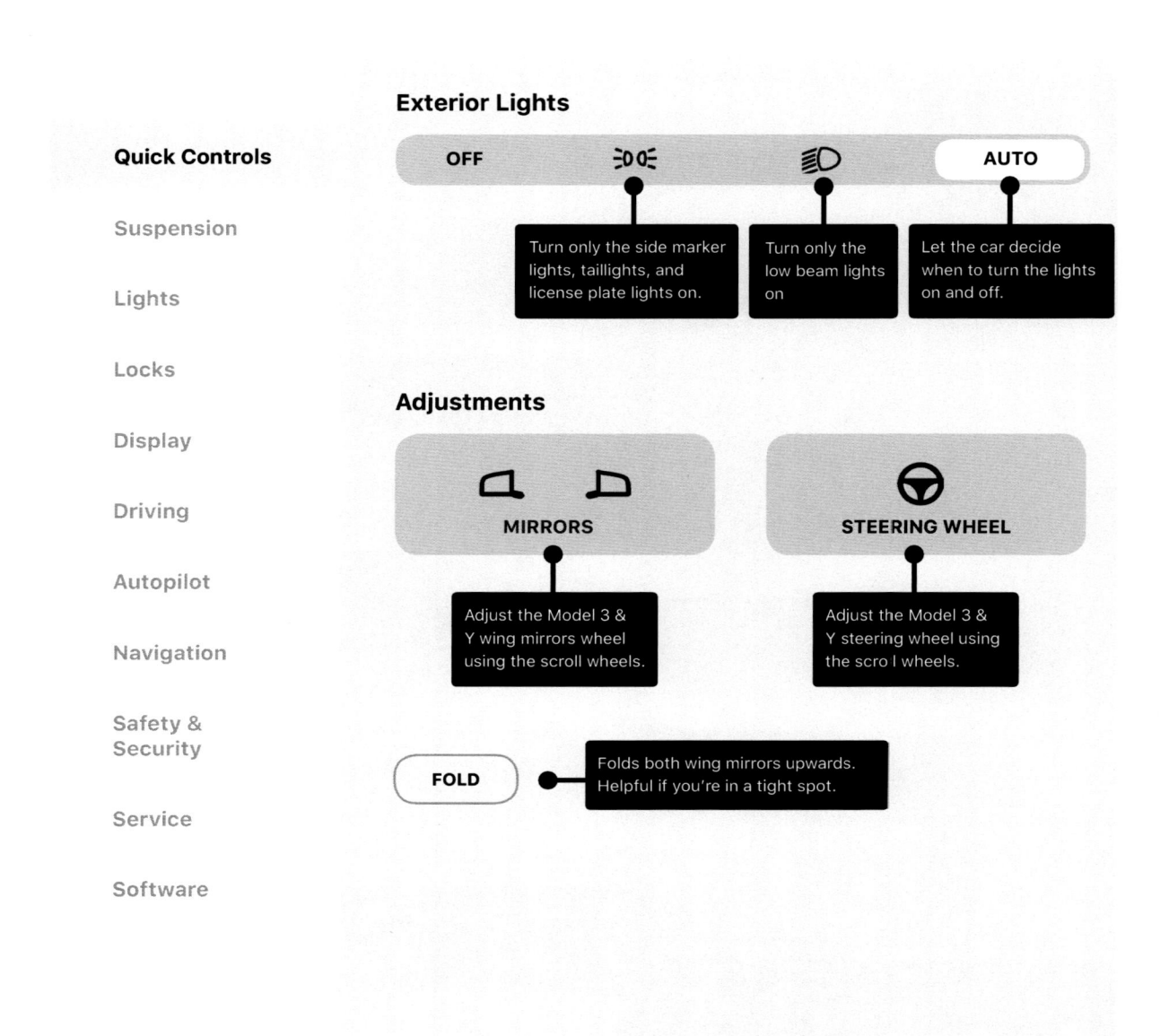

Quick Controls

Suspension

Lights

Locks

Display

Driving

Autopilot

Navigation

Safety & Security

Service

Software

Exterior Lights

| OFF | ≡O≡ | ≡O | AUTO |

- Turn only the side marker lights, taillights, and license plate lights on.
- Turn only the low beam lights on
- Let the car decide when to turn the lights on and off.

Adjustments

MIRRORS — Adjust the Model 3 & Y wing mirrors wheel using the scroll wheels.

STEERING WHEEL — Adjust the Model 3 & Y steering wheel using the scroll wheels.

FOLD — Folds both wing mirrors upwards. Helpful if you're in a tight spot.

78

Chapter 5

Suspension (Model S & X)

Raise or lower the suspension depending on terrain...

If you're lucky enough to drive a Model S or X, then you'll no doubt have noticed the Suspension menu. It enables you to raise the suspension or lower it at any time - even while you're driving. You might want to raise the suspension when you're traveling over rough terrain, or when you need to climb an uneven slope. Lowering it is a good idea when you're traveling at speed on the freeway, as the lower the space beneath the car, the lower the drag, which means you'll get more range out of a single charge...

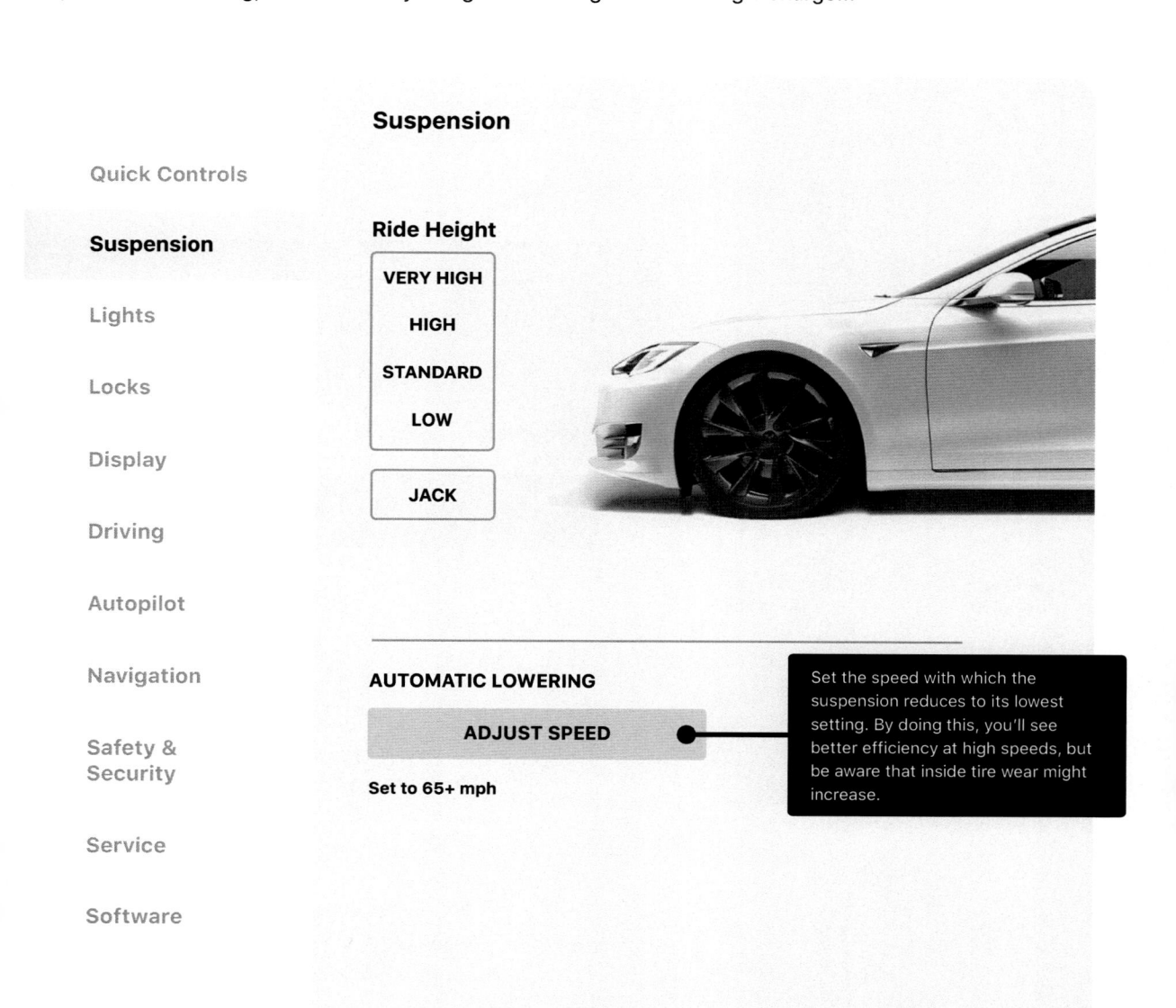

Quick Controls

Suspension

Lights

Locks

Display

Driving

Autopilot

Navigation

Safety & Security

Service

Software

Suspension

Ride Height

| VERY HIGH |
| HIGH |
| STANDARD |
| LOW |

| JACK |

AUTOMATIC LOWERING

| ADJUST SPEED |

Set to 65+ mph

> Set the speed with which the suspension reduces to its lowest setting. By doing this, you'll see better efficiency at high speeds, but be aware that inside tire wear might increase.

79

The Touchscreen Explained

Lights

Toggle ambient lighting or the high beams...

Ok, so most of the settings in this panel make complete sense. Nevertheless, here's a brief explanation of each...

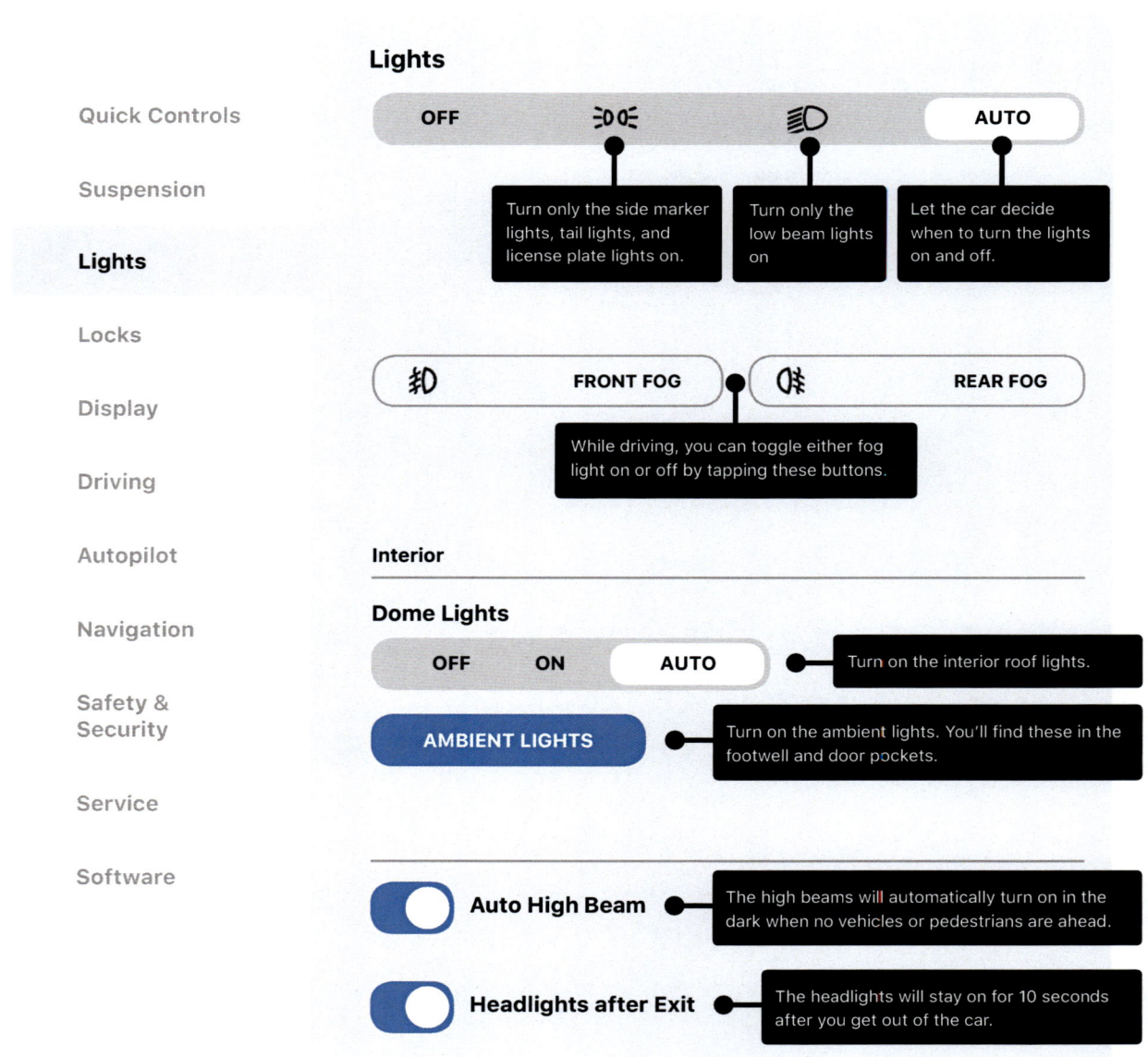

Quick Controls

Suspension

Lights

Locks

Display

Driving

Autopilot

Navigation

Safety & Security

Service

Software

Lights

| OFF | ⫶O⫶ | ⫶D | AUTO |

- Turn only the side marker lights, tail lights, and license plate lights on.
- Turn only the low beam lights on
- Let the car decide when to turn the lights on and off.

| FRONT FOG | REAR FOG |

While driving, you can toggle either fog light on or off by tapping these buttons.

Interior

Dome Lights

| OFF | ON | AUTO | — Turn on the interior roof lights.

AMBIENT LIGHTS — Turn on the ambient lights. You'll find these in the footwell and door pockets.

Auto High Beam — The high beams will automatically turn on in the dark when no vehicles or pedestrians are ahead.

Headlights after Exit — The headlights will stay on for 10 seconds after you get out of the car.

Chapter 5

Locks (Model 3 & Y)

Manage the keys associated with your car...

Both Model 3 and the Model Y come with two credit card-sized keys, but it's also possible to unlock and control both these vehicles using a mobile phone, or even multiple mobile phones if needed. All of these keys and mobile devices can be managed from the Locks menu. Here's a quick overview of how it works...

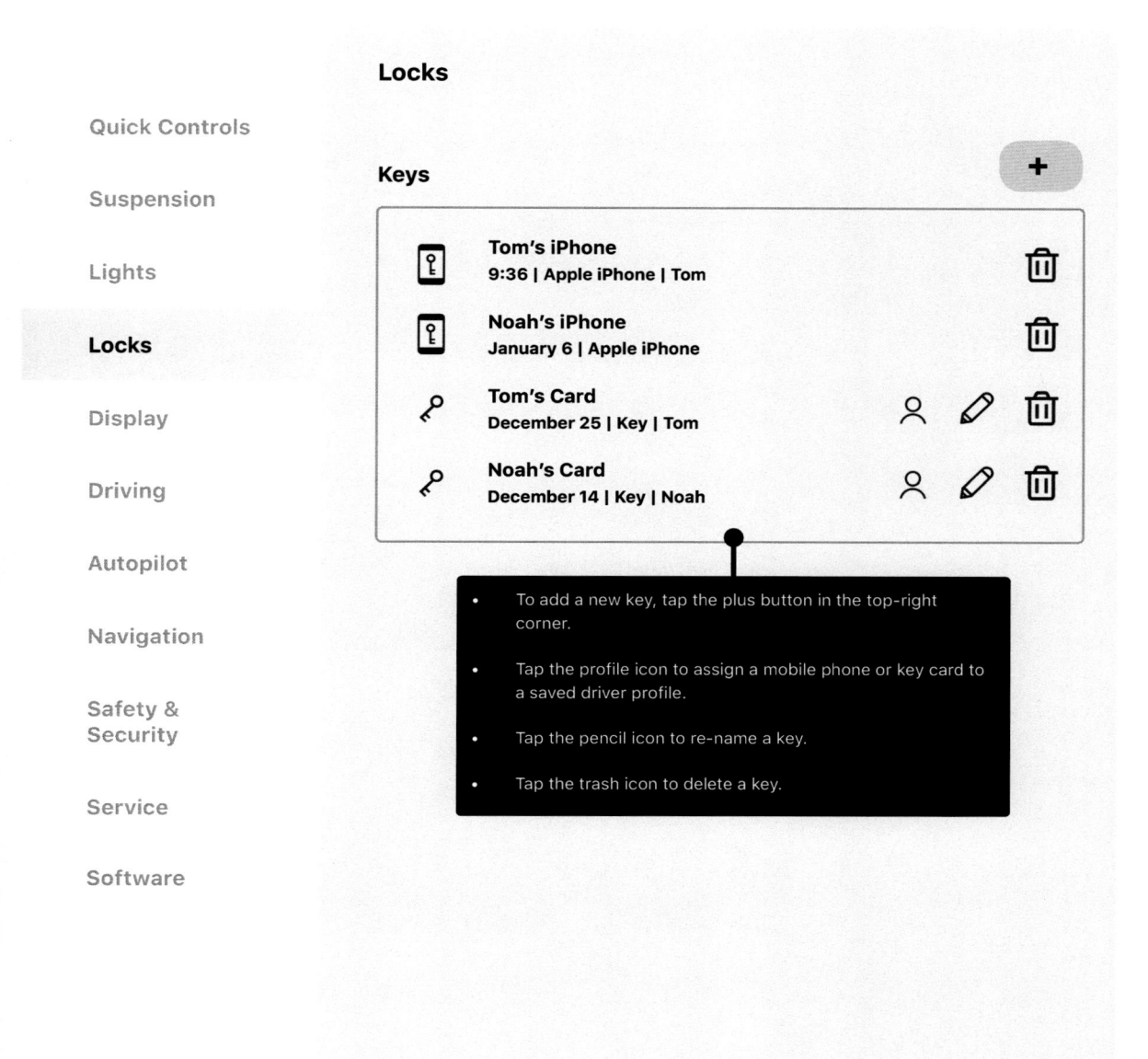

Quick Controls

Suspension

Lights

Locks

Display

Driving

Autopilot

Navigation

Safety & Security

Service

Software

Locks

Keys

Tom's iPhone
9:36 | Apple iPhone | Tom

Noah's iPhone
January 6 | Apple iPhone

Tom's Card
December 25 | Key | Tom

Noah's Card
December 14 | Key | Noah

- To add a new key, tap the plus button in the top-right corner.
- Tap the profile icon to assign a mobile phone or key card to a saved driver profile.
- Tap the pencil icon to re-name a key.
- Tap the trash icon to delete a key.

The Touchscreen Explained

Display

Alter a wide range of visual-based settings…

With the large touchscreen being such a vital piece of equipment in every Tesla, perhaps it's not surprising that the Display menu has the most wide-ranging assortment of toggles and settings. From here it's possible to switch between Day and Night mode, change languages, time formats, and even disable mobile connectivity…

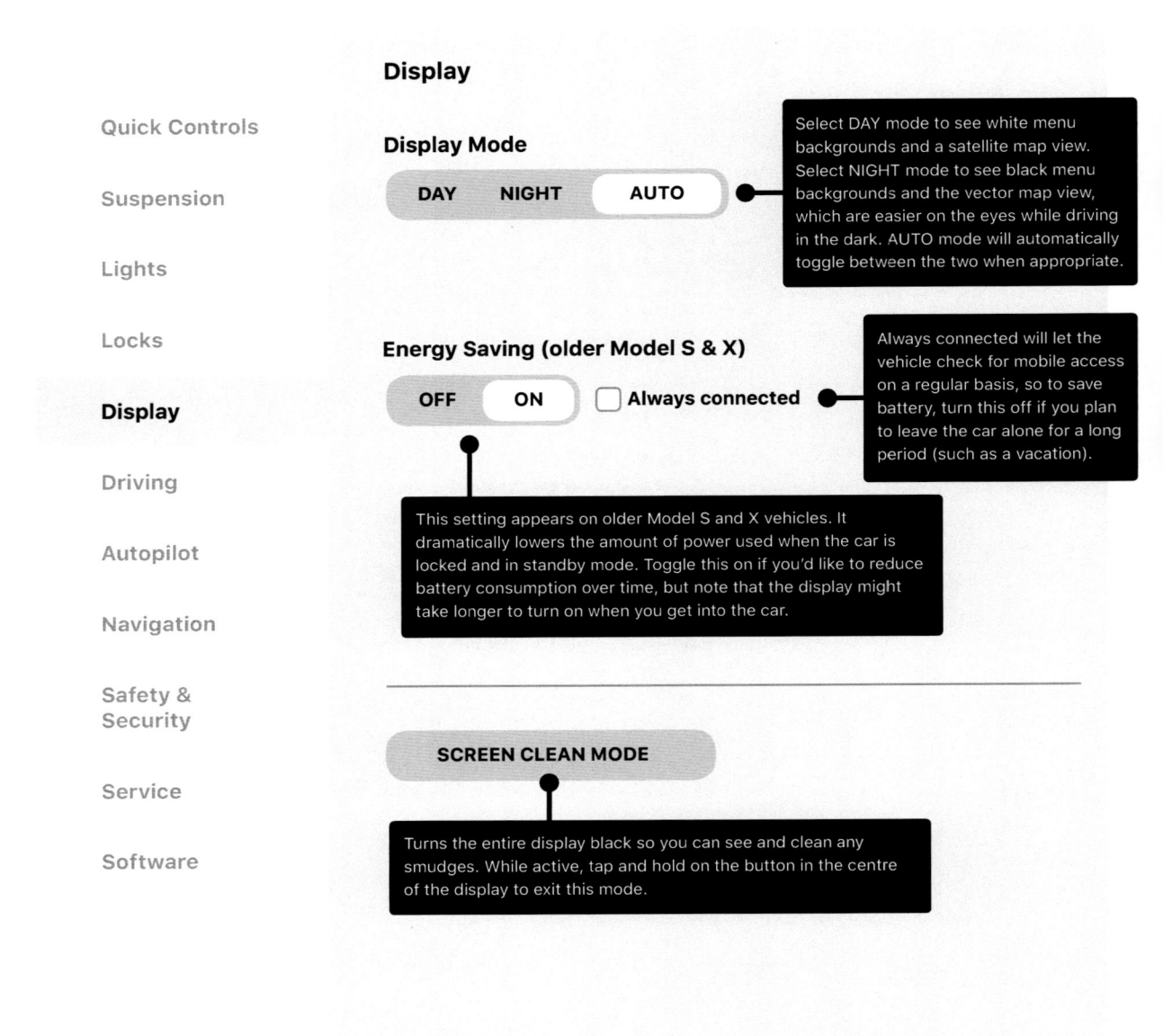

Quick Controls

Suspension

Lights

Locks

Display

Driving

Autopilot

Navigation

Safety & Security

Service

Software

Display

Display Mode

DAY NIGHT **AUTO**

Select DAY mode to see white menu backgrounds and a satellite map view. Select NIGHT mode to see black menu backgrounds and the vector map view, which are easier on the eyes while driving in the dark. AUTO mode will automatically toggle between the two when appropriate.

Energy Saving (older Model S & X)

OFF ON ☐ Always connected

Always connected will let the vehicle check for mobile access on a regular basis, so to save battery, turn this off if you plan to leave the car alone for a long period (such as a vacation).

This setting appears on older Model S and X vehicles. It dramatically lowers the amount of power used when the car is locked and in standby mode. Toggle this on if you'd like to reduce battery consumption over time, but note that the display might take longer to turn on when you get into the car.

SCREEN CLEAN MODE

Turns the entire display black so you can see and clean any smudges. While active, tap and hold on the button in the centre of the display to exit this mode.

Chapter 5

Display (continued)

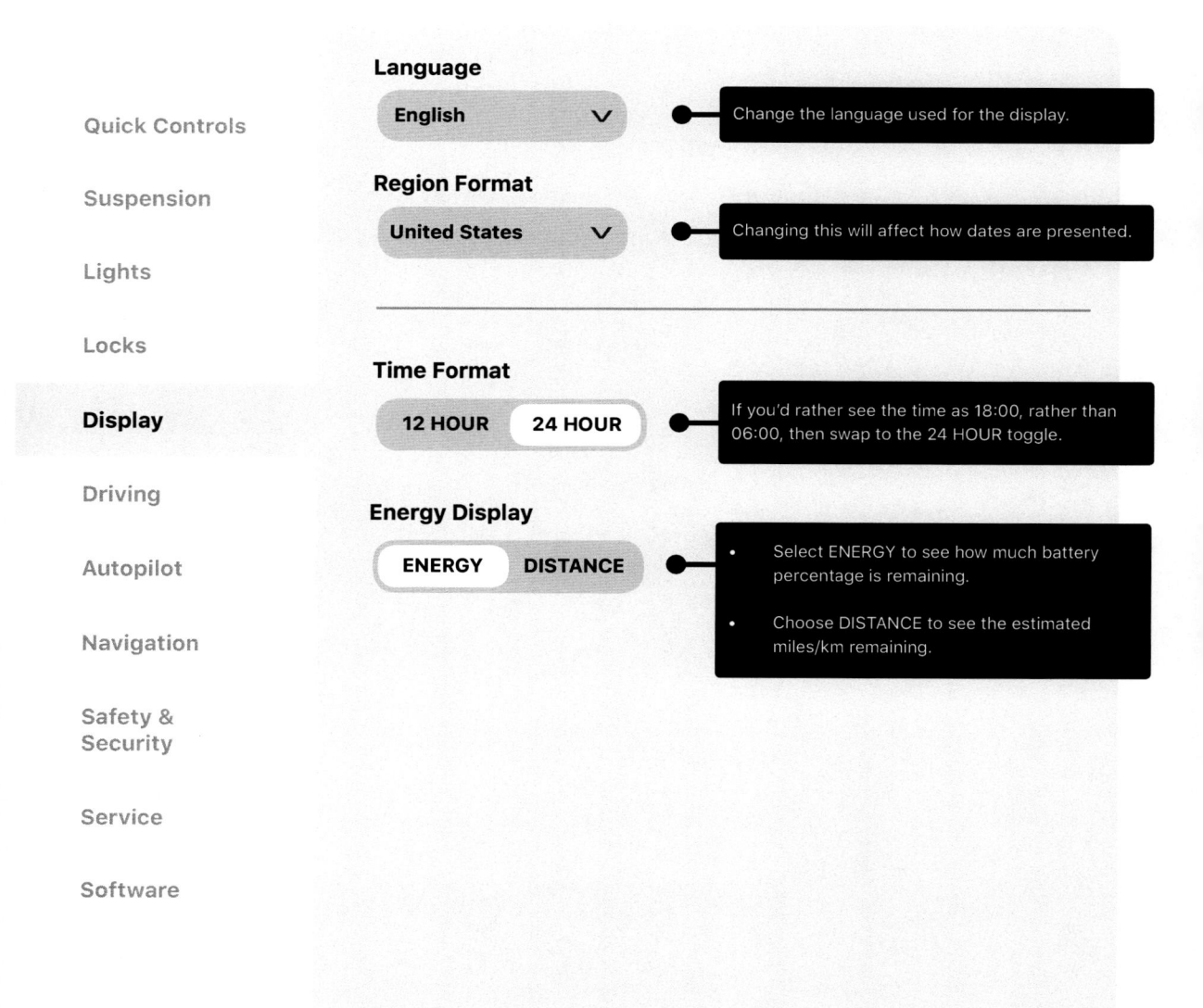

Quick Controls

Suspension

Lights

Locks

Display

Driving

Autopilot

Navigation

Safety & Security

Service

Software

Language

[English ⌄] ●— Change the language used for the display.

Region Format

[United States ⌄] ●— Changing this will affect how dates are presented.

Time Format

[**12 HOUR** | 24 HOUR] ●— If you'd rather see the time as 18:00, rather than 06:00, then swap to the 24 HOUR toggle.

Energy Display

[**ENERGY** | DISTANCE] ●—
- Select ENERGY to see how much battery percentage is remaining.
- Choose DISTANCE to see the estimated miles/km remaining.

83

The Touchscreen Explained

Driving

Adjust the strength of the accelerator and brake pedals...

Unlike traditional automobiles, electric cars can use a technology called regenerative braking to gather back energy as the car slows down. Not only does this increase efficiency, but it also enables drivers to use a single pedal to start and stop their vehicles. The Driving menu enables you to configure this technology to suit your needs, while also adjusting how strong (or powerful) the accelerator pedal is...

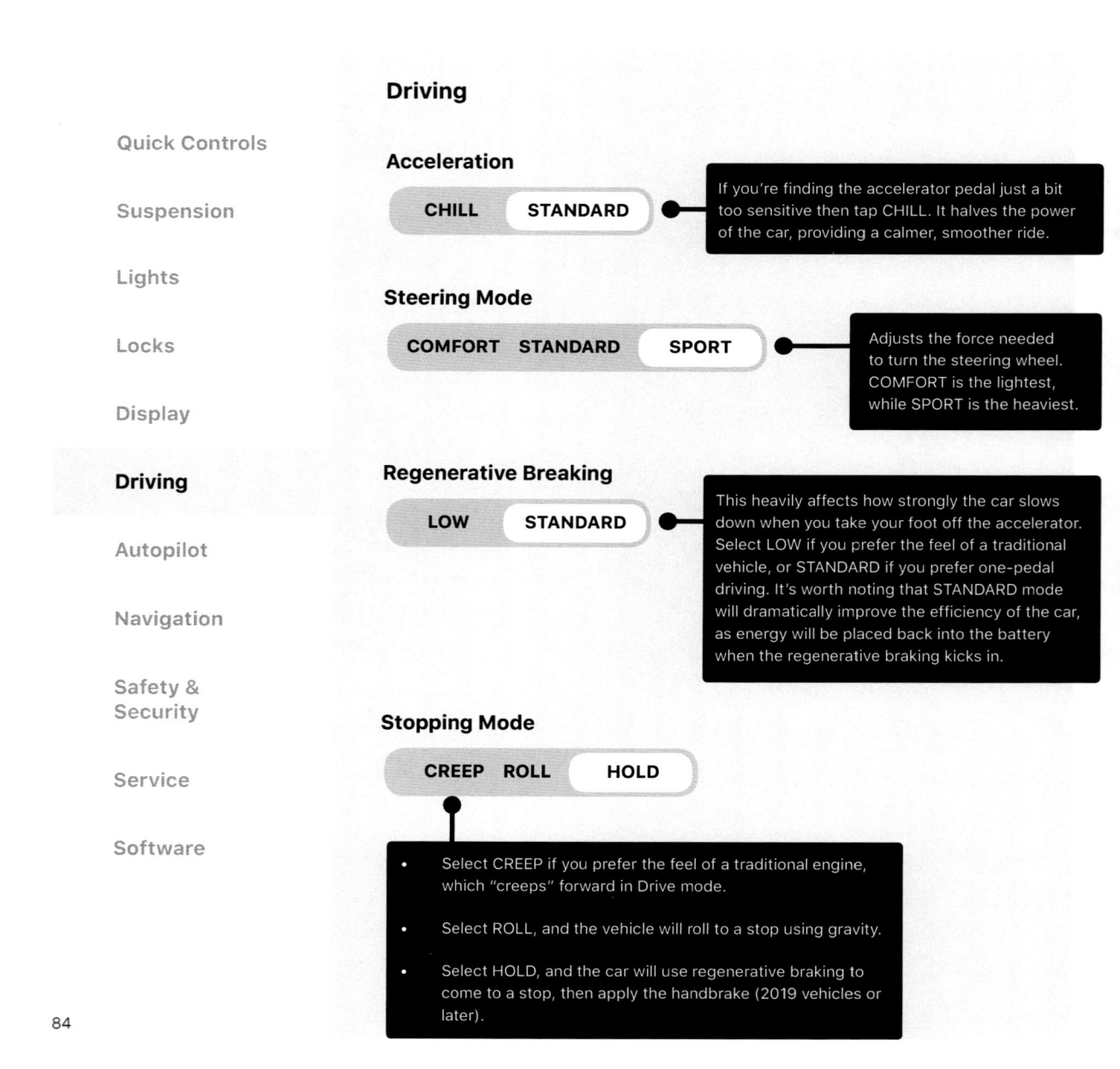

Quick Controls

Suspension

Lights

Locks

Display

Driving

Autopilot

Navigation

Safety & Security

Service

Software

Driving

Acceleration

CHILL   STANDARD

If you're finding the accelerator pedal just a bit too sensitive then tap CHILL. It halves the power of the car, providing a calmer, smoother ride.

Steering Mode

COMFORT   STANDARD   SPORT

Adjusts the force needed to turn the steering wheel. COMFORT is the lightest, while SPORT is the heaviest.

Regenerative Breaking

LOW   STANDARD

This heavily affects how strongly the car slows down when you take your foot off the accelerator. Select LOW if you prefer the feel of a traditional vehicle, or STANDARD if you prefer one-pedal driving. It's worth noting that STANDARD mode will dramatically improve the efficiency of the car, as energy will be placed back into the battery when the regenerative braking kicks in.

Stopping Mode

CREEP   ROLL   HOLD

- Select CREEP if you prefer the feel of a traditional engine, which "creeps" forward in Drive mode.

- Select ROLL, and the vehicle will roll to a stop using gravity.

- Select HOLD, and the car will use regenerative braking to come to a stop, then apply the handbrake (2019 vehicles or later).

Chapter 5

Autopilot

Customize Autopilot to drive how you like...

Autopilot is perhaps the best part of owning a Tesla. It takes the stress out of a long drive by steering and following highway traffic, monitors the vehicles around your own, and can even make an emergency stop if it thinks you're about to hit an object or pedestrian. Here are a few of the less obvious settings explained...

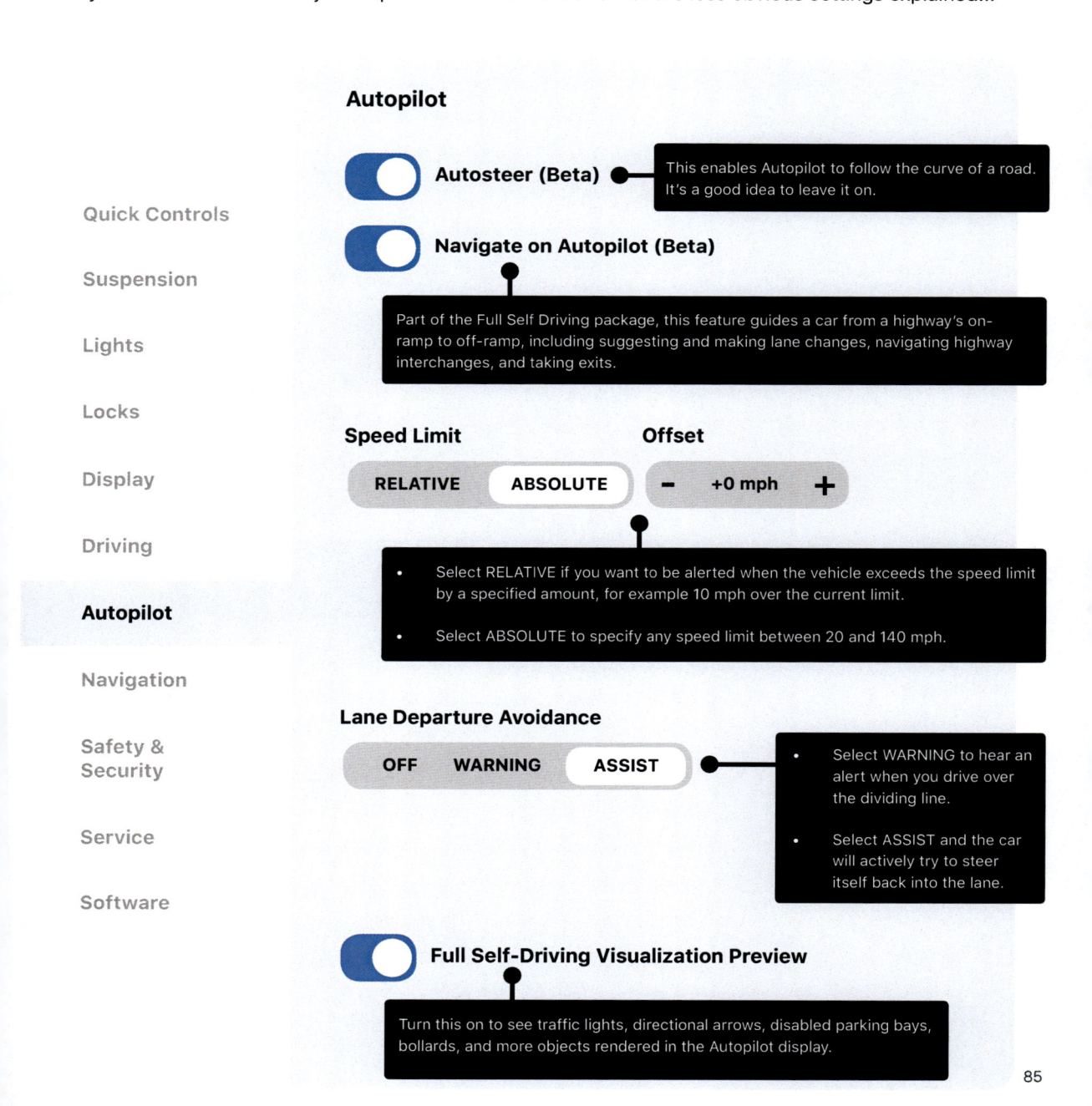

Quick Controls

Suspension

Lights

Locks

Display

Driving

Autopilot

Navigation

Safety & Security

Service

Software

Autopilot

Autosteer (Beta) — This enables Autopilot to follow the curve of a road. It's a good idea to leave it on.

Navigate on Autopilot (Beta)

Part of the Full Self Driving package, this feature guides a car from a highway's on-ramp to off-ramp, including suggesting and making lane changes, navigating highway interchanges, and taking exits.

Speed Limit — RELATIVE / **ABSOLUTE**

Offset — − +0 mph +

- Select RELATIVE if you want to be alerted when the vehicle exceeds the speed limit by a specified amount, for example 10 mph over the current limit.
- Select ABSOLUTE to specify any speed limit between 20 and 140 mph.

Lane Departure Avoidance

OFF / WARNING / **ASSIST**

- Select WARNING to hear an alert when you drive over the dividing line.
- Select ASSIST and the car will actively try to steer itself back into the lane.

Full Self-Driving Visualization Preview

Turn this on to see traffic lights, directional arrows, disabled parking bays, bollards, and more objects rendered in the Autopilot display.

85

The Touchscreen Explained

Navigation

Set Superchargers as waypoints, automatically plan trips and more...

You're going to spend a lot of time using the map to navigate from place to place, so it's a good idea to customize the navigation system for your needs. Here's a quick overview of the sliders and toggle switches found within the Navigation menu panel...

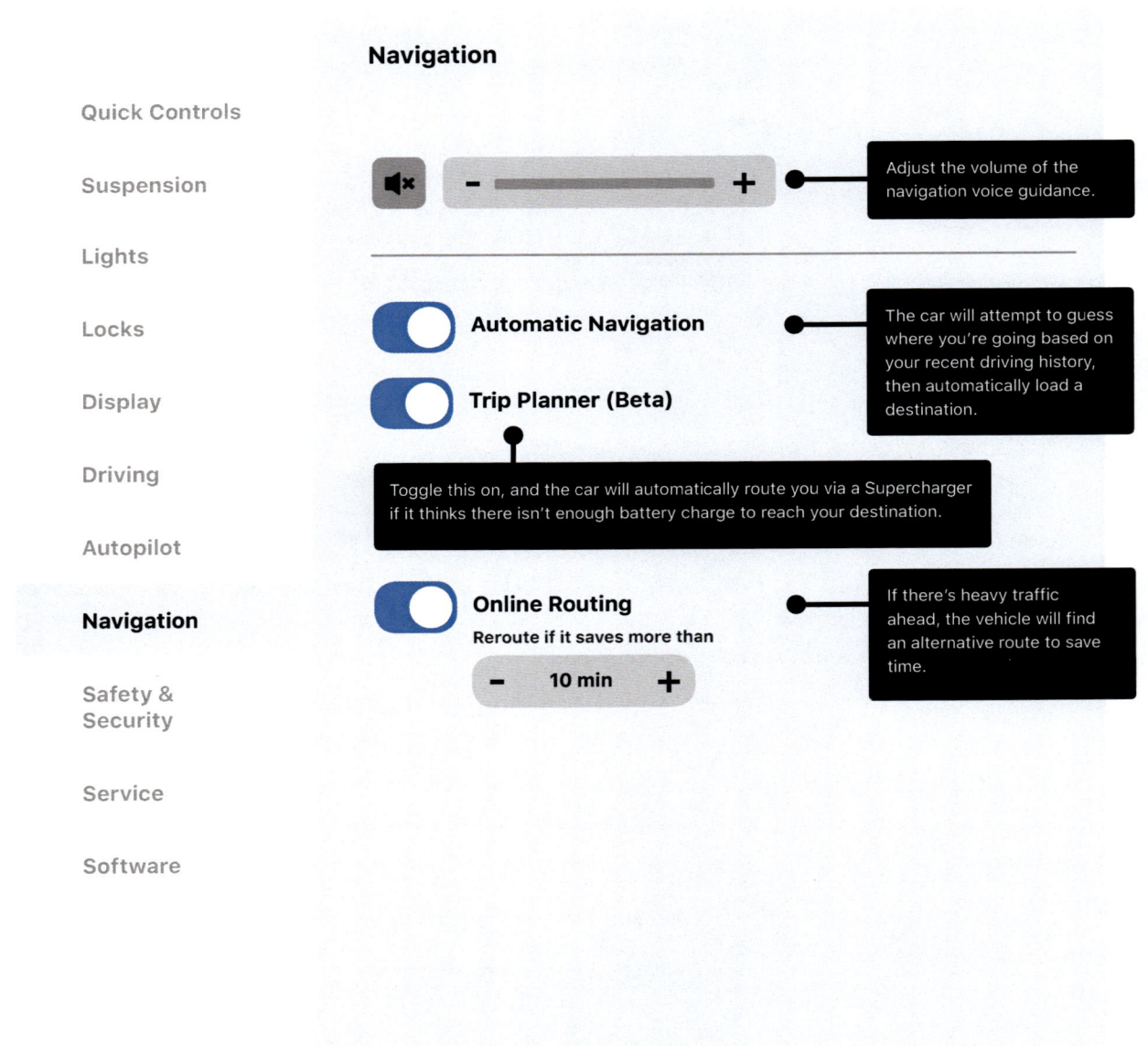

Quick Controls

Suspension

Lights

Locks

Display

Driving

Autopilot

Navigation

Safety & Security

Service

Software

Navigation

🔇 — ——————— + → Adjust the volume of the navigation voice guidance.

⬤ **Automatic Navigation** → The car will attempt to guess where you're going based on your recent driving history, then automatically load a destination.

⬤ **Trip Planner (Beta)**

Toggle this on, and the car will automatically route you via a Supercharger if it thinks there isn't enough battery charge to reach your destination.

⬤ **Online Routing**
Reroute if it saves more than
— 10 min +

If there's heavy traffic ahead, the vehicle will find an alternative route to save time.

Chapter 5

Safety & Security

Activate Sentry Mode, manage mobile access and more...

Tesla vehicles have some of the most advanced security features in the automotive world. There's Sentry Mode, which combines machine learning and the external cameras to watch for potential threats while the car is parked; then there's PIN to Drive, which prevents Drive mode from being activated without a 4-digit code...

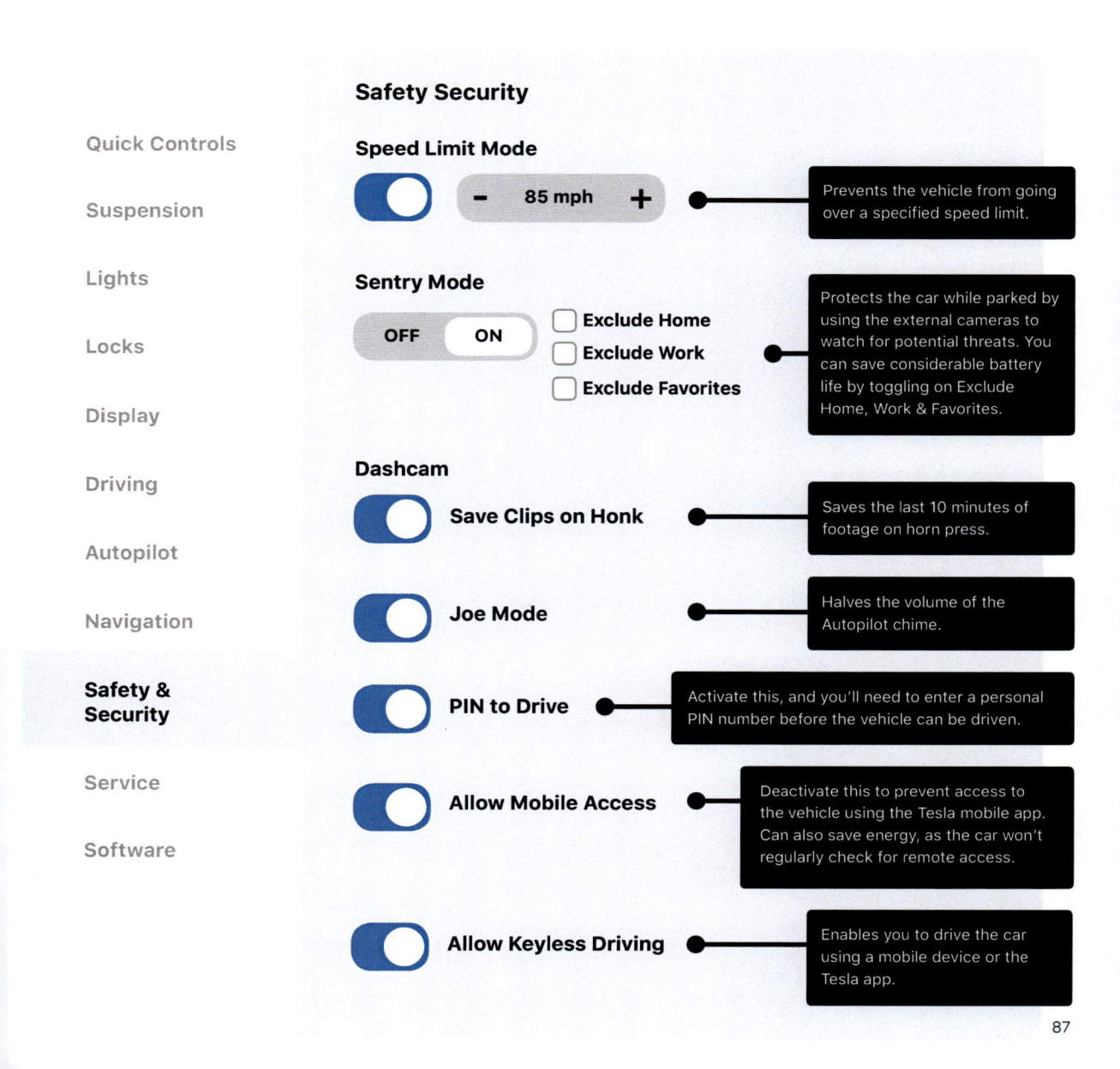

Quick Controls

Suspension

Lights

Locks

Display

Driving

Autopilot

Navigation

Safety & Security

Service

Software

Safety Security

Speed Limit Mode

— 85 mph +

Prevents the vehicle from going over a specified speed limit.

Sentry Mode

OFF / ON
☐ Exclude Home
☐ Exclude Work
☐ Exclude Favorites

Protects the car while parked by using the external cameras to watch for potential threats. You can save considerable battery life by toggling on Exclude Home, Work & Favorites.

Dashcam

Save Clips on Honk — Saves the last 10 minutes of footage on horn press.

Joe Mode — Halves the volume of the Autopilot chime.

PIN to Drive — Activate this, and you'll need to enter a personal PIN number before the vehicle can be driven.

Allow Mobile Access — Deactivate this to prevent access to the vehicle using the Tesla mobile app. Can also save energy, as the car won't regularly check for remote access.

Allow Keyless Driving — Enables you to drive the car using a mobile device or the Tesla app.

87

The Touchscreen Explained

Service

If you need to manually adjust the headlights, replace the wipers, or even tow the vehicle, this is the settings menu to visit...

You'll only need to visit this menu panel if something is wrong with your Tesla. Maybe the headlights of your Model 3 or Y need adjusting, or it's time to replace the windscreen wipers...

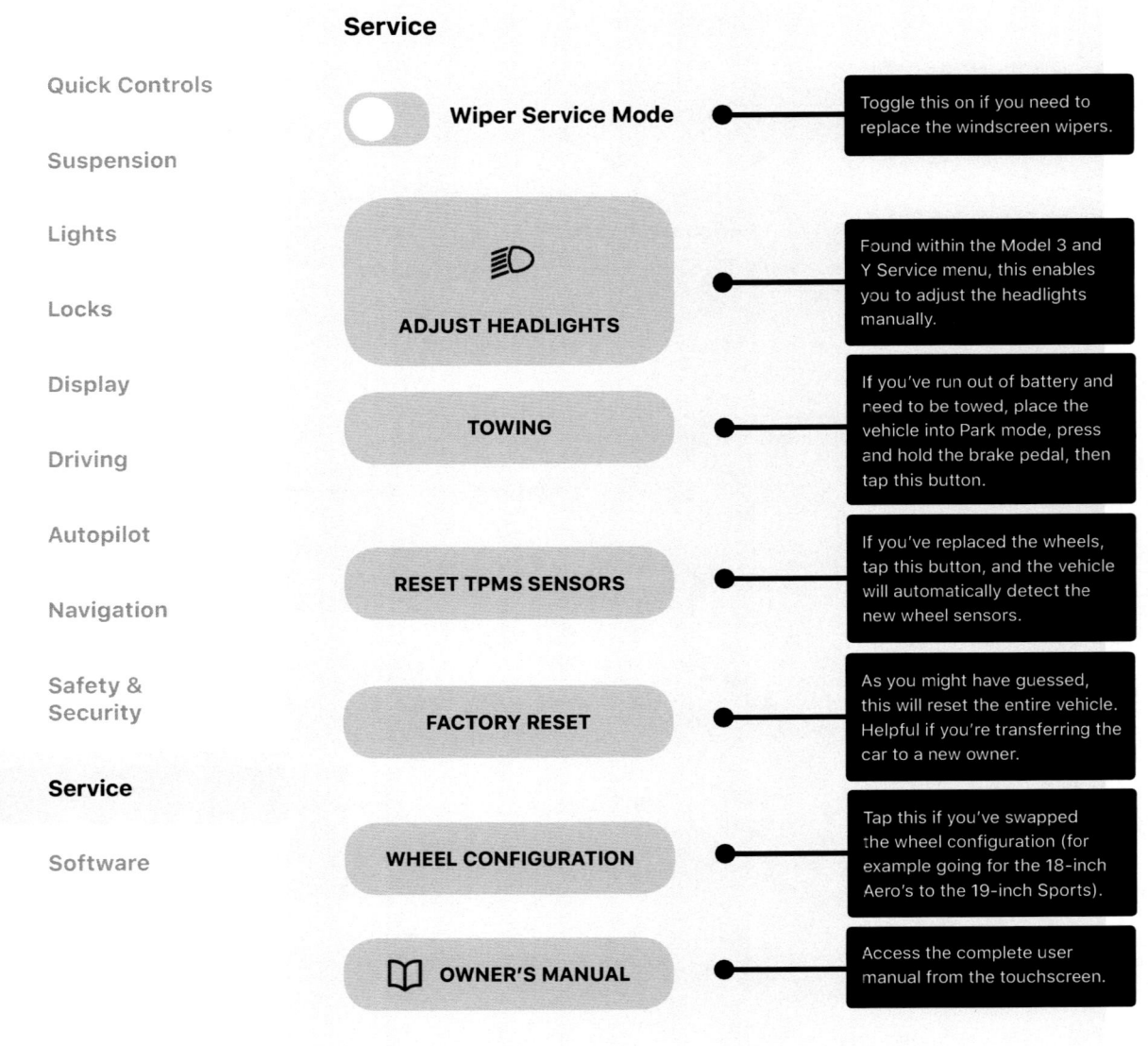

Quick Controls

Suspension

Lights

Locks

Display

Driving

Autopilot

Navigation

Safety & Security

Service

Software

Service

Wiper Service Mode — Toggle this on if you need to replace the windscreen wipers.

ADJUST HEADLIGHTS — Found within the Model 3 and Y Service menu, this enables you to adjust the headlights manually.

TOWING — If you've run out of battery and need to be towed, place the vehicle into Park mode, press and hold the brake pedal, then tap this button.

RESET TPMS SENSORS — If you've replaced the wheels, tap this button, and the vehicle will automatically detect the new wheel sensors.

FACTORY RESET — As you might have guessed, this will reset the entire vehicle. Helpful if you're transferring the car to a new owner.

WHEEL CONFIGURATION — Tap this if you've swapped the wheel configuration (for example going for the 18-inch Aero's to the 19-inch Sports).

OWNER'S MANUAL — Access the complete user manual from the touchscreen.

Chapter 5

Software

Check for the latest software updates for your vehicle...

Software updates are a regular occurrence for Tesla owners, and they can potentially introduce some massive changes. During 2019 alone, software updates added Tesla Cam, Sentry Mode, Autopilot improvements, Netflix, YouTube, 3D games, plus much much more...

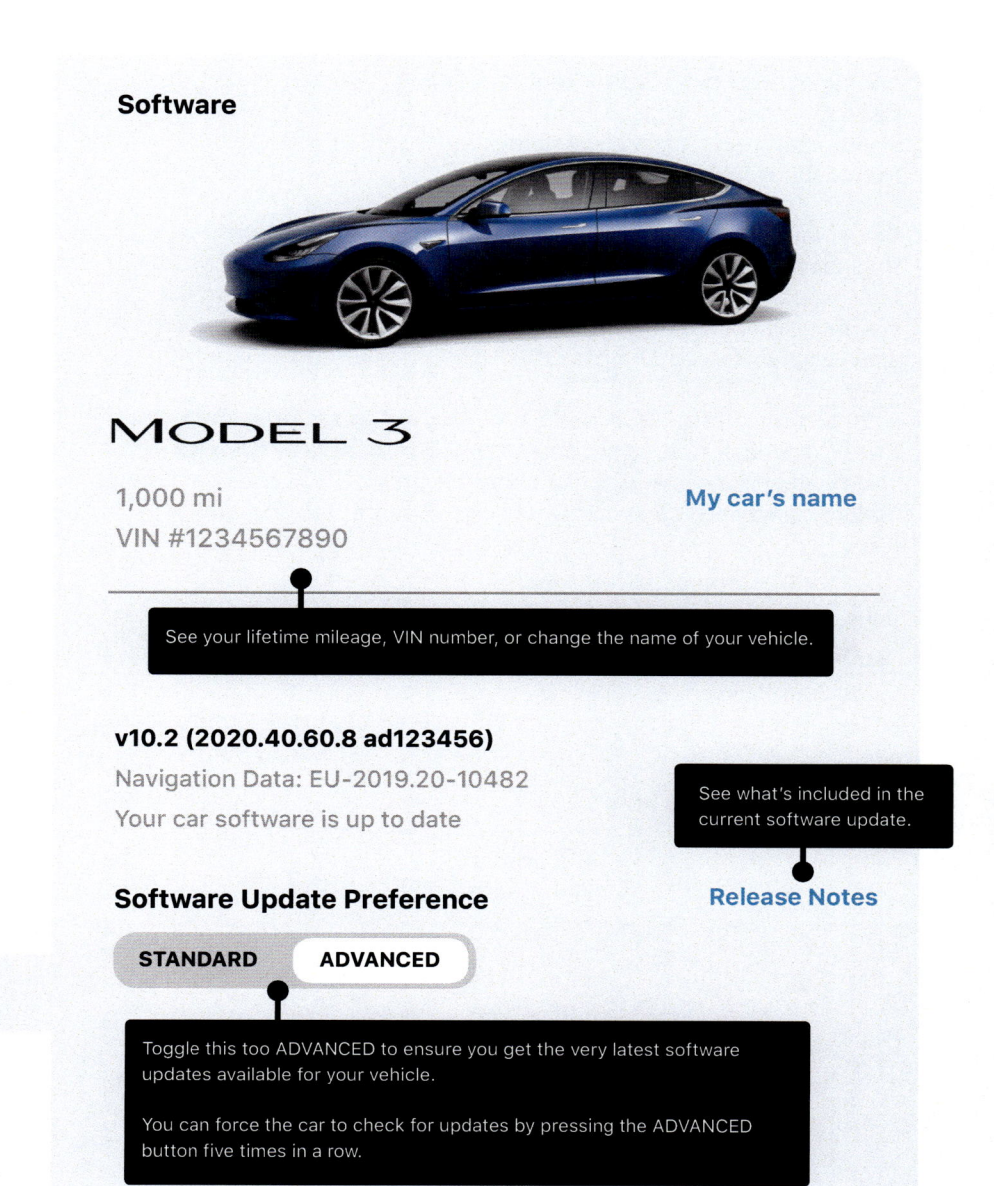

Quick Controls

Suspension

Lights

Locks

Display

Driving

Autopilot

Navigation

Safety & Security

Service

Software

Software

MODEL 3

1,000 mi

VIN #1234567890

My car's name

See your lifetime mileage, VIN number, or change the name of your vehicle.

v10.2 (2020.40.60.8 ad123456)

Navigation Data: EU-2019.20-10482

Your car software is up to date

See what's included in the current software update.

Release Notes

Software Update Preference

STANDARD ADVANCED

Toggle this too ADVANCED to ensure you get the very latest software updates available for your vehicle.

You can force the car to check for updates by pressing the ADVANCED button five times in a row.

89

In-Car Tech

Every Tesla vehicle is pretty much a computer on wheels. That's the realization most owners will come to once they've spent some time behind the wheel, because apart from the steering wheel, pedals and stalks, nearly everything else is controlled via the large touchscreen in the middle of the cabin.

These vast touchscreens offer a vast number of improvements over traditional car interior layouts. They offer the ability for Tesla to improve the user experience over time, introduce new features, improve the interface layout, and fix any bugs that might occur; just like modern smartphones, tablets and desktop PCs.

In 2019 alone, Tesla introduced Sentry Mode, a Dashcam feature, Netflix, YouTube, Dog mode, Camping mode, 3D games, AutoPilot visualizations, and so much more. This chapter will take a look at those features, enabling you to take advantage of all this new exciting in-car tech...

Voice Commands	92
The Toybox	94
Video Entertainment	96
Games	98
Dashcam	100
Sentry Mode & PIN to Drive	102
Go Camping in your Tesla	104

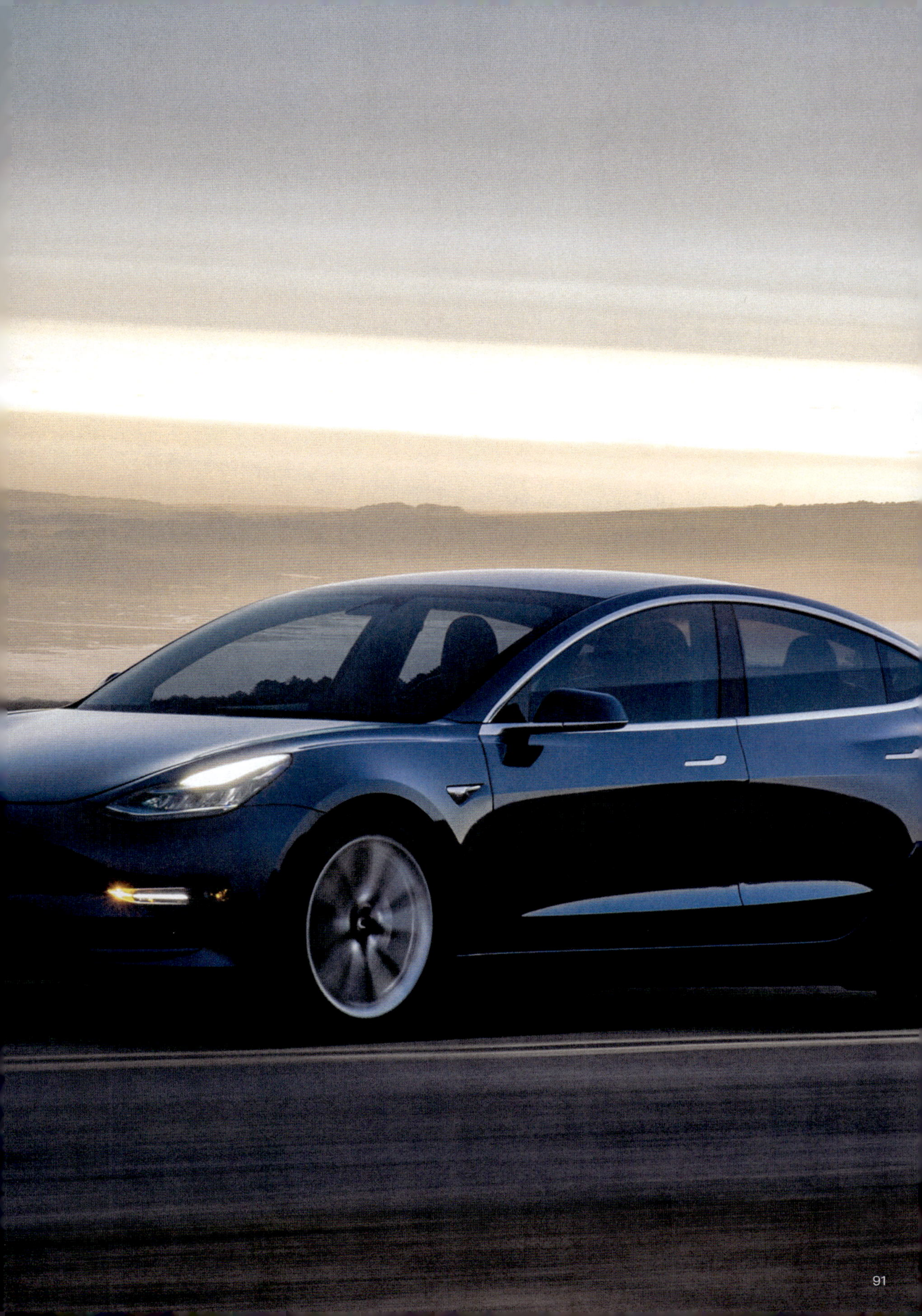

In-Car Tech

Voice Commands

Tell the car what to do, or even read your messages out-loud...

The massive touchscreen in every Tesla is easy to use when the vehicle is in Park mode, but when driving, it can be tricky to hit a button on the opposite side of the screen -- especially on a bumpy road. There's also the ethical question of whether you should be using a touchscreen at all while driving.

Thankfully, Tesla has implemented a series of voice commands which let you alter settings and toggle controls using only your voice. At the time of writing it's relatively limited, but Tesla hopes to continually improve and iterate this feature until it's the best -- and safest -- way to perform actions while on the move. Here's how it works:

To initiate a voice command, tap the microphone button on the touchscreen. Alternatively, press the right scroll button in a Model 3 or Y, or the voice command button on the Model S or X steering wheel. When you hear the tone, speak your command out loud. As you talk, the touchscreen will display an interpretation of your command. When you finish, tap the voice button again or wait for the command to initiate.

"Open the charge port"

Read out your messages:

With your phone connected to the car via Bluetooth, it's possible to view messages that you've received, have them read-out by the vehicle, and even reply using your voice.

To get started, tap the Bluetooth icon at the top of the display, and enable 'Sync Messages.' You can also choose to play a chime whenever a new text message is received by enabling 'Chime on New Message.'

To view messages that have been received, tap the arrow at the bottom of the display, choose Call, then tap Messages. You can read and reply to your messages by tapping on them in the list.

To have the car read out messages, press the right scroll wheel when a message arrives, and you'll hear its contents. To reply, press the right scroll wheel again and speak out loud. You can also view messages as they arrive via the 'Cards' section of the touchscreen.

Climate Commands:

- "Set the temperature to 70"
- "Set fan speed to 1/2/3/4/5/6"
- "Move air up/down"
- "Make it warmer"
- "Make it colder"
- "Turn on passenger seat heater"

Navigation Commands:

- "Show me nearby superchargers"
- "Take me home"
- "Navigate to Seattle"
- "Show traffic"
- "Show satellite view"
- "Zoom in maps"

Car Commands:

- "Lock the car"
- "Show me the rear camera"
- "Open the glovebox"
- "Open the charge port"
- "Turn on/off wipers"
- "Speed up wipers"
- "Adjust my right mirror"
- "Adjust the steering wheel"
- "Enable front/rear defroster"

Media Commands:

- "Play the Beatles"
- "Search for Joe Rogan podcast"
- "Pause the music"

Social Commands:

- "Call David"
- "Send a text message to Bob"

In-Car Tech

The Toybox

Keep yourself busy when charging the car...

There's no better way to demonstrate the quirky sense of humor Tesla has then by opening the Toybox in your Tesla. It's full of novel apps that serve no purpose other than to make people laugh; like Emissions Testing Mode, which enables you to play a fart noise on demand; or TRAX, which lets you create your very own multi-track songs.

To access the Toybox, tap the arrow on the bottom of the touchscreen, then choose Toybox. If you're using a fullscreen app, such as TRAX, and would like to access the brightness or volume controls, tap near the top of the screen and these will appear. You'll also see a small X in the top-right corner. This is how you close an app and return to the main touchscreen.

Chapter 6

Sketch Pad

Open the Sketch Pad app (the icon shows "Star Man" riding a red Tesla in space), and it's possible quickly doodle a note or create a masterpiece of pixels. It's a fairly basic app - there's no layer or animation support - but for passing the time it's a fun little app.

Emissions Testing Mode

Tap the whoopie cushion graphic and you'll access an app that's completely silly, but a lot of fun. To assign the whoopie cushion to a seat, simply tap on your seat of choice. Toggle "Fart on demand", and you can trigger the sound effect by pressing the left scroll button on the steering wheel.

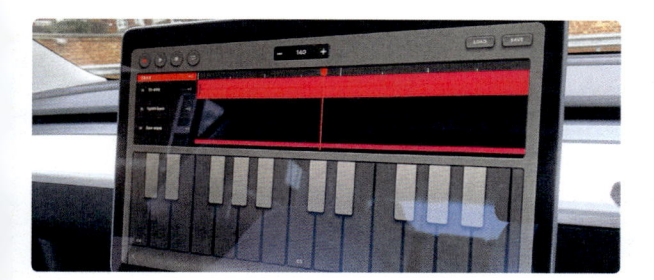

TRAX

Think of TRAX as an entire music studio, with multiple instruments and a sequencer. There's even an on-screen MIDI keyboard. By adding instruments as individual tracks, it's possible to create complex musical arrangements.

Fireplace

If you're feeling cold tap on the fire icon within the Toybox. You'll see a fireplace appear on the touchscreen, the seat heaters will come on, and the AC will turn to the max setting. Tap on the touchscreen and you'll also hear romantic music.

More Cowbell

Tap on this icon, then push the drive stalk down four times when Autosteer is activated, and you'll see the road turn into a giant rainbow — accompanied by cowbell sound effects.

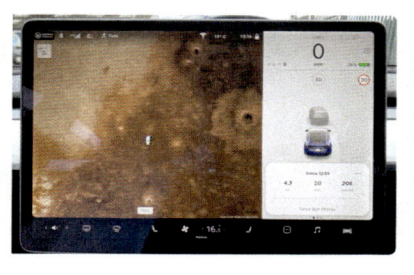

Travel across Mars

Tap the Mars icon and the touchscreen map will flip from Earth to Mars. You'll even see a little rover replace the typical red arrow.

Ho Ho Ho

If you're feeling festive, then tap the reindeer icon to turn your vehicle turn into Santa's sleigh. Other vehicles are represented as reindeer, you'll see snowfall, and you'll also hear Chuck Berry's version of "Run Rudolph Run".

95

In-Car Tech

Video Entertainment

Watch an endless stream of video content…

So you're Supercharging and have some time to kill. Thanks to the video apps in your Tesla, there's an endless source of entertainment spread across YouTube, Netflix, Twitch, and more. Best of all, thanks to the high-definition touchscreen, comfy seats, air conditioning and 15 surround-sound speakers, you've pretty much got your own cinema on wheels.

It's worth noting that you'll need to be in Park mode before any of these apps can be accessed in-car. Some of them, such as YouTube, also require a Wi-Fi connection. If your Tesla isn't close enough to your home's Wi-Fi connection, then here's how to use your mobile phone as a hot spot:

If using an iPhone:
Go to Settings > Personal Hotspot, then toggle "Allow Others to Join" ON. Next, tap on the Wi-Fi icon in the top corner of the Tesla touchscreen and select your phone.

If using an Android phone:
Open the Settings app and go to Network and Internet And > Hotspot and tethering > Wi-Fi hotspot, then turn "Wi-Fi hotspot" ON. Next, tap on the Wi-Fi icon in the top corner of the Tesla touchscreen and select your phone.

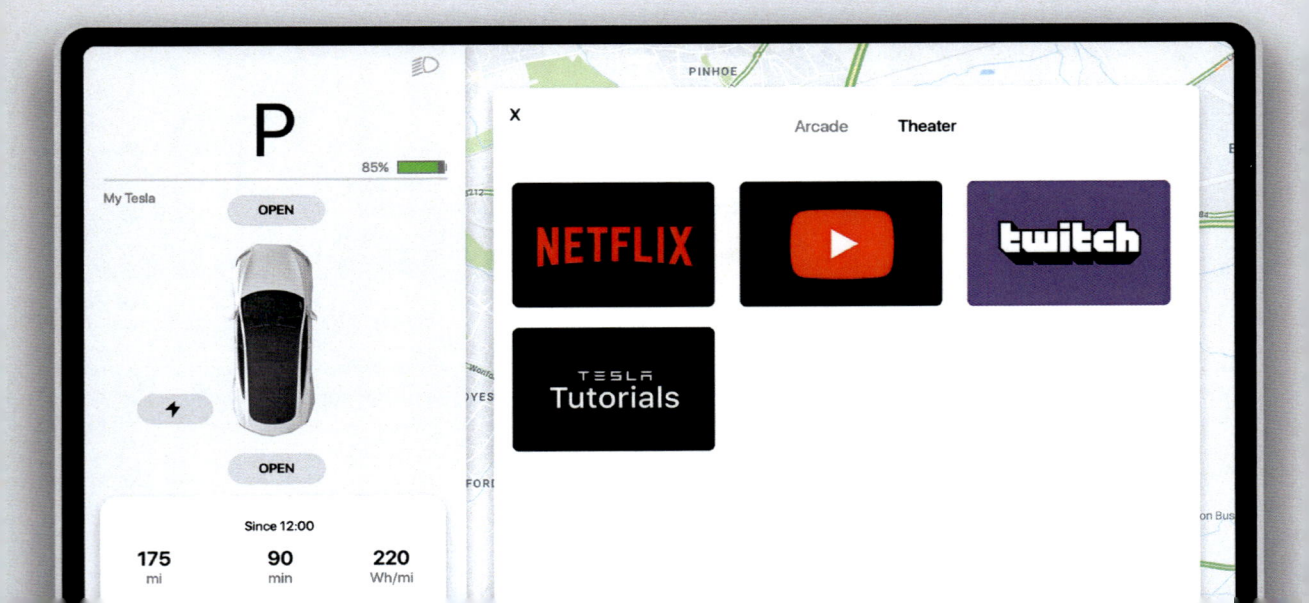

Chapter 6

Netflix

For the ultimate time killer, load up Netflix while the car is in park mode and stream your favorite TV show or movie. Thanks to the massive touchscreen and surround sound speakers you'll struggle to find a better environment to bing-watch the latest shows.

YouTube

Fire up the YouTube app and you'll find an endless source of entertainment. You'll need to be connected to Wi-Fi for Netflix to work (see the previous page for more on that), and at the time of writing it's not possible to log into your own account, but searching for content is easy thanks to the large touchscreen keyboard, and video quality is amazing.

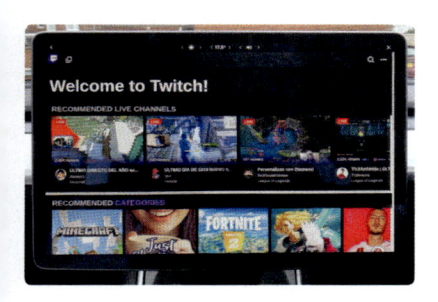

Twitch

Watch fellow gamers stream live using the Twitch app. If you're heavily into competitive gaming, then this is a great way to pass the time while Supercharging.

Tesla Tutorials

If you've only just collected your Tesla and you're a little unsure about the basics, open this app and you'll see brief videos which explain the gear selection, mobile app, key card, Autopilot, Navigate on Autopilot, Autopark, software updates, front trunk, charging adaptors, and how to schedule a service appointment.

In-Car Tech

Games

Turn your Tesla into a games console on wheels...

You might think a car is the last place people should be playing video games, but place your Tesla into Park mode, and you'll unlock a plethora of classic titles, platformers, and even a 3D racing game.

When you think about it, playing games in your vehicle makes total sense. Somewhere below the bonnet is an NVIDIA graphics card capable of rendering detailed 3D games, the vehicle has its own set of controls in the form of a touchscreen, steering wheel and brake; and there's a set of surround sound speakers for enjoying in-game audio. Here's a quick overview of the games you'll find in your Tesla:

Gaming Classics

If retro gaming is your thing then you'll find nine vintage games to enjoy. Tempest challenges you to navigate the rim of a space tunnel, Millipede challenges you to defend a mushroom forest from giant millipedes and spiders; while Lunar Lander sees you try to land a space vehicle on the moon using just a thruster and directional control.

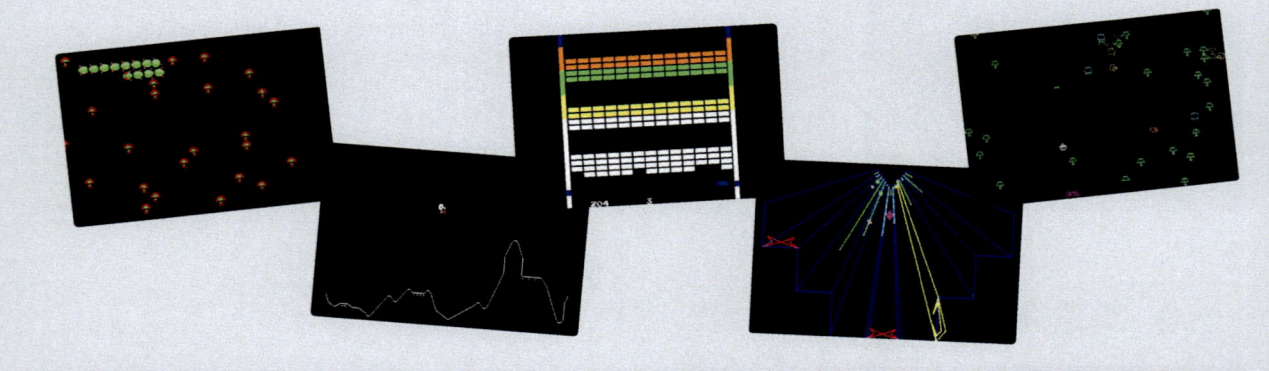

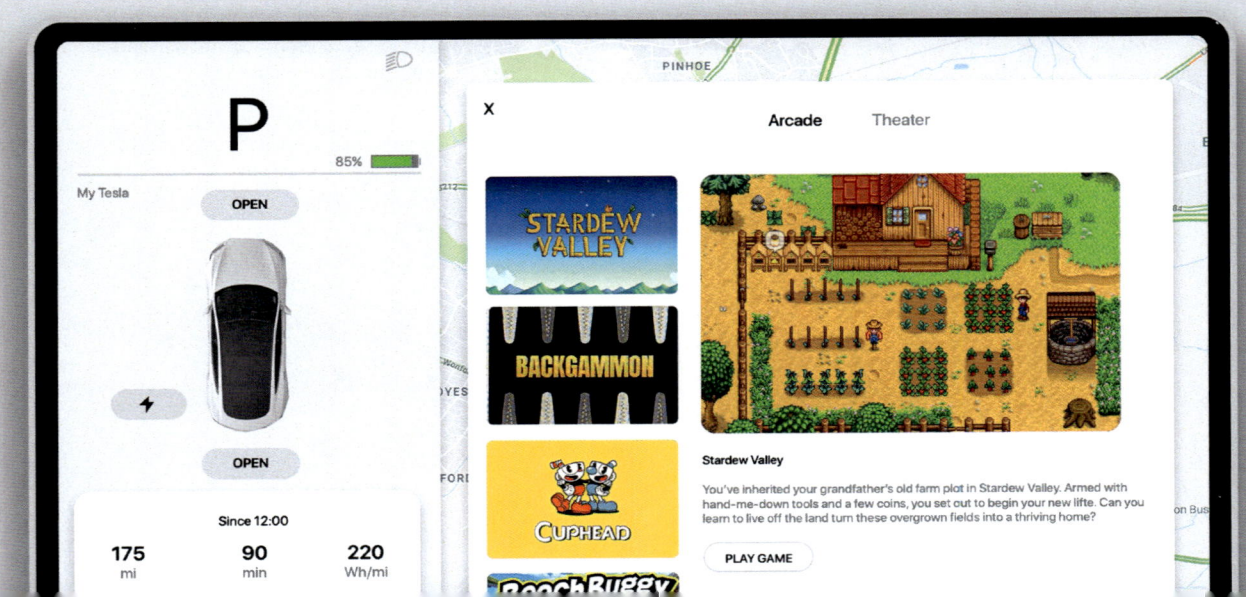

Chapter 6

Stardew Valley

A total time soaker, this cult-classic sees you manage a farm. You'll need to cultivate produce, tender to livestock and live off the land. As you progress through the game, you'll level up in 5 different areas: farming, mining, combat, fishing, and foraging. With each level up, you'll learn new cooking and crafting recipes, unlock new areas to explore, and customize your skills by choosing from a variety of professions.

Cuphead

This fast-paced action platformer is a gaming classic, and the perfect way to keep the kids busy during a supercharger or break. Just keep in mind the game requires a controller to run. Oh, and it's really difficult. It took me nearly an afternoon to get past the first level.

Beach Buggy Racing 2

A fantastic racer that's similar to Mario Kart, which means cartoony graphics, winding tracks and pick-ups to collect. It's possible to control the game using the vehicle's steering wheel and brake, but to save wearing down the tires, stick to using a controller (see more on that at the bottom of this page).

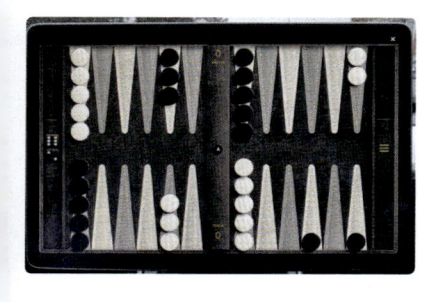

Backgammon

It's hard to believe that Backgammon has a history stretching back nearly 5,000 (archaeological records of the game have been found in Mesopotamia). It's a two-player game where each player has fifteen pieces that move between twenty-four triangles according to the roll of two dice. Admittedly the AI player in this version isn't very good, so for the best experience try playing against another real player.

How to use a games controller

Sure, you can use the touchscreen to play games, or even the steering wheel and brake in Beach Buggy Racing 2, but for the best gaming experience it's a good idea to insert a controller into the car and use it to play games. The best option is the official Xbox One Controller. Priced approximately $50, all you need to do is plug it into one of the USB ports within the vehicle, and it will be automatically recognized and available to use. Just launch a game, grab the controller, and you're good to go.

99

Dashcam

Record and save any incidents on the road...

Dashcams are becoming ever more popular thanks to their ability to capture accidents and lower any potential insurance claims. With the latest Tesla vehicles, there's no need to buy a dashcam of your own, as it's possible to insert a USB flash drive and capture footage from all eight cameras that surround the car. All you need is a properly formatted USB flash drive, and the last hour of driving will be automatically recorded and saved onto the drive. In the event of a crash or incident, all you need to do is tap the Dashcam button on the touchscreen and the last 10 minutes of footage will be saved.

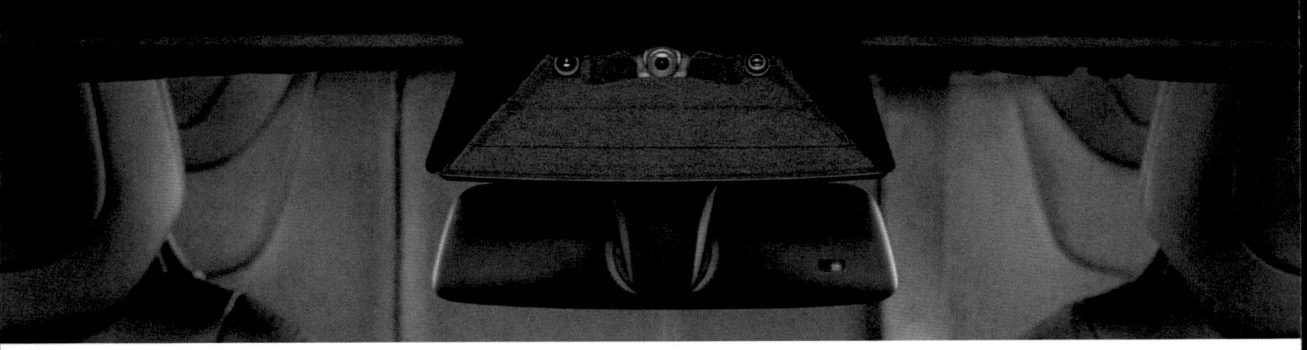

To make use of the Tesla dashcam you'll need to buy a good USB flash drive or SD card. Samsung micro SDs have been recommended for a while by dashcam companies, in particular the Samsung MicroSDXC PRO Endurance Memory Card. Opt for a large amount of storage (ideally 128 GB), as the more storage you have, the more footage you can save, and if you choose a MicroSD card, make sure to also purchase a USB to SD/Micro SD card adaptor. If you decide to use a USB flash drive, keep in mind that they can become corrupted over time as footage is repeatedly written and overwritten by the vehicle.

Once you've bought an SD card or USB flash drive, you'll need to format it to a FAT32 (if you're using Windows) or MS-DOS (FAT) (on a Mac) file system. Here's how...

If you're using a PC:

- Plug the drive into your PC and open Windows Explorer.
- Click the **File System** drop-down and choose **FAT 32**.
- Give your drive a name under Volume label, and make sure the Quick Format box is checked.
- Click **Start** and the computer will reformat the drive.
- Once completed, open the drive using Windows Explorer, then create a folder called **TeslaCam**. This is where any footage will be saved.
- You can now insert the drive into either of the front-row USB ports in the car.

If you're using a Mac:

- Insert the USB drive / SD card into your Mac.
- Open the Disk Utility app.
- Select the drive, then click **Erase**.
- Click the Format drop-down and choose **MS-DOS (FAT)**.
- Click the **Erase** button to format the drive.
- Once completed, open the drive using the Desktop, then create a folder called **TeslaCam**. This is where any footage will be saved.
- You can now insert the drive into either of the front-row USB ports in the car.

Pause the dashcam

You can turn the dashcam on or off by tapping and holding on the dashcam icon. The red dot will disappear when it's deactivated.

Save the last 10 minutes

If you've been in an accident or encountered something interesting, tap the dashcam button and the last ten minutes of footage will be saved with a unique timestamp. You can also honk the horn. To enable this feature, go to Controls > Safety & Security > Save Clips on Honk.

Supported vehicles

Any Model S or X manufactured after August 2017 will support the Dashcam feature. All Model 3's and Y's support it too.

How to view the footage back

It's fairly simple. Start by unplugging the USB flash drive from your Tesla, then insert it into the USB port on a PC or Mac. You might need a USB-C to USB adaptor if you have a new Mac. You'll see the USB flash drive appear as a separate drive. Open it, then select the TeslaCam folder. Inside you'll see two folders:

- **RecentClips.** This contains the last hour's worth of driving footage. You can open this folder then explore the clips inside. Note that each camera will have its own separate video file.
- **SavedCips.** This contains any saved footage you've recorded, alongside Sentry videos. Each will be saved in separate directories by event time and date.

Using third-party apps, it's possible to automatically stitch videos together from the multiple cameras surrounding the car, which makes it easier to watch back footage. For PC users check out "DashCam Viewer", available from dashcamviewer.com. Over on the Mac you'll find "Dashcam Viewer for Tesla Cars" in the App Store.

The dreaded "USB write speed too slow" error

You might not know it, but not all USB flash drives are created equal. To keep costs down (or to encourage additional purchases), the majority of USB drives have a limited number of data rewrites. Once you've written, deleted, then rewritten data a few thousand times, a hardware lock mechanism kicks-in to prevent any potential damage to the data stored on the drive. When this happens, the vehicle won't be able to save any more data, and it'll show the following alert on the display: "USB write speed too slow".

If this happens, you'll need to unplug the USB flash drive at the end of your journey and replace it with another. To avoid this situation happening entirely, invest in a USB flash drive (or SD card with adaptor) built specifically for dash cam use. The Samsung MicroSDXC PRO Endurance Memory Card is a good example.

Sentry Mode & PIN to Drive

Keep your Tesla safe when it's left unattended...

According to the FBI's Uniform Crime Reporting (UCR) Program, there was an estimated one motor vehicle theft (or attempted theft) every 40.8 seconds in the United States during 2017. Count car break-ins too, and you'll start to understand how important it is to keep your vehicle safe while unattended. That's why Tesla has introduced two helpful security features: Sentry Mode and PIN to Drive.

With Sentry Mode enabled, you have your very own security guard sitting in the car while you're away. It will record anyone who comes close to the vehicle, display a warning graphic on the central touchscreen, and even play loud music if necessary. Once you return the car, you'll see how many Sentry Mode events have been captured, and you can later watch them back using a computer or mobile device.

Sentry Mode works by using all eight cameras around the car to watch for movement while the car is in Park mode. If a minimal threat is detected, such as someone walking close by, Sentry Mode switches to an "Alert" state, flashes the headlights, and displays a message on the touchscreen warning that its cameras are recording. If a more severe threat is detected, such as someone breaking a window, Sentry Mode switches to an "Alarm" state, which activates the car's alarm, increases the brightness of the center display, and plays music at maximum volume from the car's speakers. If the car switches to "Alarm" state, owners will also receive an alert from their Tesla mobile app notifying them that an incident has occurred.

Toggle Sentry Mode on or off

You can toggle Sentry Mode on or off by going to Controls > Safety & Security > Sentry Mode. Make sure you have a properly formatted memory card inserted into a USB port (see the previous two pages for more on that) to save any Sentry Mode clips.

Deactivate at home, work, or your favorite locations

If you don't need Sentry Mode at home or work, then go to Controls > Safety & Security > Sentry Mode, then toggle Exclude Home, Work, and Favorites on. To add a favorite location, search for it using the map then tap the star icon when you find a result.

Save battery

Sentry Mode uses a LOT of battery. If left running for an entire day, your vehicle might lose up to 10% of its total battery life. To save energy, toggle Sentry Mode off when you don't need it. You can do this from the car's touchscreen display or via the mobile app.

How to view Sentry Mode footage

It's fairly simple. Start by unplugging the USB flash drive from your Tesla, then insert it into the USB port on a PC or Mac. You might need a USB-C to USB adaptor if you have a new Mac. You'll see the USB flash drive appear as a separate drive. Open it, select the TeslaCam folder, then look for the following folder:

- **SentryClips.** This folder will contain a library of saved clips from Sentry Mode, each labelled by date, time, and the individual camera used for the recording.

The best way to playback Sentry Mode clips is to use a third-party program. Look for one which promises to stitch together the views from multiple cameras into one movie. This will make it much easier to watch back footage, especially if multiple cameras captured a single event. If you're using a Windows PC google "TeslaCamViewer" to find a free, open-source program. If you're using a Mac, look in the App Store for an app called Dashcam Viewer.

How to use PIN to Drive

PIN to Drive enables you to set a secure four-digit verification code that must be entered before your car can be driven.

To activate PIN to Drive use the touchscreen and go to Controls > Safety & Security > PIN to Drive. Once enabled you'll be asked to create your very own four-digit code. The next time you climb into the car and press the brake pedal, PIN to Drive will appear and ask for the code.

If you forget your PIN or want to disable PIN to Drive, go back to the setting on your touchscreen. Tap the link to enter your Tesla login credentials and follow the on-screen prompts.

In-Car Tech

Go Camping in your Tesla

Turn your Tesla into a hotel on wheels with the Dreamcase...

If you've ever slept in your car then you might know how uncomfortable it can be, because no matter how far back you recline the seats, the space in the back still isn't large enough for a bed; and don't even try laying across the back seats - there's just too much aching to deal with in the morning.

Thankfully, there's a rather elegant solution to sleeping in your Tesla: the Dreamcase. Available from **www.dreamcase.eu**, it's a bed-in-a-box system that's designed to live in your Tesla's trunk. Inside is a complete hotel bed with a folding memory foam mattress, duvet, pillows and optional Mako satin covers. The mattress is designed to fit perfectly within the trunk of a Tesla S, X or 3, creating a flat surface to lay upon, and it even accommodates for the footwell of the backseats -- unlike traditional blow-up beds. Opt for the Dreamcase with hotel-quality satin covers, and you'll find yourself with a fully-fledged bed that can be set up and re-packed in just 90-seconds.

The Dreamcase isn't cheap (it starts at €649 and rises to €825 with sheeting), but it's a viable and comfortable solution to sleeping in your Tesla. If you're planning a long road trip, need to sleep overnight at the office, or want to explore the world in new ways, then the Dreamcase totally makes that possible.

How to setup the Dreamcase

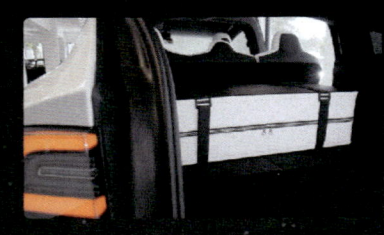

Fold down the backseats. Unzip the case and place the mattress, pillows and duvet on the front seats.

Place the case in a fully opened butterfly position, with the outer hard side facing upwards.

Unfold the mattress. Make sure the flip-down plate is on top and pointing forwards.

Chapter 6

How to enable CAMP mode

Place the car in Park mode, tap the fan icon at the bottom of the touchscreen, then tap "CAMP". The air conditioning will now stay activated unless the battery has less than 20% energy remaining. Interior lighting will also stay on, and it'll be possible to charge devices using the USB sockets. The car will typically use around 2 kW per-hour while in CAMP mode, so realistically you want to start the night with at least 60% charge, or be camping close to a charging point.

Dreamcase tips and tricks:

Take your own pillows

The Dreamcase comes with memory foam pillows, but they're fairly thin so you might want to take your own if you're used to a thicker neck support.

Quickly fold the bed away

You can put the bed away in seconds by folding it in half, then pushing it into the trunk. Put the backseats in their upright position, and you're good to go.

Use the parcel shelf for storing items

If you're camping in the Model 3, then you can use the trunk's parcel shelf to store items while you sleep. Alternatively, place your iPad or laptop on the shelf then sit back and watch a movie.

Place extra pillows against the door

If you're sharing the bed with someone else, place extra pillows in the gap between the Dreamcase and the door. This will give you some extra room to place your arms while sleeping.

Vent the windows or sunroof

If the external temperatures are moderate, vent the windows (or sunroof on a Model S) to circulate air instead of using the AC. This will save using battery energy overnight.

Sleep/camp near public amenities

You'll need somewhere to freshen up in the morning, so if you're sleeping far from home, try to park overnight within a short drive to local amenities. Restrooms can usually be found at large parking lots, hotels and service stations.

Use your cellphone as a hotspot

If the vehicle's LTE signal isn't fast enough for in-car entertainment like Netflix and YouTube, turn on your cellphone's hotspot feature, and you'll be able to connect to it using the car's Wi-Fi menu.

Buy sunshades for the windows

If you're sleeping in the car during the winter, buy a set of windscreen shades with reflective surfaces. These will help to keep heat in the cabin and the cold out. They also add privacy.

Take supplies

Make sure to take plenty of liquids and food with you, along with a fresh set of clothes and toiletries. You can store these in the lower trunk area.

Make sure to fully charge the day before

If you're planning to run the AC overnight, make sure you've got enough energy to keep the car warm and get get to your next destination.

Energy & Efficiency

Once you're comfortable driving your Tesla from location to location, you'll inevitably start to take an interest in energy consumption.

There are a few reasons why this will happen: the vehicle will continuously remind you of your driving style via the energy chart on the driver's display; you'll likely notice the energy graph tucked away in the car's menu, and you'll soon realize that the more efficiently you drive, the more range you'll get out of a single charge.

The next few pages will explain how to use the energy graph to monitor your energy use, reveal some useful driving tips for maximizing range, and what you should expect when driving in winter.

Consumption and Energy Graphs	108
Tips For Maximizing Range	110
What To Expect In Winter	112

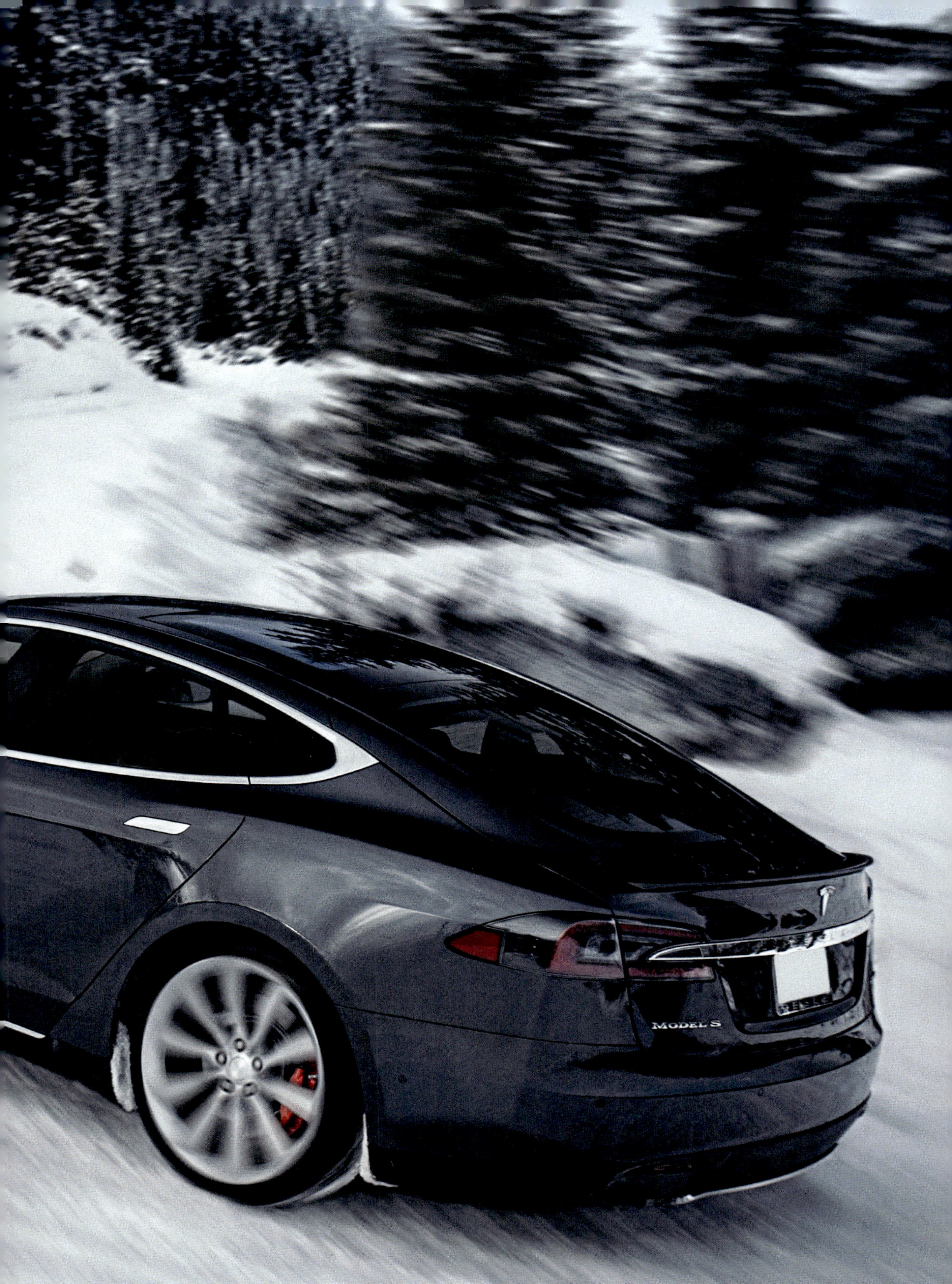
MODEL S

Energy & Efficiency

Consumption and Energy Graphs

Learn how to read the consumption and energy graphs to become a more efficient driver...

The Energy Graph

Tucked away in the vehicle's menu is a really helpful set of charts for monitoring energy consumption. To find it, tap the arrow icon at the bottom of the screen then tap Energy. You'll see a large orange chart appear, displaying the energy used by the car over the last 30 miles.

The peaks represent high-levels of energy usage, such as when the car climbed a hill or when the accelerator pedal was pressed heavily. The lows represent below than average energy usage, such as when the car was coasting or decelerating. Any green areas marked on the graph represent energy that was put back into the battery. Travel down a very large hill, and you'll see this in action.

Look below the chart, and you'll see two tap buttons: Instant Range and Average Range. Tap Instant Range while driving, and you'll see how far your car will travel if you continue to use the same amount of energy for the remainder of the journey. Realistically, Average Range is a better view to use as it takes into consideration your recent driving style.

month you get your rating (that is if you pass everything ok). I don't know yet though when I'm going. It might possibly be tomorrow. The Sargent doesn't know himself yet. Tonight, I went to Anniston and got my winter uniforms (remember I told you I was having them tailored) they fit good now. If I go to e.c.s. enlisted Cadre school tomorrow I'll have to work out some things first. I really hope I don't go until next week. I don't know about calling you now either. If I go tomorrow I don't know if I'll be able to call you Sunday. I think I will though and maybe I won't be going tomorrow anyway. By the time you get this letter I'll have either called or not called. I'm going to try my darndest to call you, because we both have been planning on it for so long now.

There's no more news honey that I can think of. It's too bad they rejected Junior Rector, I was hoping he might get sent down here. I'd like to have instructed him in carrying 60lb packs on 20 mile hikes.

Some night honey I'll try to write a real long letter. I've been writing short ones lately and I'm sorry. I start out to write a lot and I'm usually so sleepy I never get more than a page done. Anyway, you know there's nothing I like to do more than to write to my baby. I love you funny face so very much. Please take good care of yourself and don't ever forget you belong to me and me alone. No one else can ever have any part of you ever. I want you all to myself for always my precious and I always will. I love you darling with all my heart.

All my love for always, your Paul

SWAK

Sunday, Oct. 24, 1943

My Darling,

Another Sunday morning, they sure do roll around fast. Only 2 more weeks of the school. I'll be sorry when it's over in a way. We're having a lot of fun here.

The only news I can think of honey was our trip to Mooresville. We left early Friday morning. When we got there, we ate dinner (all our meals out there were K rations like I sent you). After dinner we started our problems. In the first phase of the problem I was an automatic rifleman. I carried the Browning automatic rifle, plus 220 rounds of ammunition. The rifle weighs 21 pounds and the ammunition felt like it weighed a ton. That phase of the problem ended about 9:00pm Friday night. Then we ate supper (just like the one I sent you) and after supper we went to bed. It was cold as heck. We couldn't start any fires because the situation was tactical and a fire would give away our position to the enemy. Mike, another fellow, and I slept together. We had 1 blanket under us and 1 over us. I was in the middle so I wasn't too cold. At about 1 hour before dawn we go up and got ready for the dawn attack we were going to make. It was the most realistic problem I've ever been on. We've had to capture a big hill, the whole side of the hill was covered with forest. Our firing from the day before had started a fire and a thick cloud of smoke hung over everything. All around us there were burnt trees and big holes where the 16mm mortar shells had landed. It really did look like a battlefield. At dawn we started the attack, it was cold and there was so much frost on the ground that my shoes looked as if I'd been walking through snow. At the foot of the hill there's a creek that we had to wade. The water felt like ice and it came up to my waist. (It pays to be tall when you have to wade creeks). There were heavy machine guns, 60mm mortar, 81mm mortar and light machine guns firing in back of us covering our approach. I shot about 100 rounds as we advanced up the hill. About 10:00am the whole hillside was blazing. After we got all the fires out we came back to camp. We got home early in the afternoon, instead of walking back, they brought us back by truck.

We had yesterday afternoon off, I spent most of it washing clothes and washing myself. Last night Mike and I and a couple of other fellows went to a show. We saw (Flesh and Fantasy). I liked it a lot, I'm not sure you'd like though. It certainly was different. I got 2 letters from you yesterday, sweetheart. You asked me about those ration units. The breakfast unit has concentrated eggs and ham, mixed together, the same kinds of biscuits, gum, cigarettes and coffee. The dinner has those biscuits again, and the main course is cheese, also there are dextrose and malt tablet in the dinner unit. I don't know the calorie content of any of them, but it must be high. They want us to eat them slowly or they'd make us sick.

I had breakfast at 7:30 this morning, 2 fried eggs, cereal, bread and butter and applesauce and coffee. Then I took a shower and shaved and got dressed and now I writing to you. I'm going to church at 11:00. I'm still going to the same one. Mike is Catholic, I guess all Irishmen are. He's calling up his wife this morning. I told him how quick I got you when I called early so he got up early this morning to call her.

I'm sending you our schedule for the past week. It will give you an idea of what it's like here. Also, the paper they give us when we first got here telling us what to bring and so on.

Well honey I guess that's all the news for today. I'm always talking about myself, huh? Well you know me. I really don't mean to though, but I like to tell you what I'm doing.

I'm still hoping to get that furlough when the school is over and know my rating. I should get it then. Gee I want to see you so much, my darling. I love you baby with all my heart and I always will. I'd give anything to hold you close in my arms and tell you that. Maybe I'll be able to soon. I'm going to hug and squeeze you to death I think, so you better get ready. Always belong to me darling, I'll always want you.

I have to stop now sweetheart. I still have to make my bed, shine my shoes and then walk about 1 mile to church. You see the school is quite always from my company and the church I've always gone to is over by the company.

Take good care of yourself my precious. I love you Bernie for always. All my love darling, your Paul

SWAK

November 4, 1943

My Darling,

We got back at 2:00am from the campus march, which wasn't bad. We first finished flipping coins to see who would get coal for the fire. One of the other fellows had to get it. The five of us in the hut first got back a little while ago from the movies. We saw Olsen and Johnson in "Crazy House". It was pretty good but I've seen better.

Mike and I went over to the company today to get our pay and the top Sargent told me he thought I'd have my corporal rating by the end of the week. Maybe the next time I write I'll be able to say I'm a corporal. I'll be getting $66 per month, really getting up in the money, huh?

The top Sargent couldn't say anything about a furlough. Maybe by the end of this week I'll know more about that too.

I have to make this short, honey because I have a lot to do yet tonight. I'll make the next letter a long one. I didn't get any mail from you today. They certainly barrel the mail up here at the school.

Take good care of yourself, baby. I love you funny face with all my heart, always belong to me darling and no one else. I hope and pray I'll be with you soon.

Goodnight sweetheart, all my love darling, for always, your Paul

SWAK

Friday, November 10, 1943
8:30pm

My Darling,

Boy am I mad. Honest I was never more burned up in all my life. You know I brought my electric razor back with me, well, some smart boy stole it yesterday. I left my foot locker open while I went to take a shower and when I came back my razor was gone. That's the first thing I've ever had stolen from me since I've been in the Army. It must have been someone from this battalion, not any of our men though because they don't get back from maneuvers till tomorrow night. There's not much I can do about it, but if I do find the guy he's going to regret taking it and I'm not fooling.

I got your letter to me that you wrote while I was still home. It came last night. No letter tonight though.

It's been very warm here the last few days. Right now, it's raining like heck.

Well here's one of the things I said I'd send you. I got it at the PX last night, along with a padlock for my footlocker. I hope you like it honey the pin I mean not the padlock.

Gee it sure is lonely back here. Being with you was so very nice. It certainly was a fast 10 days wasn't it. Well this time it won't be as long between times, you can bank on that.

Please take good care of yourself sweetheart and don't forget to have lots of fun when you go to see Gerald.

Please forgive the short letter tonight baby, I'm still so burned up about that razor I can't concentrate on writing. Honest I could kill that guy whoever he is, I'm hoping I find him.

Don't forget to take good care of yourself now and keep that chin up. I love you funny face. All my love my darling for always, your Paul

SWAK

November 12, 1943

My Darling,

I got my first letter today from you with Cpl. on it, it seemed good, it was Pvt. for a long while wasn't it?

Now for the latest news. First of all, I want to stress that this all can happen if I'm lucky, it may not, so don't build your hopes up to high.

I got permission from my committee chief yesterday to get my furlough starting the 29th of this month. Then I went to my company commander and asked him and he said he thought it would be all right and that he'd let me know definitely a little later. It really looks as if I'll get it, I'm hoping and praying that I do. This coming Monday one company has general inspection and that on the 17th they go on maneuvers. We'll be on maneuvers the 17th,

18th, 19th, 20th, 21, 22, and 23rd as it stands now. If it works out like this we'll be back in camp on the 23rd and I'll be able to get my furlough on the 29th, if I'm still alive after maneuvers, it's cold as heck down here and it's going to be tough out there for 8 days. Of course, if plans are changed I may not get it then, but as far as I know now it will go through.

I didn't write you last night because I went Anniston to get some train schedules and it was quite late when I got back. I don't know yet just how I'll come home, I'll let you know in a few days. I'm excited as heck about coming home and seeing the most beautiful girl in the world, who wouldn't be. If I get it on the 29th it will be just 6 days short of 6 months that I've been in the Army. That's a long time to be away from everything you love isn't it? Now please honey don't depend on this too much because it might not happen, hope and pray that it does though, because gee funny face I want to see you so much. I love you my darling with all my heart and I always will.

I hate to admit it but I've lost Gerald's address again. Please send it to me, I'd like to write to him. Don't feel so bad about him, I know it's tough, but maybe it's all for the best. Try to cheer up your mother and dad and tell them that Gerald will get over it, he's been in the Army long enough to be used to disappointment.

I don't see why your mother is working. It's really none of my business I know, but it seems foolish to me. Now don't get mad maybe I'm wrong, I probably am.

Well darling, I have to stop now. If everything works out right I'll see you in a couple of weeks. I get so excited just thinking about it I don't know what to do. Of course, I'd have rather had the furlough around Christmas but they're not going to give any furloughs from McClellan at Christmas time, so this will be the next best thing, if I get it.

Take care of yourself sweetheart, I love you. All my love for always, your Paul.

SWAK

Sunday, December 15, 1943

My Darling Bernie,

First, I'll tell you what I did over the weekend. Last night I went to a show, "Happy Land", it was very good. After the show I went to the bowling alley. I met a fellow there that I used to know at Union. The pin boys at the bowling alley are all German war prisoners. Boy that must be hard for them to take. Imagine thinking yourself a member of a super race and winding up as a pin boy in a bowling alley at Ft. McClellan? After that I went to the noncommissioned officers club for a little while, then to the library and got a book. The name of it is "Kings Row", remember we saw that picture a long while ago? This morning I got up at 9am, showered, shaved and then went to church. Came back and had a wonderful chicken dinner with hot biscuits + everything. Then I read the paper, wrote a letter to Naomi, she sent me a box of candy, a letter to my cousin Fred in Africa, one to Gerald and Millie, and one home. Then I ate supper and Mike and some of the other fellows + I went to the show and saw Betty Grable in Coney Island. It was swell. Now I'm back again. I have to shine my shoes and shave after I finish writing to you and then to bed. I like to save your letter for the last one I write. Well darling that's what I did over the weekend. It sounds like a lot but it's really not much fun without you. I got a letter from you today.

Cheer up baby, you sound as if the end of the world was coming. I want you to be happy not an old gloomy gus. It isn't going to be as bad as it was last time darling, we'll be together again and soon too. I felt awful leaving you again. It seemed so tough on you to make you go through another night of saying good bye. I realize sweetheart that it's a lot easier for me, but you keep that chin up anyway and keep smiling baby, and I'll do everything I can to bring us together again real soon.

Have a good time now when you go to see Gerald. Be cheerful and help to make everyone have a swell time.

Mike came back from maneuvers yesterday, the son of a gun had a mustache, it didn't look bad though. What would you think if I grew one? Let me know if you think you'd like me with a mustache. (just a little one like Clarke Cable of course)

Fort McClellan training details
Friday, December 24, 1943

```
           Company "B", 11Th. Training Battalion
           Infantry Replacement Training Center
                   Fort McClellan, Alabama

                                          23 December 1943

        Details For Friday, 24 December 1943

     Charge of Quarters:    Cpl. Roberts

     Latrine Orderly    :   Pvt. Boley

     Kitchen Police

     Pvts:  Bauer       Report Co. "B" at 0530
            Galimski

     DayRoom Orderly
     Pvt. Mierzwa

     Following men will report to BN. Hq. at 0730 (Fatigue Uniform

       Nicolois
       Bates
       Posage
     Matz
       Gogarty

     Following men will report to Orderly Room at 0730 (Fatigues)

       Rosenberg    Cordent
       Schipper     Moomey
       Radtke       Wallin

     The following men will report to Lt. Forstering at the
     Amphitheatre at 1830

       Wallin
       Wood
```

Fort McClellan training details
Friday, December 28, 1943

Cpl Roberts

COMPANY "B", 11TH TRAINING BATTALION
INFANTRY REPLACEMENT TRAINING CENTER
Fort McClellan, Alabama

28 December 1943

DETAILS FOR WEDNESDAY, 29 DECEMBER 1943

Charge of Quarters: Cpl. Dobbins

Latrine Orderly : Pvt. Mierzwa

Kitchen Police

Posage   "D" Company at 0530
~~Mooney~~ *Boren*

5 man Bn Detail (to be on call during day). In the evening at 1830 hours, they will be in charge of Cpl Roberts and report to Bn Hq as cleanup detail.

Moomey
~~Schipper~~ *Nicolais*
Radtke *Matz*
~~Epley~~
Rosenberg
~~Borden~~
Wallin

By the order of the Company Commander

JOHN A. JOHNSEN
Sergeant

Well baby I've got to stop now, I've still got a lot to do. Be careful now and take good care of yourself. No more blood giving either. I'm really very fond of you darling for doing so much but remember you promised not to do it anymore. I'd worry about you awfully if you did so please be a good girl now and keep your promise. If everyone was as brave and good and sweet as you it sure would be a wonderful world.

I love you baby, with all my heart for always. I'm always thinking about you or should I say us.

Good night funny face,

All my love darling,

Paul mentions his recent furlough home that he was hoping for in an earlier letter.

December 28, 1943
8:30am

My Darling,

As you can see I've been reading an Esquire magazine in some of my spare moments. I cut out some of the good jokes, or at least I think there pretty good. The "manual of arms", as done by Betty Grable, is just the way we do it with minor changes in dress of course. Seriously though I thought maybe you'd get a kick out of some of the jokes, that's why I sent them.

We're still waiting for the new trainees. I imagine they'll be here any week now. I'm writing this at lunchtime because if the train comes in this afternoon or tonight I'd probably won't get a chance to write. I won't send this until the evening though, just in case I do get some free time to write more.

It's raining like heck again today. Instead of snow I guess we get rain. Every time it rains it seems to get cold and freezes. Beautiful state this Alabama. I get 2 months' pay this payday. I didn't get any pay this month because I was home on furlough. Pay day is about 3 days away, and that doesn't make me a bit mad. I've got just one nickel between me and poverty. When I get paid I'll have a lot again though, remember I want you to let me know if you need any more money to get that cedar closet wig. I'll have more money than I need so don't think I won't have enough for myself.

There were some other good pictures in that "Esquire" magazine, but I don't think you'd be interested in them. You can't get mad at me for just looking at pictures, there was a lot of black lace things in some of them. I look at them and think how someone else I know would look in them. It's fun- are you mad at me? Or do you like to have me think about things like that? I don't think you mind, I hope not, because I can't help thinking about it, I'll bet you'll look sweet and cute too. It's not going to be too long before I find out.

I've got to stop for now, I'll finish this later on. The way I feel right now I could write longer but a whistle just blew so that means a certain corporal, namely me, better get moving. 9:00pm.

Well here I am back. Still no troops, oh well tomorrow is another day, we still haven't given up hope. We got those new insignias today, so far, I haven't been able to get an extra one but if I do I will send it to you.

I got a box of Fanny Farmer candy from your mother and dad today. You thank them for me will you, honey and I'll write them myself in a day or so. It was nice of them to send it.

I wrote a letter to my grandmother in New York thanking her for some candy she sent me for Christmas and now I can't remember her address. I know it's Lenox Ave in the Bronx but I can't remember the number. I guess the Army is slowly paralyzing my mind.

Talking about boredom, (I wasn't talking about them but that's a good way to start a sentence) I got two more pair o.d. *(olive drab)* pants (that's the kind I wore when I was home) Also an o.d. shirt and another pair of leggings from my supply Sargent, it sure does pay to stand in good with those guys. I've got 4 pair of o.d. pants now and 3 o.d. shirts and three pair of leggings.

At 7pm tonight a refresher course was held for first lieutenant and captains of the 4th regiment. The noncoms of the committee had to be there to answer any questions the officers might have and boy they had plenty. I was lucky enough to be able to answer all the questions they happen to ask me. I just got back about 15 minutes ago.

I got a letter from you today too. It was the one you wrote Sunday. That dinner sounded swell, but I don't think it beats mine by much.

The picture of Effie and George sure looked natural. She doesn't look any different in that, I guess it's the coat.

I have to stop now honey. It's 9:30 and I still have to write home. My grandmother sent me another box of candy and stuff, so I better tell her I got them. I only write home every other day now. I just can't think of enough to say to write every day.

Please take good care of yourself darling, don't forget to answer the questions on the other of this page. Maybe you won't every let me look at you just in black lace things? I remember once you wouldn't even let me see you in a bathing suit. By now your either mad or laughing so I better stop. If your mad I shouldn't say anything more, if your laughing, well, that's the purpose of my letters to make you happy. I love you darling for always.

All my love my sweet, your Paul

SWAK

Right here

December 30, 1943
9:00pm

Hi Honey,

By gosh I'm really getting good, this is the second letter of the day and it's not Sunday either. We finished with the work for tonight so I thought before I went to bed I'd write you again, the first letter was kind of short, as this will make up for it. Cpl. Halion (his c.o. tonight just yelled lights out) they all have to have these lights out at 9:00pm, boy are they are a mixed up bunch of guys. They don't know if their coming or going. The train Mike is on hasn't come in yet, he should be here sometime tonight though. All together there was 4200 men who arrived at the fort today, that's quite a few in just one day.

You know what, I'm still thinking about you in that new black dress. Gee you looked nice in it, and you felt nice in it too. I liked it an awful lot honey, and I love what was in it, namely you. You're a cute little thing, you know it, and I love every bit of you from head to toes. Remember every bit of you belongs to me too, and no one else. I love you funny face, and I want you all to myself.

This is another short letter but with the first one it makes one long letter so that's not so bad.

I'll be waiting to hear if it's ok to call you a week from this Sunday. Be sure and let me know now. And if it is ok you be sure and wake up when the phone rings. When you and I are married we'll sleep late mornings but until then you can't be an old lazy bones. You know, I dream about that. When I get up about 5 in the morning and it's freezing cold I think to myself, someday I'll be able to stay right in bed under the warm blankets with you right in my arms. That would be just like heaven. I'll do my best to make that day come soon baby.

Take good of yourself now, that's an order.

I'll love you funny face for always, your Paul

SWAK

Tuesday, January 4, 1944
8:00pm

My Dearest Bernie,

I have the very doubtful honor of being CQ (charge of quarters; guarding the front entrance to the barracks) tonight. It isn't so bad though, I really don't mind it. So far tonight there's been about 25 guys asking questions. Some of them are sad, some funny, some dumb, and some fairly intelligent. We have a little of everything in this cycle. I don't know much about the men, but here's some interesting things just about the 3rd platoon (that's my platoon). One man has 4 children between the ages of 5 and 13 (I wonder when they're going to start drafting fathers, what a laugh the papers are), another fellow can't read or write English, another one was born and brought up in Germany, right now he has 3 brothers fighting in the German army, another man spent 9 years in the French foreign legion, you can see it's an interesting bunch of men that we have. Some of them are just barely 18, others are about 38, all sizes, shapes and lengths. They were all issued rifles and bayonets today, and were they tickled to death to get them, in about 1 week they'll wish they never saw a rifle. (just had to answer the telephone, it was the battalion headquarters wanting to know if we had put up our posters on the venereal disease for the benefit of the new men. I said yes maybe we have, and he said thank you corporal, and that ended that conversation). I forgot to mention that we have one conscientious objector. He refuses to carry arms although he doesn't refuse military service. He's a Mennonite or something like that. I don't know what they're going to do with him yet. This morning at revelry one man dropped unconscious. Don't know what was the matter with him yet either. That's just a few of the things that go on at the beginning of a new cycle.

Hey! I'm mad, I didn't get any mail from you today. Dog gone the old US mail anyway, gee I miss it when I don't get a letter from you. Guess why, you little monkey I love you, so much I just can't tell you because words can't say it.

Interruption

(Fellow just came in to ask what time he had to get up in the morning for K.P., I told him not to worry about it, just go to bed and he'd be waking up in time, I hated to tell the poor guy he had to get up at 4:30. I'll have to get up about 4:15, I hate to think of it).

As I was saying, ok heck, its 9:00pm. I've got to go around the company and call lights out. Be back in a minute.

Back again, all the lights are out now, the little boys should be safe in bed. I hope I can finish this without an interruption now.

You know what I think about every night, you. Also, every day I think about, you. I love you baby that's why. I love everything about you, your eyes, your nose, your mouth, your hair, every bit of you. I love the way you kiss me, the way you snuggle up close to me, and a thousand other little things about you. All and all I think your pretty darn swell.

Do you ever think about the first night we're going to be together after we're married sweetheart? I do a lot, lots of times I go to bed and fall asleep thinking about it. I'm never going to do anything in the world to hurt you honey, just things to make you happy. I hope you think about it to, I even think about those black laced things and how you're to look in them. You'll have to let me see you then you know. I'm going to have the minister say to love, honor and obey. You'll just have to do whatever I tell you to then, will you want to? I don't ever want you to do any of the things that I'll want you to do for any other man but me. You're my property baby, no one else's ever. Don't ever let anyone else ever touch you. I want to be the first and only one to love you in every way. I know you want that too.

Now there's something I want you to promise me. 1.)that you'll eat good, don't be trying to get thin, your just right now, 2.) go to bed early nights, none of this 11 and 12 o'clock stuff, and 3.)you'll be careful crossing streets, careful when you drive, and just plain careful wherever you go or whatever you do. Promise me that you'll do all those things. I almost forgot, this one more thing I want to promise me, and it's very important too. Don't be doing everyone else's work as well as your own. You've got plenty to do, when you're just doing your own so let the other people at the bank do their own jobs, their getting paid for it. Now don't be a little dope and go helping everyone out because you think you should. You listen to what I say, I'm the boss.

Don't think I've forgotten any of my promises funny face. I haven't, how could I when I love you so much. I'll do everything I can to get us together soon. You should know that I want you with me, life without you isn't much fun I can tell you that. Just be a little patient and be happy. Every time you feel blue or unhappy just stop and think of all the happy years that are ahead us. I'll do my very best to make you happy. I promise. Remember all those things I told you when I held you close to me, those things that I whispered to you then are going to come true someday real soon I promise. I love you my darling, there's so many reasons for loving you I just can't name them all. First of all, I love you because I like the kind of person you are, because your pretty, your sweet, your pure and good, and because, well, you're just my kind of girl. I've loved you for a long-time funny face, even longer than you've loved me. As long as you loved me now with all your heart, and want to belong to just me and no one else, I'm the happiest guy in the world, and I can take anything.

Well it's about 10:30, with all the interruptions I've had I've done pretty good. At 11 o'clock I have to make a bed check, so I guess I better stop now. I'm going to bed about 11:15 or 11:30 as soon as I get through that bed check. 4:30 comes awfully quick.

Don't forget now, I want you to promise me all those things I asked you. And darling don't ever forget that I love you more than anyone else in all the world. Take good care of yourself my baby. I'll have you with me soon.

Goodnight my precious, I love you with all my heart, for always.

Your Paul

(SWAK) RIGHT HERE

Tuesday, Jan. 11, 1944

My Darling,

No letter today. When I don't get one I feel as if part of my day (the nicest part) is missing. Well I guess all I can do is blame the old US mail again.

There's not much new news. The trainees are getting ready for their first bivouac this Thursday night. Boy I hate to think of it. We just heard today that the 14th Battalion, which is at Mooresville for the last two weeks now, is just about all shot. They brought back about 20 guys with pneumonia. It's been awfully cold down here and sleeping with just 2 blankets and an overcoat on the ground doesn't tend to improve your health any.

I just found out today from one of the men in my platoon that he fought with the Italians against Ethiopia. He was in Italy when the war broke out with Ethiopia and at that time he wasn't an American citizen. He was forced into the Italian Foreign Legion for 13 months. His name is Nini Vagi. You certainly meet some interesting people in the Army.

There's another kid in this cycle, he can't be more than 18 at the most, and a real nice guy. Tomorrow he leaves for the stockade for 6 months of hard labor. He went a.w.o.l. for one day. He'll have to work 18 hours a day for 6 months, and have 2/3 rds. of his pay taken away from him, for being absent without leave for just one day. They ought to try something like that on some of the guys going on strike.

Ever since this cycle started I've had charge of the whole 3rd platoon by myself. Sargent Johnson who is the platoon Sargent went home in furlough and Corporal Davis who is the corporal with me with the 3rd platoon has been on committee work.

That's left just me to the care of the whole platoon. I've been acting platoon Sargent, besides being platoon corporal. I'm still on the mortar committee but it hasn't started to function and it probably won't till the 6 or 7th week of the cycle. In some ways it's an awful job being over these men. If one drops his rifle or moves in rank I have to ball him out and then make the poor guy work in the kitchen at night. I hate it really, but I guess that's the way it has to be done. If you let down on them even a little they'll walk all over you and that just doesn't go in the Army.

Well honey as usual I'm tired as heck and it's not even 10pm yet. I guess I'm getting old or else McClellan is sort of wearing me out. Anyway, tonight isn't one of my better letter writing nights, so forgive me for not writing the kind of letters I really like to write to you. Maybe tomorrow after I hear from you (I hope I do at least) I'll be more in the mood to write the kind of letter I really like to.

I love you my sweetheart, I want you to always belong to me, and I want you to please take good care of yourself. I hope and pray I'll be able to have you with me soon.

Good night sweetheart,
All my love for always,
Your Paul

SWAK
Right here

Tuesday, January 18, 1944
10:00pm

My Darling Bernie,

I'm writing this at the guard house, remember I told you in last night's letter I was Corporal of the guard tonight. I came on duty at 6 P.M. and stay on till 6 A.M. It's not hard at all but you don't get much sleep. It's the first time these boys have ever walked guard. Every four hours I have to get up and post the new guard relief. There are two corporals on duty and one Sargent, the Corporals do the posting of the guard, every two hours a new guard is posted, but because there are two of us we only have to get up every 4 hours.

I didn't get any mail from you today. I certainly do miss it when I don't get a letter from you. Maybe that's because I love you, think so? Boy I'll be glad when this war is over. I can't help feeling that I'm just wasting my life away, there's not one thing that I'm doing in the Army that will ever be of any good to me in civilian life. All I've learned is how to kill, and a knowledge of the weapons that are used to kill. I guess the Army has given me a sense of values though that I never had before. I never did realize before how much a home meant to a person, or how much personal freedom meant or how much being able to be with the people you want to be with most. I bet I sound like a dope saying all these things but sometimes it helps to say them.

I'm glad you got the raise honey. I'd still rather have you working at the branch than at the G.E. The G.E. is too much of a grind, and besides you just don't belong in a place like that.

As usually I'm awful sleepy. Tonight's going to seem awfully long. Tomorrow night I have to go out on a night problem, oh woe is me.

We've got a new battalion commander Major Dahl, and boy is he an old crank. No one likes him. The other night he had a meeting of all the officers and none came and he told us he expected every man to work even harder than he has been. Then he said, if any of you are getting tired of being here, I can very easily arrange to have you sent to combat, just let me know. That burned everyone up. He made it sound as if we were all afraid to go to combat or something. If he keeps that up he'll have all the officers and non-coms asking to leave. I don't like the guy at all. Well maybe he won't stay long, I hope not.

In one of your letters yesterday you asked me to take it easy in some of the things I've said in my letters, then in the second letter you asked me if I hadn't dreamed about black lace. Now I don't know if you want me to "take it easy" or not. Which is it? I could say a lot more, that I'd like to say, ok?

You know I think of you in other things beside black lace. You know what I dreamed about doing? I bet you'd never guess. I don't know if I should tell you or not, but I think I will. Here I go getting fresh again. In that house of ours beside having a very nice fireplace in the living room and a nice big soft couch, and besides having a nice bedroom (without a fireplace) with a nice big soft bed, we're going to have a beautiful bathroom, with a great big bathtub. It's going to be nice and warm in there all the time, with nice soft lights, and do you know what I'm going to do? Some night before we get in that big bed I'm going to fill the bathtub with water nice and hot, then I'm going to pick you up, and you're not going to have even those black lace things on, and I'm going to put you in the tub and give you a bath. No fooling, I'd love to do that. I'm going to get you all covered with soap suds, then I'm going to rinse you all off and then dry you with a great big bath towel and then just put you in that big bed of ours. Gee I'd like to do that, would you like me too? I hope you would, if you wouldn't I would be disappointed. Don't forget to tell me now if you'd like it or not.

I hope you're not still mad at me, and I hope that you don't think that when I do something you don't like that I'm doing it to hurt you. I never want to hurt you darling, you should know that, I love you too much. I never think anything that's really bad or that should make you think that I don't love you. At least I don't think I do.

Well baby I've got to post a guard so I going to stop. I love you, I always want you to belong to just me, no one else ever. Don't ever let anyone else ever touch you baby, you belong to me and me alone. Take good care of yourself now funny face, and don't ever doubt for a minute that I love you with all my heart.

All my love darling,
Your Paul

January 18th, 1944
7:00pm

My Darling,

Guess what, I didn't have to go on bivouac tonight. It's hard to explain but here goes. You see wherever the committee you're on is functioning you don't have to be with the company. Well my committee was working this afternoon till 4:30 and the company left on bivouac at 3 o'clock. That's the reason I couldn't go with the company on the bivouac. Of course, it made me feel very bad, but I guess I can bear it.

I was just told by the top Sargent that I'm C.Q. for the weekend. Well that's the way it goes, you get out of one thing in the Army and run smack into something else. I guess I'm still ahead though I'd rather have C.Q. on the weekend, then go on a bivouac tonight. Mike didn't have to go either because he's C.Q. tonight.

I was talking with the fellow in my platoon today who refuses to fire a rifle. His name is Mattson and he is really very intelligent. He's being transferred tomorrow to Camp Grant in the medical corp. I guess I told you he said he wouldn't kill anyone but he wanted to help some live. He's 23 years old and married. We talked for quite a while. I really like the fellow I think he's honest about what he believes. I asked him what he would do if a Jap or a German were going to kill his wife and he had a rifle in his hands. He said didn't believe god would ever put him in such a situation as that. Well maybe he's right, he certainly believes in the things he claims. I'm glad they transferred him to the medical corp.

I've been giving lectures all day today. The committee I was on was the interior guard committee and we were teaching the new men how to walk guard and also how to learn their general order. You want to hear my speech, well here it is ready or not. First as the men come up to my platform I tell them to form a semi-circle around me. At my side I had a big chest with the 11 general orders on it. After their all around this is what I said (I dreamed this up all by myself too, don't flatter me too much now after you read this.)

Speech

All right men first of all I want to see how many of you know your 11 general orders. (about 10 hands go up.) Only 10 men out of a whole platoon, that's not very good. Now I'm going to give you a little warning, if you men want passes this Saturday night you're going to have to know your 11 general orders. Besides that, this coming Saturday morning you'll have inspections and the inspecting officer will definitely ask you at least 1 of your general orders. If you don't know the 1 he asks you, you'll be quizzed and if you are quizzed you know that means extra details for you over the weekend, so I strongly advise every one of you men to learn all these orders by Saturday morning.

Now let's look at the first general order. (Here I point to the chest) #1. To take charge of this post and all government property in view. #2. To walk very fast in a military manner keeping always on the alert, and observing everything that takes place within sight or hearing. (then I stand in front of the chest and ask one man to give me the first 2 orders.) (then I do the same thing for 3 + 4) Then comes #5. To quit my post only when properly relived. This will be a hard order for some of you men to carry out. (now comes a big joke by yours truly, and it always gets a big laugh, although I don't imagine you'll laugh) I say, now men no matter what happens you have to obey this order, even if a beautiful blonde comes walking up to you, you just first say no thanks. I don't want any and keep right on walking your post (laugh!)

Well I go through all 11 orders this way and then that 50 men move on to another instructor and I get 50 new men. I did that for 8 hours today. It's fun for the first couple of hours but after that it becomes awfully tiresome.

I write the darndest things, don't I? I try to write interesting letters so you'll have to forgive me. I'm sitting in the day room writing this letter and Tommy Dorsey is playing (I'm getting sentimental over you) on the radio. It's the same record I use to have. Remember that Tommy Dorsey album I had with Marie and Mike. Boy that sure brings back happy memories.

Just before I started writing I took a shower, shaved, washed hair, shined my shoes and washed my cartridge belt. I'm all nice and clean now, it feels just like getting ready for Saturday night, the kind we use to spend together. All that's missing is civilian clothes, my car, home, and most of all you. When I think of it I guess everything is missing.

I got the letter you wrote me Sunday evening today. The one you sent by regular mail. The letters I've been getting lately have been longer so I don't have that to bawl you out about that. I know I give you heck quite a lot but I only do it because I love you. It makes me mad to think of you working too hard, or staying up late nights and taking a chance of getting sick. You need someone to bawl you out though because in a lot of ways you still act just like a little girl. And an awful sweet and cute one though, and I love you because are like that.

I'm glad you've been thinking about that "First night", I want you too. Just think of all those nights, hundreds of them that we'll have together. Gosh it's nice to think about things like that isn't it. Don't forget about that room with the fireplace and that nice big bed. And above all don't forget all the things we're going to do together, just you and I all by ourselves.

I guess I'll stop now sweetheart. I'm going to bed real early and catch up on some sleep. I won't be able to get much over the weekend because of being C.Q. One good thing about it as you said, I can write long letters when I'm C.Q. so that's something.

Take good care of yourself sweetheart I love you baby, for always.
Your Paul
SWAK
Right here

Paul explains his recent hospital stay because of a bout with pneumonia.

Sunday, February 6, 1944
3:30pm

My Darling,

This is going to be a long letter honey and one with a lot of explanation too. For a whole week now, I've been debating whether or not to tell you something and now I finally decided to. It's nothing serious so don't get excited.

First of all, I didn't go out on maneuvers Sunday as I told you. I went to the hospital with pneumonia. I'll tell you the whole story. Last Sunday morning (a week ago today) I woke up about 6 o'clock and I felt awful sick. I was shaking like a leaf and I was awful sick to my stomach and I had pains in my chest. I thought I had the grippe so I just stayed in bed all day. Late Sunday afternoon I was still feeling awful and Mike and some of the fellows went to the orderly room and told the Captain. He came up to the hut and ordered me to go to the dispensary to find out what was wrong. I walked up, Mike went with me, and they took my temperature. It was 103 so they decided to send me to the hospital. I didn't want to go but I didn't have much to say about it. They sent for an ambulance and I climbed in and rode down to the fort hospital. They examined me, sent me to the ward and put me to bed. That meant I didn't get a chance to write to you Sunday. Monday, I felt pretty tough, I had a temperature of 106 which is kind of high. They started giving me Sulphur drugs on Monday. Well I didn't get a chance to write Monday either. On Tuesday I felt a lot better, good enough to write but I had to think up something to tell you so you wouldn't wonder why I hadn't written Sunday or Monday. I thought of the bright idea of saying we went on maneuvers for a week. I didn't want you to worry darling. I wrote the same thing home. Well Wednesday my temperature was down to normal and by Friday I was out of bed. Here it is Sunday again, I'm still in the hospital but I think they'll let me out and in a couple of days. I feel fine and there's nothing wrong with me now. There just keeping me a few more days to make sure I'm ok. I would have told you about it sooner sweetheart but there was no reason to worry you needlessly. It's ok to tell you now because I'm all ok now and there's nothing to worry about. By the time you get this letter I'll probably be back with the company on duty again. I hope you're not angry with me but I thought it was best to do it this way. I've been getting you're mail, although it does take a little longer as it goes to the company and then they send it from there to the hospital. I hope you're getting my mail all right.

Now darling I don't want you to say anything about this to my grandmother or father. They still think I was out on maneuvers this past week and I want them and everyone but you to keep on thinking that. I don't want you to tell anyone about me being sick, that's just between you and I. There's no sense having my grandmother knowing anything about it, because she'd only worry even though there's nothing to worry about. I know you're too sensible to do that.

I didn't know whether or not to tell you but after thinking it over I decided I wanted to tell you. I love you darling and I don't ever want to keep anything from you, just as I don't want you to keep anything from me. Please don't worry now, I'm all well again and as I said I should be released from the hospital in two or three days. There just keeping me now to get my strength back. Those Sulphur drugs make you pretty weak. I don't know how I ever got pneumonia. I guess it was being out on the range for those three days, I had a cold and then I had to lay out there for three days in the rain and I guess that didn't help things any.

The x-rays they took here at the hospital showed that I had a very slight case of pneumonia, nothing very bad.

(Time out, the mail just came)

I just got a letter from you, my grandmother, Mildred McCullough, and Dr. Larrabee at Union. Quite a lot of mail for one day.

In your letter (written Thursday morning) you said you hadn't heard from me, but in my grandmothers, she said you both got letters Thursday (her letter was written Thursday night). I'm glad to know your getting my mail from here. I'm sorry to hear Dr. Malber is leaving for the Army, you certainly need him around there. Tell Effie I still can't picture her as a mother, it just doesn't seem possible.

I wrote a letter to Gerald today also one to Ward. I didn't say anything about my being in the hospital to them, you're the only one that knows it, tell your folks if you want to but be sure and tell them not to let my family know about it. I'd rather you just keep it to yourself darling, just let everyone think as they do now that I was out on maneuvers.

That picture you sent me of Freddy's car is good. He had that when I was home though. I saw him with it down at Browns garage. I'm sending it back to you in this letter.

Mike and some of the fellows are coming down to see me tonight. I'm going crazy trying to find something to do with myself. The nurse in charge of this ward is a 2nd Lieutenant, (not bad either, are you jealous?)

Keep on addressing your letters to the company because they forward them right to me the same day, and as I said before, I shouldn't be here more than two or three more days.

Well honey, I guess I have to stop now if I want this to go out on this afternoons mail. Take good care of yourself my darling and don't worry about me,

I'm feeling fine and that's the truth. I love you baby and I always will. You belong to me funnyface for ever and ever, don't forget that.

Good bye for now sweetheart, I love you,
All my love darling,
Your Paul,

S.W.A.K.
RIGHT HERE

February 27, 1944
9:30am

My Darling,

How's this for starting to write early in the morning. This is going to be a long letter so I'm starting it now.

A bunch of us went to the movies last night and saw the "Bridge of San Luis Rey." It was pretty good. When we came back to the hut we all sat around talking. Guess what we talked about? Remember I told you Joe Di Cosmo was going to get married, well some of the married fellows were telling him about the first night of his married life. We talked till about 1 o'clock in the morning. Joe should be well advised after talking to the fellows last night.

I'm going to church at 11 o'clock, then eat dinner and after that we may go bowling. It's raining out right now, as usual, no fooling it's rained every day for the past two weeks. I'm beginning to get waterlogged.

Colliers Magazine has a good article in the last issue. I think I'll cut it out and send it to you. What do you think of it? I bet they don't look half as nice as you do.

Well Mike is home by now, I bet he's one happy guy. Here's hoping May comes around fast. I'm going to start applying for my furlough on the 1st of May. I should get it sometime during that month. That's only two months away. I'll be coming home in *(illegible)* this time. That will make it a lot easier to get ready. I won't have to bother with an overcoat, blouse or things like that.

You should keep on taking those music lessons Honey. Of course, if you just don't have the time or if it makes you tired doing it, that's different. You'd be a swell player, though, you can't expect to get it the first lesson. I hope you keep on taking them.

Well Baby it's time for me to go to church so I'll finish later. I don't know if I ever told you or not but the Protestant minister of our chapel (Captain Hogglan) used to be a Methodist minister. He's been a chaplain in the army for the past 15 or 18 years. I like him a lot. When I first came here he was a first lieutenant. About two weeks ago he got his captain's commission. He goes on hikes with the men, even stays out on bivouac with us sometimes. I'd say he was a man of 55 or so. Well I've got to get ready to go now, you're just about getting out of Sunday School. It's 10:45 my time, 11:45 yours. Don't eat too much for dinner now Funny Face.

1PM - Just finished eating, boy it was good, chicken, mashed potatoes, bread and butter, beets, tea, and ice cream. I went to church, it was a pretty good talk. I'm sending you the program in another envelope. I didn't write much on the program because you would probably like to show it to your father.

The bowling alleys open at 2 PM so we're going down at 1:30 so we'll be sure to get an alley. I really like to bowl a lot, you and I and Gerald and Millie will have to go when we're back together again. By then I'll be an expert, oh yeah. Today I've got to get 200 or bust. The fellows are ready to go now so I'm ready to stop again now. Be back in a while.

5PM – We bowled till 4 o'clock, 162 was my best score. I won't tell you what I made on the other 3 games. I just finished eating, so here I am writing to my Baby again. Four or five of us are going to the movies at 6 o'clock. Bob Hope in "Let's Face It." We saw the previews last night and it looked good.

After writing about all this running around today you're probably thinking I'm having a swell time. It is fun to go to the shows and bowling but Darling nothing in the world is so nice as being with you. The way I spend my Sundays now is an awfully poor substitute for the way I used to spend them when you were with me. Gee what I'd give to be able to ride up to your house and take you for a ride, or if no one was home to sit in your front room with you cuddled up on my lap. What happy Sundays those were, I was with the sweetest and prettiest girl in all the world. Those days will come again for us my Precious only they'll be even better because you'll be my wife.

Here I go again, it's almost 5:45 and the fellows are ready to go. I'll finish the letter after I get back. I'll only be gone a couple of hours so don't go away.

8:30PM – Hello Darling, I'm back again. The show was good, you can't beat Bob Hope. Tomorrow I have to get up at 5 AM. Our committee (the one I'm on) gives all the instructions on the Browning Automatic Rifle, Hand Grenades, and the mortar. Starting tomorrow we teach Hand Grenades. We've already finished the B.A.R. Next Friday starts the mortar. Here's how the instructors work for tomorrow. There's six of us on the committee plus 3 lieutenants. Each of the noncoms is in charge of a pit. The men come in to the pits one at a time. We hand them their Hand Grenade (they're the real thing). The trainees pull the pin, then release the handle. He then has 5 seconds before the grenade goes off. He's supposed to hold it for two seconds and then throw it, and duck down in the pit, so the shrapnel won't hit him. We have to coach each man through all that. I hope some of these dopes don't get excited and drop one in the pit. If one does, don't expect a letter from me for a while. They'll be putting the pieces together for the next six months.

I didn't get any mail from you today but I got one yesterday.

It was a real warm day today, this afternoon the sun actually came out. It felt just like spring at home.

Well Baby I guess it's about time I started talking about what I like to talk about. Namely you. I'm only writing on one side of the paper because it's too fine to write on both sides.

I miss you Bernie an awful lot. I miss holding hands, kissing you, holding you in my arms and telling you that I love you. I miss our Saturday nights together, Sunday afternoon + night, it's been a long while since I've fell asleep with you holding me. I know you miss me the same way Darling and I'm glad you do. I still dream about my first night home on furlough and walking up to your house. I actually felt weak when I got to your house and when you came out and when I held you in my arms, it was a wonderful feeling. To have you again close to me, to be able to feel you, to my face alongside yours and realize it was really you. Sometimes it seems as if I've been away from you and have for years, and then sometimes it seems as if it was only yesterday that I drove up to your house that last night before I left for Upton.

This is my ninth month in the army, and it's the 15th month that I've actually enlisted in the army. It's a long while to be away from someone you love, I've found that out. Even though I don't especially like the army or army life I wouldn't want to be anywhere else but in the army. If I were home I couldn't be happy, the only time I want to leave the army is when this thing is all over. Then watch me make a beeline back to good old civilian life.

Hey you'd better be a good cook. You said you wanted to be, boy you'd better. I think you're "pretty" good now. I'll always be a good guy and help you dry dishes, well for the first month or so.

Gosh, I hope May comes around fast, it would be swell if Gerald would be home then too. Well maybe it will work out like that, we'll all keep our fingers crossed.

I love you Darling or did you know, you're mine Funny Face, you belong to me for always. Take good care of yourself and always keep that chin up. Keep smiling and I'll keep smiling too. We love each other, we belong to each other and we both know that. That should be reason enough for both of us to be happy at least. I know it is for me. Keep yourself for me Darling, I want to be the first and only one to ever have you for my very own in every way. That's what you want too isn't it Darling? Tell me so, it makes me feel awfully good.

It's 9:30 Sweetheart so I'd better get ready for bed. Dream about us Darling, I do.

I hope I get those pictures soon, I want to see my sweetest girl in a sweater.

Good night Darling, I love you Bernie, I want you, and I promise that just as soon as possible.

I'll do my best to make all our dreams come true. When you answer this letter my Precious, tell me that I'll be the first and only one in your life. I just want you to say it, it's one of the reasons why I love you so much Darling. When you marry me I know you'll be the purest and sweetest girl in all the world and that you'll never give yourself to anyone but me. I'll never want anyone but you Baby, I mean that, honest. Don't forget to tell me now, I want to hear you say it.

Once again Honey, take good care of yourself please. Don't ever let anything happen to you. I love you Sweetheart for always and always.

All my love my Precious,
Your Paul

S.W.A.K.
Right Here

March 6, 1944
7PM

Hi Baby,

You know how I feel tonight. Just like necking like heck. If I were with you tonight you'd have a lot of trouble with me. I don't know why I feel the way I do, but boy I sure do feel that way. I haven't been eating olives either. This is going to be a long letter, I feel like writing a lot tonight, it's the next best thing to being with you.

Well I better get the news out of the way first then I'll be able to write just about you & I. I got a letter from Gerald today. He told me about Millie going home when she had her baby. He's been lucky to have had her with him for so long. I wish they could stay together, but I do think she's doing the right thing by going home.

It's raining like the dickens out right now. Thunder and lightning and everything.

The company commander got a V-mail letter *(Victory Mail, a secure process used to correspond with soldiers abroad)* today from one of the boys from the last cycle. Two months after they left here they were in Italy. Some of them have already been killed and the fellow who wrote the letter was in a hospital somewhere in Italy. The C.O. read the letter to the trainees as a warning for them to take their training seriously.

I guess that's all the news Honey except that I got a letter from my Baby today.

Now I'm going to talk about us, O.K.? I feel first like talking about black lace, and bedrooms & things like that. Do you mind if I do? When I used to hold you on my lap and whisper things to you, you used to like it, so I'm to talk about them now, only I won't say everything I'd like to, you fill in between the lines, I think you know what I would say if I were holding you and whispering to you.

First of all, I want to tell you, that I love you an awful awful lot, and that I want you all for myself. You'd never want to belong to anyone else but me, would you Baby? I promise that when we're married I'll make up for all the time we've both spent away from each other. And Honey, I'm never going to stop making love to you, no matter how long after we're married we'll still push, and I'll still hold you on my lap, and tell you what a cute little thing you are. I mean that Funny Face, we're not going to slow down any that is unless you want to. I don't think you will, you hadn't better.

You know what I think of every night? The first night of our honeymoon. Where would you like to go? Where ever it is it's going to be a wonderful night my Precious. On that night, I want you to be the same sweet girl you are now, from then on you'll really belong to me in "every" way for always. Tell me often Baby that I'll be the only one. That's one of the reasons why I love you so much Bernie, because I know you'll never belong to anyone else and that you want me to be the first and only one to ever have you. Every man wants that kind of a woman Darling and I'm the happiest fellow in the world because I know I have that kind of woman. Hey! The lights first went out, they came right back on again, boy is it raining, it's coming right in the hut, these rat traps we live in have cracks in them big enough to drive a truck through anyway.

You know what else I think about a lot. The house we're going to have. I don't ever want to live in the one I have now. We'll have a little place with nice big chairs, a warm fireplace, and a nice white kitchen and bathroom. No, I haven't forgotten the bedroom, and by the way we're not going to have twin beds. I wouldn't stand for that.

After supper nights we would go in the front room by the fireplace, there would be a nice warm fireplace going and we'd have the radio on. Then we'll turn out all the lights, lock the front door, pull down the shades, and take the telephone off the hook, so no one can bother us. Then around 10 or 11 o'clock we're going up to "our" bedroom. I'm going to carry you up in my arms and when we get along side of "our" bed I'm going to put you down on it and kiss you and kiss you. After that Baby we're going to be close together all night, very close, then I'm going to kiss you and hold you all night long. When morning comes we're just going to ignore it. I won't let you get up till 10 o'clock at least. When we do get up I'm going to stay home with you all day and kiss you and tease you all day long. Then we're going to do the same thing all over again at night and every night for years and years after that. Of course, I won't be able to stay in bed till 10 every morning but gee I sure would like to. You are probably saying to yourself that I'm just dreaming again. Well Darling, I'm not. It's all going to come true, if I have to stand on my head to make it come true. I'm not having pipe dreams Baby, we're going to have that home, and we're going to have each other and I promise I'll do everything I can to make it come true as soon as I can, please believe me Sweetheart and have faith in me, I was never more serious in all my life.

Baby, tell me something. It's not that I don't have the answer or anything like that, but I want to have you tell me. Did any of the fellows you ever went with mean anything at all to you? That may sound like a funny question but let me explain. Before I went with you I went out with other girls and had a good time and that was all. But when I started going with you Sweetest I know that it was the real thing and that I was in love with you. No other girl ever meant anything to me, you're the only one that ever has and I know you're the only one I'll ever love or want for my wife. Tell me how you feel about it. Was it the same way with you? I hope so Darling, I'm sure it was but I want you to tell me about it. And don't forget Baby to tell me often that you belong to me and that I'll be the first and only one in your life. It helps my morale more than anything else anyone could tell me. When I get home on the furlough we're going to definitely make plans, I promise that. I've taken it just about as long as I can without you, I want you and I to know you want to belong to me too. I promise Baby we're going to do something about it and soon too. May will be here soon, then we'll be able to decide what to do.

Well Honey, it's 8:45 and I should get ready for bed (8:45 is late for me now) but I still feel like writing so here I go again.

You haven't told me yet when you'd like me to call you. Maybe tomorrow's letter will tell me.

Remember the fellow I used to tell you about at college. His name was Mintline. I never liked him and he used to follow me around all the time. I get a V mail letter from him the other day, he's in the South Pacific someplace. The poor guy, 2 to 1 he never gets back, I can't understand why they ever sent him overseas, boy that's just plain murder.

Oh, I almost forgot. One of the corporals (this comes under the heading of news) in A Company got his hand blown off today. He had a 50-caliber shell in his left hand and he was trying to get the powder out of it and it went off. It blew most of his hand off. It was an awful mess, I saw his finger lying on the ground with a wedding ring on it. Boy it was a little tough eating lunch after that. He's in the hospital and I guess he'll be alright. When he gets well he'll come up before a court martial for having live ammunition in his possession. It was his own fault but I feel sorry for him.

Well I guess that really is all the news. Lights just went out again but only for a couple of minutes.

You know something, I love you. Do you know how much? Well I'll tell you. You know how much you love me, well add a little more to that and that's how much I love you. Honest Darling I'm crazy about you. I love every bit of you from head to toes, and every bit of you belongs to me, don't ever forget that.

You know Bernice I've never lied to you about anything that really mattered. I couldn't lie to you and any time that I ever did I always told you the truth afterward (like being in the hospital and things like that). Well what I'm driving at is this. When I tell you, I love you and respect and adore you more than anyone in the world, I mean it from the very bottom of my heart. You're my woman, you're my kind of woman and I love you and want you to be my wife more than anything in the world.

I have to stop writing now Baby. Please be careful and take good care of yourself. If anything happened to you Sweetheart I don't know what I'd do. Take care of yourself for me. I love you Bernice for always.

All my love my Darling,
Your Paul

S.W.A.K. RIGHT HERE

March 8, 1944
Wednesday, 8:30PM

Hi Darling,

I was just looking through Collier Magazine and I saw this picture. Not bad, huh? I know someone who would look just as smooth in something like that. Guess who. I really think you would Baby and I'm not fooling. I'm expecting to see something like that so don't disappoint me. In fact, I'm expecting to see something much prettier than that, and I know I will too.

I'm looking forward to calling you Sunday Darling, first to hear you helped a lot. I hope we don't have to go on the range, but I'm almost certain that we won't have to. Gosh, I love you Sweetheart, I think about you all the time, night & day. As you said, it is nice to be in love, especially when you know that the one you love, loves you and belongs to you.

This is one of those nights when it's hard to write. Everyone seems to be making a noise and it's hard to think. It's funny but sometimes I feel as if I could write for hours and then other times it seems as if everything I write is wrong. I guess you feel like that sometimes too, you just can't seem to get started.

Well anyway Baby I can always think of one thing to write about and that's how much I love you. It's an awful lot my Precious, I think you know that. I hope so.

Here's something kind of interesting. We have a lieutenant in our company by the name of Haney. He spent 18 months on Guadalcanal. Then they brought him back to send him to O.C.S. *(Officer Candidate School)*. He tells us quite a lot of the things that happened over there. Here's one of his stories. One day about 10 of them were going along in a single file when they came upon a wounded Jap. The first man looked at the Jap and he told the second man to kill him with his bayonet. The second man didn't care for the idea so he told the third man and so it went down the line. Haney was the last man so he had to do it. He said he didn't want to but he was the last man so there was no one he could palm it off on. He said he first stuck his bayonet into the Jap's throat, pulled it out and walked on. He's certainly seen a lot. He was decorated with the Silver Star for gallantry in action. I like him a lot.

Well Baby I guess I'll stop now. Take care of yourself Darling, you belong to me funny face and I love you very, very much and I always will.

All my love Darling,
Your Paul

S.W.A.K.
Right Here

Paul, to his surprise, has been awarded the Good Conduct Medal.

Sunday, March 26, 1944 9:30AM

Hi Darling,

How's this for writing early, only 9:30 in the morning. I guess you can tell who I have on my mind 99% of the time.

I just finished showering and shaving so now I'm already to go to church at 11 o'clock. (It will be the first time in 3 weeks that I've had a chance to go.) Next week I won't be able to because we'll be at Talladega on maneuvers. We leave this coming Thursday morning and come back one week later. I'm not looking forward to it one bit. I'll do my best to write you all I can while I'm out there, Honey. You write every day because they'll bring our mail out to us.

You can't call me Itchy because I don't itch anymore. It's all gone away I guess it was just a heat rash.

Big happenings yesterday. I was awarded the Good Conduct Medal. The order came down yesterday that I was to be awarded the Medal and that Major Dahl, the Battalion Commander would present me with it Monday (tomorrow). Why they gave it to me I don't know, it doesn't mean very much anyway, but it's something new to wear on my blouse, that is, if my best girl doesn't take it away from me.

I got a letter from Gerald yesterday, he spoke of their new baby. I better answer your letter now. First about the graduation picture, sure you can have it if you want it. I'm afraid my grandmother's jealous of a lot of junk on you that you don't really want but have to take to be polite.

The fellow you saw with the patch like mine may have been from any I.R.T.C. not just McClellan. You should have asked him. I never heard of Dothan, Alabama, no one in the hut ever heard of it either.

I guess that answers all the questions. That joke was pretty "good," kind of corny though.

I have to shine a couple pairs of shoes Baby so I'm going to stop for a while now. I've got a lot more to write about so don't go away.

8:30PM

That was quite a while to wait, wasn't it? I'll tell you what I've been doing. After dinner a bunch of us went bowling. My first game was 170, the lowest 145. We bowled 5 games, that took till about 5:30. After that we had a sandwich and a Coke and then went to the show. It wasn't a very good picture. I just got back from the show, after I finish this letter I'm going to bed because I have to get up at 4:15 tomorrow.

I had a very nice dream last night, all about you. I can't tell you just what it was but it was awfully nice. I'll tell you about it when I come home, it's easier to whisper it to you than write it.

I miss you Baby an awful lot. In fact, I'm always thinking about you, I guess maybe it's because I'm head over heels in love with you. Think that's it?

I still don't think you're too big for shorts. When I get home, we'll settle that. At least I know I'm going to see you in them, to see you in them sometime, or else. When we're married I want to see you in more than shorts, or should I say less than shorts. I'm getting kind of fresh, huh?

I don't think you mind though do you Baby. After all it is your future husband that's being fresh.

It's 9:30 Funny Face so I think I'll go to bed. Take care of yourself now. Rest up good for May, I promise you'll need it. I love you Darling with all my heart for always.

All my love forever,
Your Paul

S.W.A.K.
Right Here

P.S. Here's the church program from church this morning.

Paul has a close call on the artillery range.

Monday
March 27, 1944
9PM

My Darling,

I came very close to not writing tonight. I'll tell you about it now that it's all over. Today we were on the range shooting the mortar again. Everything was going along fine till about 4:30 this afternoon. We'd finished firing the company so they decided to put on a demonstration for the trainees. I was gunner and Lt. Carr was my assistant gunner. When you fire the mortar after you once hit your target you fire for effect, that means fire about 5 rounds as fast as you can. Well we hit our target and we were given the order to fire for effect. Carr dropped the first three rounds in O.K. but on the fourth one he did it a little too fast. Before the fourth shot had cleared the tube, he started to drop the fifth shot. The fourth hit his hand as it comes out of the mortar, luckily the head of the shell missed his hand and the pin of the shell hit it. If the head had hit it would've exploded and we would have both been killed. As it was it broke three of his fingers and cut his hand up very badly. One quarter of an inch difference and we'd have both been dead tonight. He's in the hospital now, we called an ambulance right away. Besides his hand being

Original letter from Sunday, March 26, 1944

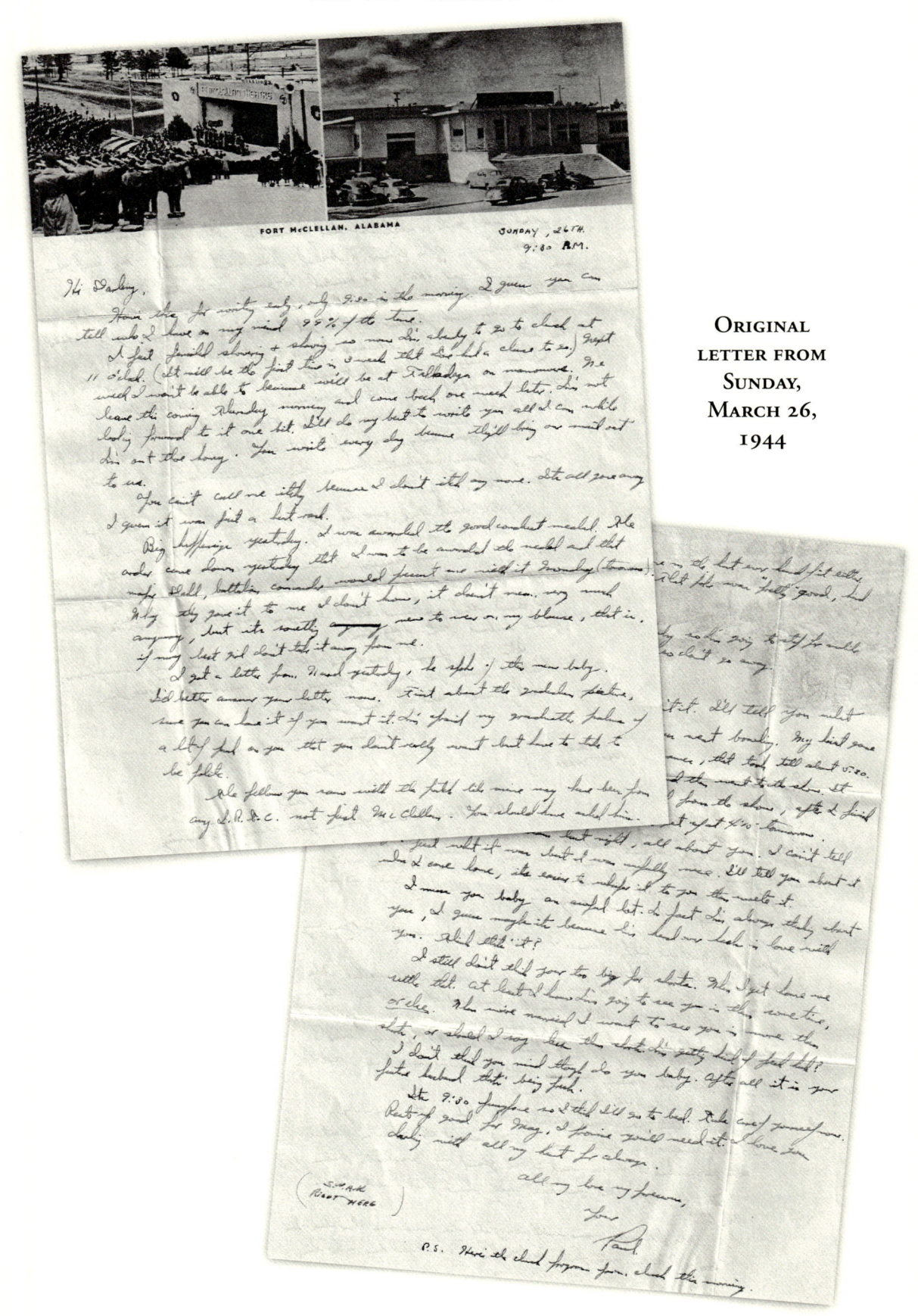

badly hurt he's suffering from shock, but I guess he'll be O.K. Well all's well that ends well, but that was a little too close for comfort.

I got your letter today Baby, the one where you said you felt blue. I know how you feel Funny Face, I feel the same way myself plenty of times. I wish it was May too Darling, keep saving those hugs and kisses for me, I want lots of them. When you marry me, I'm going to want lots more than hugs and kisses. O.K.? The answer to that question better definitely be YES. You know what Baby, I love you very much. You're the cutest little girl in all the world and Sweetheart, you belong to me every bit of you forever and ever.

When you feel blue Darling remember this. When we're married we're going to have years and years of happiness just the two of us. We'll make up for all the time we've been apart, I promise.

Well Funny Face it's 9:30 so I'd better go to bed. Tomorrow morning is the last one I have to go on the mortar range. I sure do hate getting up at 4:15.

Good night my Precious, with all my heart and soul. I love you and I'll never love any other woman but you. Belong to me for always Precious, I'll always want you.

All my love my darling,
Your Paul

S.W.A.K.
Right Here

Paul has returned from a furlough home.

May 29, 1944

My Darling,

Well I got back at about 1'oclock this morning. As usual the trains were late & boy they were crowded. I had to change trains in Washington and when the train left there it was 1 and ½ hours late already. People were sitting on newspapers in the aisles.

The letter you wrote me was waiting for me when I got here. It was nice Darling. By the way I sat with a soldier most of the way back, from Atlanta to Anniston. I sat with a girl, but it couldn't be helped.

This picture was taken before a parade one day down here. From left to right is me, Sergeant Smith, Mike, & Neville.

They certainly made a lot of changes while I was home. Mike, Owen, Carry, and Halion have gone. They all went to Mead to be shipped overseas. Mike was the last one to go. He left Saturday morning and I got back Saturday night. It doesn't seem like the same place without those fellows here. We've got three new men in, two sergeants & one private. They seem like pretty nice fellows.

I couldn't send the telegram last night because it was too late, so I waited and sent it this morning. So far, I haven't heard anything about the sergeant rating, he's not planning on it too much.

This afternoon we all went swimming in the pool. Boy it sure it did feel good.

The new cycle starts tomorrow. The men are all here and everything is ready to go. I'm on the same committee that I was on the last time. This time I'm cadre chief. That means I'm the head of the cadre on the committee. Lt. Gallenfer is committee chief.

Well I guess that's all the news Darling. I still can't quite believe Mike has gone. None of them got a delay in route, so he didn't even get to see his wife and baby. Well maybe we'll meet again sometime, I hope so.

This isn't going to be a very long letter Honey. I don't feel much like writing. I think my morale isn't so hot today. I want you to know though that I had a wonderful time when I was home, being with you has always meant having a wonderful time.

Please be a good girl now and take good care of yourself.

All my love my Precious,
Your Paul
S.W.A.K. RIGHT HERE

Original letter from Sunday, May 29, 1944

June 2, 1944
9:30pm

My Darling,

I'm writing early while it's still cool. I don't think it's going to get so hot today though, there is a nice breeze out now. The latest news is that I take my physical tomorrow morning at 8 o'clock. I'll be glad when tomorrow morning is over. I'm really scared of that eye exam, don't forget to keep those fingers crossed for me. If I pass the physical there's a good chance of my leaving for Benning sometime this week.

I ate the whole bottle of olives before I went to the party at the cadre club. They didn't seem to affect me any though. I wouldn't have had to eaten olives if I'd been around when you wrote me the letter I got yesterday. I can just imagine you laying on your bed, in your birthday suit, writing it. I like to think of things like that. I guarantee I wouldn't need any olives.

Pat wasn't at the club and it isn't anyone else now, wise guy. Here's a picture they took the night of the party, it's not very good though.

Well we're all finished with the range, I hope that's the last time I ever have to see it.

You said my letters for the last few weeks have been indifferent and indefinite about August. I know they have but after all it's kind of hard to be definite about something when you don't know how what's going to happen yourself. I don't think I've been indifferent. I said if I were home I wanted you to come. I still don't know if I'm going to be or not, so it's hard to make definite plans.

I don't know why you said you made a fool of yourself while I was home. I don't think you did. In fact, I think you were awfully sweet to me. I don't suppose you believe that.

The next part of your letter is kind of hard to answer. To tell you the truth I don't know what to say. I don't blame you for writing what you did. If it's true I must seem like a washout to you. According to what you say I've got about as much backbone as a worm. Some of those things are true, I admit it. I send twenty dollars a month home, maybe I'm foolish for doing it, I probably am. I sold my car, that probably was foolish also, although it doesn't matter much to me whether I sold it or not. I probably won't need a car for a long while, because if I don't go to O.C.S. I'll be going overseas within weeks not months. It's hard to write just what I mean. When I was home even for those short 10 days I was fed up with family. All my life all my relatives except one person, my mother, have been selfish and all for themselves. So, you see I agree with you on a lot of things. But don't think anyone is putting something over on me, it's just that I really don't give a damn. Excuse my language but that's the way I feel. You also mentioned about you going to New York to visit me, and going there for a couple of days together and about joining church etc. You can blame me for those things. If I had wanted to have done them I would have. Don't think the reason I didn't do them was because I didn't want to be with you, it wasn't that. If we had gone to New York for a couple of days, what would we have done. We couldn't very well have gotten a room, together could we? We would have gone to shows and things like that, we could do that at home, the only difference would be that I wouldn't be able to be with you as much in New York as I would be at home. If you had met me in New York at 1AM what could we have done, we could have *(illegible)* for the next train to Albany as I did and been with each other for 4 more hours on a dirty train. I don't think you'd have enjoyed that as much as you think.

I guess the last thing you mention was the ring. I think you're absolutely right in expecting it. The reason I haven't given it to you is not because of my father. And it's not it's not because I don't love you. I'll try to do something about it real soon.

Well I guess that answers everything. I know I haven't done such a good job in answering your letters, but what I've said is the truth, believe it or not. You probably don't.

They just brought today's mail in, there's a letter from you, wait till I read it.

That's kind of funny, just after I finished answering yesterday's letter you say you're sorry you wrote it. Well I'm really glad you did, I had it coming I guess.

I'm awfully glad Gerald is home. I wish I could have been there when he was.

I'll finish this letter, I'm going to get ready and go to church now. Once in a while I do something you like, such as going to church.

1PM

Back from church, it was pretty good. We just finished dinner, ham, mashed potatoes, salad, broccoli, lemonade, and ice cream. Lucky me.

Now to answer your second letter. As I said before I'm awfully glad Gerald got home. That's a nice long furlough too.

I'm glad he hasn't changed any. From the way you talk I must have changed an awful lot. Well I guess maybe I have. Another year in the army and probably no one will know me.

A bunch of us are going swimming this afternoon, it's a swell day for it.

I'm going to try and send your letters home this week, if I pass the physical I might leave at any time and I know you want the letters. I'll put them all in a small bag and then just that in a box and send it. I may not get around to it for a few days so don't expect it at any certain time.

Well we're going swimming now so I'm going to stop. Be sure and have a good time while Gerald is home. I guess I don't have to tell you that. Take good care of yourself. Don't forget to keep your fingers crossed for me.

I love you Sweetheart for always,
Your Paul

S.W.A.K.
Right Here

Paul is writing the day after the D-Day invasion in Normandy, France.

June 7, 1944

Hi Darling,

I got a swell letter from you today. The one you wrote Sunday. It sure was long but better than that it had some awfully nice things in it.

I didn't write last night because we had training films till about 11 o'clock and I was tired as heck. Forgive me?

Everyone down here is interested in the invasion of course. It seems to be going O.K., so far, here's hoping.

If everything goes O.K. and I'm still here in August I'm sure I'll be able to get a 3 day pass. It would be swell wouldn't it. Please don't plan on it too much though Baby. I don't want you to be disappointed if it doesn't work out that way.

Tom and I went to the show tonight, it wasn't very good though, I'm sorry I went now.

I miss you Baby an awful lot but as long as I know you're taking good care of yourself and being a good girl then I feel better. Please don't get any thinner, I don't like the girdle. When you weigh between 120 & 125 you're just right. I don't want to feel your ribs. You'd better get up to at least 120 pretty soon or I'll get mad.

You don't have to send me olives Honey. Every time I think of my furlough and being with you, I don't need olives. You're all I need, I don't have to have anything additional.

I love you Sweetheart very, very much & I always will. Be a good girl now and be careful and take good care of yourself.

All my love my Precious,
Your
Paul

S.W.A.K.
Right Here

Paul has been promoted to sergeant.

June 9, 1944
9:00pm

My Darling,

I got your letter with the big news today about Gerald and Millie's baby. Boy that's swell. I bet you're all pretty darn proud. Ask your Dad how he's going to like being called Grandpa. I'm glad they had a girl, maybe I'll be able to get a date with her in a few years. See if you can fix it up for me.

Today was the first day I received letters addressed as Sargent. I got one from my grandmother, one from my father and one from you. I've had about 5 sets of ribbons sewn on so far, still have about 10 to go.

A bunch of us went to the show tonight. The picture was "The Eve of Saint Mark." It was very good. If you see it you'll cry, I'm warning you.

I'm glad you got the pins O.K. The next one will have a rocker underneath it. I'm just fooling, I don't expect to make Staff Sargent for quite a while. I'm what you call a back Sargent or a line Sargent, they both mean the same thing.

It's been awfully hot down here today. But I'm not complaining, I like the warm weather, I guess I always will.

I can't get over Gerald and Millie being proud papas and mommas. Gerald and Pete and George are sure beating my time, aren't they? Well someday I'll catch up, that is if we have two at a time.

Be sure and tell Millie I was asking about her. I hope she feels alright soon. I knew about it before I got your letter because my grandmother's letter came this morning and yours this afternoon. I know how excited you all must be, I wish I could have seen the new member of the Getter family. Here's hoping she's not all grown up by the time I see her.

Well Baby I'm tired so I guess I'll go to bed early tonight. Take good care of yourself Funny Face. I love you Darling, even if you are getting pretty old. An aunt, my! my!

Good night my Darling.
All my love for always.
Your Paul

S.W.A.K.
Right Here

June 28, 1944
10 PM

Hi Darling,

Another day on the range over, only the 3 more to go. This getting up every morning at 3:30 and going to bed at 10:30 is getting me down.

I got a letter from you today. I sure am glad Millie and the baby are home. Tell Dawnne I'd like a date in about 18 years from this Saturday night.

An order came down from Battalion tonight saying I was to report before the O.C.S. Board at 8:30 Friday morning. Wish me luck Baby, Friday will decide whether I go or not. The Board consists of colonels & superiors and if they say O.K. I'll go to O.C.S., if they say no I don't go. Keep those fingers crossed.

To tell you the truth I'm kind of excited about it, after Friday I'll feel more like writing.

Please forgive the short letter Baby. I love you with all my heart. Be a good girl and take good care of yourself.

Good night Darling. I love you.

All my love Darling,
Your Paul

S.W.A.K.
Right Here

July 3, 1944
9:30pm

My Darling,

I'm Sgt. of the Guard tonight, I always manage to get chosen for the horrible job. I go off duty at 6 A.M. and go out with the company at 7:30 A.M.

I mailed all your letters back today. Let me know if you get them O.K. I think they're all there even the ones I got when I was on bivouac. They're not in order or anything and there are some papers from Larrabee, keep them for me, will you?

Well I took the physical for the O.C.S. this morning and I passed it. I almost didn't though. The lowest eye vision they would accept was 20/100 and mine was 20/200. The major down there said I'm sorry I can't accept you. I asked him to let me try it again and with a little cheating on my part I managed to have 20/100 vision. It was a close call though. Thanks for keeping your fingers crossed for me, it helped. I may leave at any time now for O.C.S. that is if everything continues to go well. Don't uncross those fingers yet. If I do get there you'll have to cross them for 17 weeks.

I don't know what to tell you about coming down with Gerald, Darling. If I knew I were going to be home I'd say come but as it is now I might even leave this week. I hope you understand Honey please don't think I don't want you to come. I do.

I suppose you're all having a swell time. I sure do hope so. I haven't heard yet whether or not I'm going to get a date with Dawnne. How about asking her old man? I promise to be a gentleman. If the girl is doubtful she can ask her aunt about me. O.K.?

I'm kind of anxious to hear about O.C.S., in fact I haven't been thinking of much of anything else for the past week or so. Yes, I have to. I've been thinking of you. Are you surprised or did you know I think about you all the time? I do you know, maybe because I love you huh? I do love you Sweetheart an awful lot.

Be a good girl and take good care of yourself. You belong to me alone, remember that always.

Good night Darling,
All my love,
Your Paul

S.W.A.K.
Right Here

July 9, 1944
10 A.M.

Hi Darling,

I got two big letters from you yesterday and one was really big. They made me ashamed of the small ones I've been writing.

I wasn't angry with you about that letter Darling. I just think you had a perfect right to say what you did.

I think your new plan about going to see Gerald and then me is a good one Honey, I sure do hope it works out.

I just got another letter from you. A bunch of us are going to see "The White Cliffs of Dover" this afternoon. It was funny you're mentioning it in your letter.

Hey you, did I ever say I thought anyone else's legs were as pretty as yours? Yours are definitely the nicest ones I've seen Baby. They're the only ones I'll ever love.

You haven't mentioned getting the letters yet. I hope they get there O.K. Let me know as soon as you get them.

We always said Gerald would make a good father. He's the type for it I guess. I know he must love his daughter very much.

I guess I told you that I'm a platoon sergeant now instead of working on committee. I have the second platoon. I've got 10 men out of the platoon on Sunday K.P. for having dirty rifles. It sounds mean doesn't it? I guess it is, but it has to be done. One of my men was in prison for 5 years before coming into the army, some of them are married and have 2 or 3 children, some are only 18 years old. They're all kinds, but they're a pretty good bunch of fellows. My platoon had the best record on the rifle range. There are some wise guys, they're the ones in the kitchen right now.

I've got about 50 chigger bites on my legs. Boy they're awful. They itch worse than mosquito bites.

I hope I'm forgiven for writing short letters Sweetheart. These O.C. S. things have kind of got me going. I still haven't heard any news. It will be one week tomorrow since I've taken the physical. Something should happen soon if it's ever going to. If news does come I'll call you right away.

I'm going to get ready to go to church now so I guess I'll stop. I miss you Darling very much. I'd like to be sitting with you on that bench you were talking about. I love you Sweetheart an awful awful lot, I always will. Please take good care of yourself Baby and always remember you belong to me.

I hope I'll be seeing you soon, I will if our plans work out. Bye for now Baby, I love you.

All my love my Darling,
Your Paul

S.W.A.K.

July 10, 1944
9:30 P.M.

Hi Darling,

I know I must be in the dog house after reading the letter you wrote Saturday. I'm glad you got the letter. Now please let me explain Peg. I hope you believe this, it's the truth. She was the girl that worked at the store that one summer. She worked for Elaine. I told you about her I think. Well when I first came in the army she wrote me asking me how I liked it etc.

I never answered it, then later on she wrote again so I answered it. I don't know how her letter sounded it was a long time ago (look at the postmark) anyway the letter I wrote her was about like the kind I've written Naomi Connors or someone like that. Believe me? I hope so. It's the truth no fooling. Her name is Peggy Colby and they live in Schenectady.

Now for Irene. I don't know any girl by that name except Irene Hunter and I'm sure I wasn't writing to her. You'll first have to take my word for it, that I wasn't writing to any girl called Irene.

It is nice to have more than one friend and I hope I have more than one, but Darling I only want one Sweetheart. That's you. I'm either out of that dog house by now or farther in it. I hope you believe me Honey, you should. I'm glad Pete got home while Gerald was still there. I wish I could have seen both of them. Gerald and Millie and the baby must be on the way back by now. I hope they have a nice trip.

I haven't made O.C.S. yet. I'll say I've made it when I arrive at Benning. I've been accepted but that doesn't mean I'm definitely going. There still has to be a quota. I always heard that girls preferred enlisted men to officers. And some people I have heard it said, prefer the navy with their nice white uniforms to the Army with the dull colors. I hope that such rumors aren't true though.

Oh, by the way you mentioned in your letter that Bill Pierce was home for 10 days. Gerald sure did get to see more of the fellows than I did.

Here's the schedule we had today. Each platoon Sgt. gets a schedule each morning for the day's work.

I know this letter has been just a little bit on the "smart" side but then yours was a bit like that too. Seriously Sweetheart I hope you do understand. Peg doesn't mean a thing to me, she was first someone I met and I had to answer her letter to be polite. I still can't figure out who Irene is, but believe me I don't know anyone by that name.

If you were trying to make me jealous when you mentioned how nice Bill Pierce looked you succeeded. I've always been a little jealous since you told me you like the way he kissed. I hope a certain Sgt. in the infantry does a better job. Does he? I want to know.

I love you Darling, no one else, only you. You're the one and only woman I want. You've got everything I want Baby. I'm still dreaming about the last furlough and the evenings we spent together. It was wonderful. I love every bit of you from the tip of your head to the tip of your toes. I want all of you for myself Darling, I'll never share you with anyone. I've got to be the first and only one in your life or not in it at all. I know you want that too. I'd feel awful if you didn't.

Well I guess I'll go to bed now. I hope I'm forgiven for all my failings.

I love you Darling, with all my heart for always.

All my love my Darling,
Your Paul

S.W.A.K.
Right Here

Bernie has celebrated her nineteenth birthday.

July 13, 1944
10 PM

Hi Darling,

You've probably been thinking that I'd forgotten about your birthday. I hadn't Honey, in fact for the last 3 nights I've been looking for something to get you. Darling I just can't seem to find anything. I couldn't even get a birthday card that I liked. I think I've looked in every store in Anniston for something, but they just don't have anything nice. I'm sending you your present this way although I know it isn't half as good as getting a real present. Forgive me Darling but there just isn't anything else I can do. I want you to be sure and spend this right away on anything you want. Don't save it, spend it all on yourself right away. I know it isn't much Baby, but I think you know that I'm also sending all my love and devotion, to you, the one and only girl I'll ever want.

I want you to think of this present as just a tiny bit of what I want to give you soon. As soon as I have enough money and where I can get it I want to get you a ring. There's nothing I've seen down here that I like and to be truthful I don't have enough money to buy a nice ring. Money and I seem to part company awfully fast for some reason. I'm not trying to offer excuses for not getting the ring for your birthday, I just want you to know that I want to get it for you and that I'm going to as soon as I can. You see Sweetheart, even though you found a letter written from another girl to me, and even though you sometimes think I'm a pretty awful guy, I love you with all my heart. I know I always will. You're not getting any bargain when you get me, but I hope you'll always want me, and want to belong to me. One of the many reasons why I love you so much Bernie is because I know that when I marry you I'll be the first man and the only one to ever have you. That means an awful lot to me Darling. I hope you know how much.

I'm going to try to call you sometime this week whether I know about the O.C.S. thing or not. I want to talk to you, that's the next best thing to seeing you. I told you I guess that we go on the B.A.R. range Sunday so I probably won't be able to call you on Sunday. Maybe I'll get a chance to call before Sunday.

Have a happy birthday my Darling, I hope and pray that long before your next one we'll all be together again for good.

We have to get up at 4 AM again tomorrow. We go on a patrol, have to have faces blackened and things like that. Some fun.

I've been thinking of you more than usual lately Honey. You seem to be all I can think of, at least all I want to think about. I wish I could be there for your birthday. I'd like to give you 19 good solid wacks. Don't think I could do it, do you? You just wait, I'm going to win a lot of bets from you. That one special bet we have is as good as won right now. The way I feel when, I'm lying with you on the couch, there's not a doubt in my mind that I can win. I'll have you asking for "time out" you just wait and see. I don't mean by that that you won't be able to satisfy me in every way. I know you can, do that Baby, you're all the woman I'll ever want, and that's a lot.

I better go to bed now. I'm tired as usual, it will be wonderful to be tired from something other than revelry. I think you know what I mean.
You'd better.

Good night Sweetheart. Don't forget to me, and that I love you with all my heart. Happy Birthday my 19 year old Darling, I love you.

All my love forever and ever,
Your Paul

S.W.A.K.
Right Here

July 15, 1944
9:30 P.M.

My Darling,

This has to be a short letter because I've got to get up at 3:30 in the morning. We go on the range tomorrow (Sunday) to fire the B.A.R. Oh what fun.

I didn't write last night because I had a cleaning detail that lasted till 10 o'clock, I was so darned tired I went right to bed.

You asked me what a platoon sergeant does. Well to be brief I'm in charge of 49 men. I'm in charge of the 3 huts these men sleep in and I'm also responsible for their drilling, giving them passes if I think they should get them, putting them on details such as Sunday K.P. etc. Whatever they do I do it right with them. I march with them everywhere they go. It's a little harder work than committee work was. (I do what the Sgt. did in "See Here Private Hargrove")

I hope I'll be able to make that call soon Honey. I'm beginning to doubt if they'll ever call me. Keep your fingers crossed Baby.

I'll write a long letter tomorrow night. Take care of yourself Funny Face. I love you my Precious.

All my love my Sweetheart,
Your Paul

Paul has been accepted for Officer Candidate School.

July 20, 1944
10 P.M.

My Darling,

Well my orders finally came through today. I leave the 31st of this month for Fort Benning, GA. Wish me luck Darling, I'll need it.

I didn't write last night because we had training films till 9:30 and by the time I washed and showered it was about 10:30 and I was awfully tired.

You'll probably get this letter Monday, don't write to me after next Tuesday or Wednesday. Wait until you get my new address. I'll telegraph it to you as soon as I know it myself.

Naturally I'm excited about going to O.C.S. It will seem funny leaving here. 14 months down here, that's a long while. You'll have to keep your fingers crossed for me for 17 weeks of O.C.S. I'll do my best but I need you backing me up.

I've got to make this a short letter Darling. I'm awfully sleepy and 5 o'clock comes early. Be a good girl now. Remember I love you with all my heart. You belong to me Precious.

All my love my sweetheart,
Your Paul

S.W.A.K.
Right Here

July 21, 1944
9 P.M.

My Darling,

I didn't write last night because I was getting ready for the O.C.S. interviews this morning. I went to I.R.T.C. Headquarters this morning for the interviews and I passed it. The board was made up of two colonels and 2 majors. These were the questions they asked me.

How old was I, was I married, how long had I been in the army, what college I went to, I said Union and the colonel said that's a fine school, why didn't I finish college, had I gone to E.C.S., my academic average at E.C.S. Then I had to give some commands to an imaginary platoon, tell him the organization of an infantry regiment. After all that he said we approve your application.

All I have to do tomorrow is pass the physical and then I'm all set to go to Benning. I'm worried though. I've heard that to pass the eye exam your eyes have to be at least 2100 without glasses and I think mine are 2200. Keep your fingers crossed for me Baby, if they stop me from going just because of that I'm going to be one mad guy. I may get the physical anytime now, in fact there's a possibility that if I have it within the next few days and pass it, I stand a chance of leaving for O.C.S. next week sometime. Keep hoping for me.

I got two letters from you today. I was sorry to hear about Eddie. He was a swell guy. Missing in action doesn't always mean they're dead though. It seems like only yesterday that he and Gary and I sat together at fraternity meetings. What a nutty world this is.

Gerald should be home by now. If he is I bet he's really one happy guy. Ask him if I can have a date with his daughter. He'll probably say no, he knows me too well.

About the only thing I can think of is that eye exam. I wish they'd call me tomorrow and get it over with. Boy I was nervous this morning, if you do one little thing wrong you're out.

If I am lucky enough to go to O.C.S. at least I'll be able to say I did the hard way. I've never had anything handed to me on a silver platter yet in the army.

Tomorrow is the last day on the range, it's been a long week.

I can always tell when you're going to write a nasty letter. They always start out with "My dear Paul." You're very good at saying nasty things in a nice way. I hope Norma and her Pfc will be very happy, I think they might have been a little wiser if they had waited until she grows up to the ripe old age of say 18 at least.

As soon as I've had the physical I'll let you know how it came out. Keep on hoping with me Baby, everything has gone O.K. so far, keeping those fingers crossed really helped.

Take good care of yourself now. Be sure and tell Gerald I was asking about him.

We get paid tomorrow, it will be the first sergeant's pay I've got and boy I can use it, I've been broke for the last 3 days.

I love you Sweetheart with all my heart for always. You belong to me Funny Face and no one else.

All my love my Precious,
Your Paul

S.W.A.K.
Right Here

(Sent as a Western Union Telegram.)
Paul is leaving for Officer Candidate School.

July 26, 1944

Miss Bernice Getter

Leaving tomorrow morning for Ft. Benning. Will send new address as soon as possible.

Love,

Paul

Chapter 2
Officer candidate school at Fort Benning, Georgia
July 28, 1944 to November 8, 1944

July 28, 1944

My Darling,

I haven't got much time so this has to be short.

We left McClellan at 11:30 A.M. yesterday morning and arrived here at Benning at 11:30 P.M. last night. Twelve hours to go about 150 miles.

We didn't get to bed until 2:30 this morning then up again at 6 A.M. We've been taking tests all day.

Don't write me at this address. It's only temporary and we're not allowed to have mail sent here. I'll tell you my mailing address as soon as possible Darling.

We took all our stripes off today. Tonight, we have more tests starting at 6:30.

So far, I don't like it but that's natural I guess. It's about as bad as being a trainee again. I'll still keep my ranking and get Sgt. pay but we don't wear our stripes.

Tell my grandmother I'll write as soon as I get settled.

It's going to be tough down here from what we've already seen and heard. Keep your fingers crossed Baby, I'll need it.

I hope you got my telegram from McClellan O.K. There's no way of sending one from here that's why I haven't.

Take care of yourself Sweetheart. I love you very much. You belong to me.

All my love my Darling,
Your Paul

Paul explains the challenges of Officer Candidate School.

July 29, 1944

My Very Own Darling,

This thing gets worse and worse every day so far. All we've done is take tests, fill out forms etc. We're just like a bunch of trainees. In our group there are two master sergeants, 4 first sergeants, three warrant officers (why they want to be 2nd Lts. I'll never know) The rest of us are all sergeants and corporals. Everyone without his stripes looks just like a trainee again. We haven't finished our processing yet. Probably by Monday we'll start our classes, I hope so.

From all we've heard it's going to be plenty tough. Only about 50% finish the 17 weeks. They can wash you out even on the last day. A lot of the fellows are wondering if it's worth it. I'm going to do my best, I can't do any more than that, if it isn't good enough you'll just have to keep on loving a sergeant instead of a second Lt. They have a stiff math test the 5th week. You know how I'm looking forward to that. I wish I had your brains Darling, well anyway those twins of ours should be smart. And if they take after you they'll not only be smart but beautiful too. I mean that.

You still can't write to me. Probably by Monday I'll know my mailing address. If I can possibly do it, I'll write it to you.

We have to fall out in a little while so I can't write much more.

Forgive me for not writing much Sweetheart, I just don't have the time. Keep your fingers crossed for me Baby, I've never needed it more than I do now. I love you Darling and the happiest day of my life will be when I'm a civilian again and can be with you always.

I'll always love you Bernie, don't ever forget you belong to me.

All my love Darling,
Your Paul

S.W.A.K.
Right Here

July 30, 1944

My Darling,

Another day almost over and we're finally finished our processing. Tomorrow we start the first day of our 17 weeks. We filled out forms and took tests all day again today. I definitely don't like it here as yet, I don't think any of the fellows like it. We've talked to fellows who have been busted out in the 15th week for just little things. It looks as if it's going to be plenty tough. Well I can't do any more than my best.

You can start writing to me now. Here is my address:
    O/C Paul E. Roberts, C.S.N. 12170404
    14th. Co. 2nd. S.T.R.
    Fort Benning, Georgia,
    U. S. Army

I'm in the 14th company, the second student training regiment. O/C means officer candidate.

Guess what my class number is. #366. Remember that number on the old Ford? Maybe that's a good luck sign.

If you don't get a letter from me every day Honey please don't worry or be angry. I don't know yet how much time I'll have to write but you know I'll write every day I possibly can. I haven't had any mail forwarded from McClellan since I've been here. I sure do miss your letters Darling. Maybe because I love you so much, think so?

I miss you more and more every day my Darling. You were made for me Baby, I've known that for a long, long while. Be a good girl and be happy, have fun, & take good care of yourself. We'll be together again soon.

I'll love you my Precious, I always will.

All my love my Darling,
Your Paul

S.W.A.K.
Right Here

P.S. Keep those fingers crossed on both hands.

August 3, 1944

Hi Darling,

Still no mail forwarded from McClellan, so I still don't have any letters to answer. If this pace keeps up for 17 weeks and if I last that long, I'll probably have grey hair. By the way I had my hair cut short again. About 1 ½ in. high. Still love me? You'd better.

It's rained every day we've been here so far. Georgia is worse than Alabama as far as weather goes.

They inspect our barracks every day. If you're foot locker is unlocked that's a star gig. Three-star gigs and you're washed out. There's a lot of other things you get star gigs for, then there are about 999,999 regular gigs, such as dust on floor, not dirt just dust.

The first meeting of the board comes in the fifth week. That means you can be washed out as early as your fifth week and any week thereafter. I don't think there's a man in the class (over 200 of us) that is confident of finishing.

It looks about hopeless at times. I'm depending on your keeping your fingers crossed for me Baby. I definitely need it.

The food here can't compare with McClellan. Most of us feel like we're starving to death. I guess we'll survive though.

Well I guess I've kicked enough for one letter. You probably think I'm dying from the sound of my letter. Well it's not quite that bad. The physical training program is brutal. I'll kick about that in my next letter.

Take good care of yourself my Darling. I love you very much Baby, I always will. I'll do my best to write longer letters as soon as I can.

By for now Honey. I love you.

All my love Darling,
Your Paul

S.W.A.K.
Right Here

August 6, 1944

My Very Own Darling,

On our day of rest, I've worked harder than the other six days. Here's what I've done so far. Get up at 7:30 had breakfast. Started studying map reading at 8 o'clock till 10:30. Wash clothes from 10:30 till 12:15. Had dinner 12:30. Studied from 1 P.M. till 3 P.M. Cleaned rifle from 3 to 3:45. Now I'm writing to you, then done, then I'll eat supper. Then shine shoes, shower and shave, study till 10 and go to bed about 10:30. Gee Darling when this war is over I'm going to make up for these Sundays especially. I'm going to take life easy all day long or get dressed in slacks and ride and ride and guess who's going to be with me every minute. YOU. We'll make up for all these months we've missed Darling, I promise.

I got a letter from you yesterday. It was forwarded from McClellan, the last one you wrote to me there. It sure was good to get one.

Next Sunday I'm going to try to go to church. The chaplain talked to us the other day, he seemed very nice. He's the first chaplain with the rank of major that I've seen. There's a lot of high ranking officers around here. The men instructing us in our different courses are all captains, majors and Lt. Colonels.

There's not much news to write about. Starting tomorrow I'm assigned as platoon leader. That will be for 3 days, then someone else gets a turn at it. (Platoon leaders are 2nd Lt.) That way each man in the platoon acts as lieutenant of the platoon and of course they watch every move you make to see if you do anything wrong.

I was showing the fellows in the hut your picture a little while ago. They think you're very pretty and sweet. They'd be crazy if they didn't. I think you're the prettiest and sweetest girl in all the world and I always will. I have your big picture up on my shelf and the little one (the one I was showing them) in my foot locker. Don't worry I didn't show them one of you in your shorts. I'm the only one permitted to look at that one.

I wrote a letter last night to the fellows at McClellan. I miss them quite a lot but I've made a lot of new friends here. In a way it was a good thing I left McClellan when I did, even if I don't make it here. Someday I'll tell you about it. It has nothing to do with women so don't get angry.

The water is running off my chin faster than I can wipe it off. Don't mind the blots. You just can't help sweating down here.

I'll write Sgt. DiComo to send me a pennant from McClellan and then I'll send it to you O.K.? I am sorry for not having it before.

I've still got my fingers crossed about finishing the next 16 weeks here. Sometimes it looks almost impossible. I'm depending on you to help me along don't forget. You'll get awfully tired keeping your fingers crossed all that while but I sure do need it. I'm jealous Baby, I wish I had half the brains you have. Well as I said before, our twins should be smart, that's something.

It's about time for supper Honey so I'm going to stop. We probably won't have anything to eat, they're slowing starving us to death, but I guess I'll live.

Please take care of yourself Darling. You belong to me, don't ever forget that. I'll always love you Bernie and only you. Be a good girl now. And above all be happy and have all the fun you can. I love you Darling.

All my love for always,
Your Paul

S.W.A.K.
Right Here

August 13, 1944

Hi Darling,

Here's that man again. I'm writing this one from the service club. It's not as nice as the one at Fort McClellan but it's a lot better than the hut. Frank Dergin (he's from McClellan too) took a walk down here to have supper. I had roast beef, peas, mashed potatoes, ice cream and cake. Not bad huh? Frank and I had basic training together at McClellan only he was in A company and I was in C. Then when I went to B-11 he went the same day to A-11. Then we were both ordered down here at the same time. He's a swell guy, came from *(illegible)*. I've still got a couple of more hours of studying to do. After I finish this letter I'm going back to the company and study & then go to bed. It started to rain a few minutes ago that's why I'm writing here instead of at the company.

On that card that Marie Van Horn sent me she said you were looking good, and that she thought you were feeling much better. Have you been sick again? Please tell me Darling, if anything is wrong I want to know about it. You certainly look O.K. to me in that picture but if there's anything wrong tell me about it. I'd be angry if you didn't.

I hope you're writing me a long letter today. If you didn't by gosh after my writing twice I'll sure as heck be mad.

I hope you send some more of those pictures. Please do if you have them. That one you sent really did things to me. I've got those favorite pictures of you now. Really 4. One in that summer dress, one in your den with the pin on it, the one in the bathing suit, and the one of you and I together when I was still a civilian. Remember the one we took up at Millie's? Did I ever tell you that you're the cutest, most adorable, sweetest girl in all the world?

If I didn't there was something wrong with me because Darling you're all of those things plus a lot more. You know something, I'm in love with you. I sometimes wonder how you could love me but as long as you do that's what counts. (I hope you still do)

My hair has grown in quite a lot. I can almost comb it again. I guess I'll let it get long again. Another thing I forgot to mention was your permanent. I bet it looks swell. I still like your hair best when it's long but I like it the other way too.

I've been gigged three times so far. Once for dust, once for leaving a button unbuttoned, and once for having a manual out of place. If I keep that up I'll have the record for the most giggs. Those giggs don't count too much though. Their class three giggs. Class number 2 and one are what you have to watch out for. Class one or a star gigg is the worst. 3 of those and your worked out. If you get a class 2 gigg you have to go before the company commander.

You can see by this letter head that we're in the Sunday church area. This area is 8 miles from the main fort. So actually, I haven't ever seen Ft. Benning itself as yet. The paratrooper's school is here at Benning also. We can see them every day jumping. It sure looks like fun. Benning is, I think, the biggest Fort in the South. It's at least 5 times bigger then McClellan. There are all kinds of things going on down here. There are two or three regular divisions, the paratrooper school, Officer Candidate School, cooks and bakers' school, I.R.T.C., Commission Officers School, and about two or three more things. So far all I've seen is the Harmony Church area. I haven't even been to the main post.

I guess I've written just about everything I can think of now. You're probably tired of reading all this anyway. I wouldn't blame you.

Do you mind if I talk about my favorite subject for a while? Do you know what my favorite subject is? No! Well I'll tell you. It's about 5 feet 2 or 3?, weighs about 120 pounds, has dark hair, very soft and beautiful, has an awfully cute mouth, nose and eyes and two little ears that I like to bite. Soft hands and little feet? To sum it up my favorite subject is very sweet, very pretty, and in a bathing suit even more so. You recognize yourself, that's what you're like to me Darling only I can't help explain the way I feel in words. The most I can say in a few words is that "I love you." Don't ever doubt that for even a second. Maybe one of the reasons why I do some crazy things that I'm sorry for is because I can't have the one person who means everything to me with me. Darling I miss you oh so very much. We'll make up for these months, I've told myself that a million times it's just got to come true. Keep yourself for me my Precious, you'll never regret it. I want you to be mine and mine alone. You're my woman Darling and I'll never love anyone else as long as I live.

Good night Funny Face. Take good care of yourself.

All my love forever and ever,
Your Paul

S.W.A.K.
RIGHT HERE

August 16, 1944

Hi Darling,

Boy what a day this has been. This morning we learned how to load vehicles on trains, in fact we even did it for the practical experience. That's in case you were a transportation officer when your outfit moves someplace. This afternoon came the real fun. We had physical achievement tests for 4 hours. I'm really tired and that's no fooling. First hour we had to do pushups, chin-ups, 300 yd-, grenade course (350 yards) creep and crawl under barbed wire. That was the first hour. I passed everything with a very satisfactory rating so that's not bad. The second hour we had log drill. A team of 8 men were on one log about 30 ft. long. The third hour was the obstacle course, it has to be run under 2 minutes. I did that in 1 minute 50 sec. The last hour we ran for 45 minutes straight. I haven't got enough pep left to raise my hand.

I didn't get any letter from you today, so I don't have to answer. Don't forget I'll call you Sunday morning. If something should happen and I don't please don't worry.

We haven't got the company picture yet. I'll send it to you as soon as I get it. I've got one of the pins we wore on our hats at McClellan, would you like it? If you would I'll send it to you. Maybe I can dig up an extra O.C.S. patch too if you want one.

Well Baby I guess that's all the news for now. I'm getting awful sleepy and lights go out in about 10 minutes.

Going under the barbed wire today we had to go as fast as we could of course by crawling. I was unlucky enough to raise my head a little too high and I got the barbed wire right across the top of my head. It cut a little but not bad. Next time I'll put my nose in the ground further.

This is the third week already, I sure hope I'm still here the 17th. Don't uncross those fingers whatever you do.

Take good care of yourself Darling. I love you Baby more and more every day.

Good night Darling,
Your Paul

S.W.A.K.
Right Here

August 23, 1944

My Darling,

I haven't much time to write this, I've still got some studying to do and lights go out at 10 o'clock. Tomorrow we have the math test. Boy how I wish I knew as much as you do about math. Keep your fingers crossed Baby.

So far, I have a B in Map Reading, a B in the M1 Rifle, a B in the Light and Heavy Machine Gun,

a Very Satisfying in Leadership and a Very Satisfying in Physical Training. If I can only get a good mark tomorrow I'll be happy. So just I'll be very happy so far.

We ran the obstacle course for time today. I did it in 105 seconds. That's the average company time so I'm O.K. in that. I think I could have done it faster but when I was jumping over one obstacle I hurt my foot. For a minute, I thought I broke my ankle but I guess I just sprained it. It's swollen like heck tonight but I can still walk on it so it will be O.K. I guess. Maybe the swelling will be down by tomorrow, I hope so.

I just looked at my two pictures of my bathing beauty. You know what, when we're married I'm going to pick out some of your clothes. There are some things I'd like very much to see you in. Guess what they are. Are you going to always wear pajamas? I like them but I'd also like nightgowns and if I have my way there are going to be times when I won't like nightgowns or pajamas. Am I going to get my way or will I have to act like a cave man? You know when I think of cold winter nights and how you and I are going to be all tucked in in our big bed with you just as close to me as you possibly can be, I feel wonderful all over. When 5:30 comes in the morning we'll just turn off the alarm clock, pull the blankets up over our heads, kiss each other and ---- I don't think I have to finish that sentence. Then about 11 o'clock we might get up, remember I said "might." It's going to be hard on you losing bets all the while Darling, but I promise you'll like the way you'll lose them.

Well Baby I have to stop now. Take good care of yourself Darling. I love you Bernie. Forever and ever.

All my love my Darling,
Your Paul

S.W.A.K.
Right Here

August 24, 1944

My Darling,

I won't forget this day for a long time. Everything seemed to go wrong. We had the math test today and I definitely didn't do very good. In fact, I'm awfully doubtful about passing it. I'll know for sure in a day or two. Besides that, my ankle hurts like heck, and this afternoon they gave us shots. They gave me 3 different ones. Typhoid, small pox and tetanus. I'll probably feel as if I'm paralyzed by tomorrow. Keep your fingers crossed for my passing that test Honey, if I don't I'll have as much self-respect as a worm.

I didn't get any mail today so I don't have any letters to answer. I'm really not in a very good mood to write. Sometimes I think I'm the stupidest guy alive. Can you imagine going 3 years to college and still not be able to do simple mathematics? Boy that is just plain stupid.

We don't go on the bivouac tomorrow, instead we go on a 10 miles hike. I hope my ankle is better by tomorrow morning. 10 miles isn't going to be much fun. I guess the only time I'll ever have fun again is when I become a civilian. I guess I sound pretty low but don't mind me, I'll try to make the next letter more cheerful.

There's not much more news Darling. We're going to eat in a few minutes so I'd better stop.

Take care of yourself Baby. I love you like everything.

All my love Sweetheart,
Your Paul

S.W.A.K.
Right Here

August 27, 1944

My Very Own Darling,

First of all, forgive me for not writing Friday or Saturday night. I really couldn't help it because we stayed out from Thursday till late Saturday night on the bivouac.

I got three letters from you on Saturday so I have a lot to answer. I'm glad your trip is all settled Honey and it's swell that Nomie is going with you. That makes me feel a lot better. Be careful in those slacks now. You're making me jealous, I think I'd better write Nomie for sure now and tell her to keep a careful eye on you.

I'll stop writing on the 29th. I'll write a few letters to your Florida address. You're getting to sound pretty ritzy.

Now for the second letter. I think I'm going to vote for Roosevelt. Are you angry? You mention my father hitting the jack pot. What did he do, win a race or something? I sent him the $50 I owed him maybe that's where he got all the money. We get paid again in about a week for August. My father sent me a card for my birthday.

I think that was our best telephone call Darling. I know it sure made me feel good. It was really cold here today, I guess we're getting some of your weather. I bet Midgie's kids are cute. I know Faith is, if the other one is half as nice as her, he's O.K.

I got another test back yesterday. It was a B. That makes 5 B's I've got now. I still don't know about the math test though and I'm really worried about it, I really don't think I passed it. Well keep hoping with me there's still a small chance.

I sent you the class picture. I forgot whether I told you about it or not. I'm on the right side of the picture as you look at it, kneeling down. I haven't got my glasses on and my hat looks too small, in other words that funny looking guy in the picture is me.

My ankle feels O.K. now. It really hurt for a couple of days.

Well I guess that answers all the letters Honey. Now comes some orders.
1.) Please be careful on the trip.
2.) Have a real good time
3.) Sit with Nomie no sailors, soldiers or Marines.
They're all wolves.
4.) Be careful where you wear that play suit. And when you do wear it have some pictures taken and send them to me.

I went to church this morning. They had Communion. Here's the program. It was really very nice. Before I met you, I would never have thought of going to Communion. I know it seems perfectly natural and I really wanted to do it.

Well Baby I have to stop now. Boy it is really cold tonight. When I'm married to a certain somebody, namely You, I'm going to enjoy cold nights. I'll have you to keep me warm. Will you?

The answer had better be yes, or else. I love you Sweetheart an awful, awful lot and I always will. Be a good girl now and be careful.

Good night my Darling,
Your Paul

S.W.A.K.
Right Here

Paul talks about the high attrition rate at Officer Candidate School.

September 3rd, 1944

Hi Darling,

I got your telegram last night about 10:30. I'm glad you had a nice trip, now be sure and have lots of fun while you're there. Tell Gerald and Millie I was asking for them. I sure do wish I could be with all of you. Someday, my girl going to Florida for her vacation. I guess I'm going to have quite an experienced wife to support.

We got the math test back. I got a D, but that's passing so I'm feeling pretty good. So far, I have 5 B's and one D. Next week the O.C. S. Board meets. It meets the sixth week, the 12th week and the 16th week. That's when they kick you out if they want to. We don't know for sure yet who has to go before the board, here's hoping I won't have to. About 60 men are sure of going because of low numbers. Next week this week time our company will probably be about 120 instead of 180 as it is now. We have already lost about 20 men. They resigned for the most part. One guy was caught cheating on a test and they shipped him out in less than 2 hours from the time they caught him.

I've been busy as heck today. We had to make out rating sheets. Each man has to rate 24 other men, as to how good they'd be as combat platoon leaders. Boy what a job. I went to church this morning.

Last night they had a company party with sandwiches, beer, soda etc. I drank Coco Cola about 5 of them and nothing else. Of course, I did eat enough for three guys.

Well Honey I've got to get back to work. Have a swell time now. I'll be thinking of you in that play suit. Take good care of yourself my Darling. I love you.

All my love,
Your Paul

S.W.A.K.
Right Here

September 4, 1944

My Darling,

I got two letters and a card from you today. I'm glad you had a nice trip. Tell me something, how did you get warm when the car got cold? You've got me worried.

The O.C. board meets this Thursday. I'm very grateful I'm not meeting with them. About 70 to 90 men have to go before the board. We started out with a company of 204 and by the end of this week we'll be lucky to have 120 men left. Keep your fingers crossed I've still got 12 weeks to go.

If I ever sound discouraged when I write to you don't worry about it, it all passes over sooner or later.

I suppose you're getting all nice and tan running around in a play suit. Some class. Tell Millie and Gerald I want them to watch you pretty close. With all those air corps guys around there I know there's a least a few thousand wolves. Remember you belong to a guy in the Infantry.

Seriously though Baby, have a swell time and take good care of yourself.
I love you very much my Darling. You belong to me and me alone remember that always.

All my love my Darling forever and ever,
Your Paul

September 11, 1944

My Darling,

I got your telegram today. I'm glad you had such a nice trip and I know you must have had fun in New York. I'm glad you went Darling, have all the fun you possibly can.

Tomorrow we go on bivouac. It's been raining all day and it's still raining now. Here's hoping it stops by tomorrow. We'll be back Friday night, so that really isn't so long. I doubt very much if I'll be able to write out there, if I don't, don't worry. If everything goes O.K. I'll call you this coming Sunday. Now if I don't call please don't worry. I'll try my best to, probably between six and seven Sunday morning. If I don't you'll know I just couldn't make it and I'll call you the following Sunday.

I got my war ballot today. I've just about definitely made up my mind to vote for Roosevelt. I suppose that makes you mad. You think I should vote for Jim Gage? He said he'd appreciate it in that letter he sent me.

There's nothing new to write about Sweetheart, the same old thing day after day. Work and more work.

The next time you go to New York I'm going to be with you, should we stay at the Taft? I'm going to close the door, lock it, put a sign out Do Not Disturb, and then take you in my arms and hug and hug you till you can hardly breathe, then I'm going to do a lot of other nice things, that is if I get the proper confirmation. You told me once if I coax hard enough I might get you to not wear those pajamas. I'm a pretty good coaxer.

Well Baby I have to go to bed now. We get up at 5 o'clock tomorrow and that comes early.

Be a good girl, have fun, and don't work hard. I love you Honey, with all my heart for always.

All my love my Darling,
Your Paul

S.W.A.K.
Right Here

Paul makes a prediction about when the war will end.

September 16, 1944

My Darling,

Guess what I'm doing. I'm on C.Q. Went on duty at 6PM this evening and don't get off till 12 noon tomorrow. We pull company charge of quarter by roster number, my roster number is 157 and my number came up for tonight. Of course, that made me very happy. Well anyway it gives me a chance to catch up on my letter writing. There's a radio here in the orderly room, it's the first time I've had one since I've been here.

We came back from bivouac Friday night late. I'm sorry I couldn't write to you while I was out there Sweetheart but I didn't have time. Boy we really worked. I don't know if I explained it to you or not but each O.C. class is made up into a company. The candidates act as platoon leaders, platoon guides, squad leaders, company commander and so on. When you're got one of those jobs they watch you like a hawk to pick up any mistakes. So far, I have been Platoon Leader, squad leader, instructor, physical training instructor, and tonight C. Q.

I don't get off till noon tomorrow, so I don't know what to do about calling you. I'm going to try to sneak off for a few minutes in the morning and call you. If I don't though you'll know I just couldn't help it. I'm going to try my best to call you though Honey.

Well today ended the 7th week. 10 more to go. You've still got 10 weeks to keep your fingers crossed.

Hit Parade just came on. Frank is now singing "Is you is or is you aint." I bet you're listening to the same program. Do you feel faint at the sound of that voice? I can hardly hold myself in my chair.

When we were on bivouac I slept with a fellow in my platoon named Ritz. He says he's going to write you and tell you not to marry me if you ever want to get any sleep. He says I whirl around in my sleep like a top. Looks as if you're going to have a tough time.

They're playing "I'll Be Seeing You." Boy how I'd like to be seeing you. Gee that would be swell.

Oh yeah, another new habit I've acquired. They all tell me in the hut that I talk in my sleep. That, is definitely not good.

The number 9, "It Had to Be You." I hope you're listening.

I was just interrupted. One of the fellows brought in a pint of ice cream, so I just finished eating that.

They're now playing "Swing on a Star." It's good isn't it?

I won't be able to go to church tomorrow. That will be the second time I've missed since I've been down here. I really do enjoy going.

Hey! Here comes number 1. It's "I Walk Alone." That's your favorite isn't it? It is a swell song. I guess it's my favorite too.

They told us today that it cost the government approximately 10,000 dollars to train one second lieutenant. Boy I really am costing the government a lot of money huh.

Well that's the end of the Hit Parade. I'll probably get a chance to hear it again about six months from now.

Did I tell you my prediction about the war? Of course, I may be wrong, although I hardly ever am, but I think it will all be over, German and Japan, by the 5th of June 1945. That's a little less than 9 months from now. I don't mean everyone will be out of the army by then but I do think the fighting will be over by then. I'll have been in active duty two years by then. It really doesn't seem possible that it will have been that long, although sometimes it seems I've been in 15 years now instead of 15 months.

It's 10 o'clock so I guess I'll go to bed. I'll try my best to call you in the morning Baby. Take good care of yourself now, be a good girl and remember I love you more than anyone else in the entire world. Good night my Darling, I love you.

All my love my Sweetheart,
Your Paul

S.W.A.K.
Right Here

September 17, 1944

Hi Darling,

Well I guess my sneaking off to call you was O.K. nothing happened while I was gone.

It was swell talking to you sweetheart. We could have talked a little longer, I had 50 cents left after paying for the overtime. I only had 4.50 in change that's why I was afraid to talk too long.

I'll be looking forward to seeing those pictures. They sound exciting. You'll know when I get them alright, my letters will probably be too hot to handle. You do that to me, I wonder why.

Four more hours and I'll be over my time of duty in C.Q. I have to clean my rifle then, shine shoes, and study for tomorrow. It seems we work harder on Sunday than any other day around here.

I was just talking to a 1st Sargent a few minutes ago. He's retiring in December. He'll have been in the Army 30 years by then, 17 ½ years of it being overseas. He was in the last war and war in the landing on Africa, Sicily and Italy in this war. They sent him back to the U.S. two months ago after he was wounded in Italy. That fellow has really seen and done things.

I could hear you very well over the phone. It's funny that you couldn't hear me so well. Had you been waiting long when I called? I always try to call between 6 and 7 because I never have to wait more than 5 minutes to get the call through then. If you try to call through New York in the afternoon you have to wait from 5 to as much as 15 hours. This is an awfully big camp and just about every other guy wants to call someplace on Sunday. McClellan wasn't ¼ as large as Benning. Benning covers 274,000 acres, that's big. They even have a railroad right here on the Fort. The engines and cars are about the size of a large automobile. The tracks are narrow gauge and they go all over the post. Besides that, they have big trailer buses and what we call shah buses for the O.C.'s. They put 77 of us in one truck. These trucks take us to demonstrations, problems and so on. One demonstration of artillery that they put on for each O.C.S. class cost about $20,000. No one can realize what this war is costing, I don't believe there is anyone who can count that high.

Yesterday we saw another O.C.S. class number 396 and the day before class 350. That means there are at the very least 46 O.C. classes going on right now. Each class starts out with at least 200 men so that's at least 9200 men. There are probably a lot more. There are at least 30 classes that have started after ours and we've only been going 7 weeks. There must be a lot of 2nd Lt.'s getting killed someplace.

General Lear visited us when we were on bivouac. You know he's the one the papers made so much fun of that time when he made his men march for whistling at some girl. He's a 3 Star General. He asked each of us how long we'd been in the army. Then he watched us go through a tactical problem. There were 2 two Star Generals with him and a couple of lowly colonels.

Well Baby I've got to make out the morning report so I'm going to stop. As I've said over the phone keep those fingerss crossed. That 12th week board is the hardest of all to get by. We've had 10 examinations so far, I've got all B's except for the math, I got a D in that, but that's passing so it's O.K. Of course, the tests don't mean everything. They rate you on leadership and things like that. Leadership is as important as the exam.

Take care of yourself Darling. Be a good girl, don't work too hard. I'll try to call you in a couple of weeks.

I love you Sweetheart.

All my love for always.
Your Paul

S.W.A.K.
Right Here

October 5, 1944

My Very Own Darling,

I got a swell letter from you today Sweetheart, it was the one you wrote me Sunday. I'll try to answer it better tomorrow night.

A bunch of us just finished doing pull ups, pushups, sit ups etc. We're all trying to get ready for the next physical achievement test that comes in the 12th week. We have to do better in this one than we did in the one in the 5th week. I did 25 pushups then, tonight I did 30, I did 70 sit ups then and tonight I did 72. That's not much of an improvement. In the next 2 weeks I've got to lose about 8 pounds of fat, if I want to make a good showing. You ought to see me, we look like a bunch of nuts lying on the floor doing physical exercises.

I've got a lot to do to get ready for tomorrow before lights go out so I'll write a long letter tomorrow night.

Good night Baby, be a good girl, I love you with all my heart, my Darling, I always will.

All my love my Precious,
Your Paul

S.W.A.K.
RIGHT HERE

October 7, 1944

Hi Sweetheart,

Study Hall just started so here comes my big two paragraph letter. I know some of them are awfully short but I just can't help it.

I didn't get any mail from you today so I don't have any letter to answer.

I've been building bridges today, setting off dynamite blowing down trees etc. That's no fooling we were actually taught how to build a bridge strong enough for a 30-ton tank to go over. We even built it. We also learned how to use dynamite, TNT, and nitro starch. We really had a lot of fun. I'll make a good gangster after the war, it will be a cinch to blow open a safe.

That 12th week board is getting closer and closer and everyone is getting more and more nervous. If we're still here at the end of 17 weeks we'll all be nervous wrecks. Our hut looked like this 10 weeks ago.

(Drawing of how the beds were laid out.)

Now it looks like this.

(Drawing of where the beds are now laid out.)

I'm a pretty good artist huh?

Well Baby I have to do some studying so I'd better stop. One of the fellows in the hut is engaged to a girl and he's only written her 7 times since he's been here. See how lucky you are.

Keep your fingers crossed Baby. Eight weeks isn't very long. I love you Darling with all my heart for always.

All my love my Precious,
Your Paul

S.W.A.K.
RIGHT HERE

Paul learns that his friend Mike O'Connor has been killed in action.

October 10th, 1944

My Darling,

I don't feel much like writing tonight Sweetheart, I got news today that Mike O'Connor was killed in France. I can hardly believe it yet. You know he left McClellan the day I came back from my furlough. I'm still hoping it isn't true but I guess it's pretty definite. I thought an awful lot of Mike. He was one swell fellow. I never told you but if I hadn't been on furlough I would have gone with Mike. We both knew we were going to be shipped so we asked the captain to send us both at the same time. When the order came down for two sergeants and two corporals to be shipped, Mike and I would have gone together. It just happened that I got back from my furlough about 5 or 6 hours too late. It's pretty awful when you think about his wife and baby, he certainly loved his family, he used to tell me about that little girl all the time. Boy this is a crazy world. What a bunch of fools we all are. My feeling like that won't help matters any I guess. I still can't imagine him being dead. He was such a big strong guy and such a darn good soldier. If any one of us got through O.K. I thought it would be him.

I guess might as well not talk about it anymore, it won't do any good now. I didn't mean to write a depressing letter but I know you'd be interested. I got a letter from you today. Darling, once and for all, nothing is wrong. I love you more than ever, and I still have plans for us. A lot depends on what happens in the next seven weeks and where I go if I do graduate. There are three things that can happen. I could be sent to an IRTC (Infantry Replacement Training Center) like McClellan, I could be sent to a division here in this country, or I could be sent directly to combat overseas. I don't have any idea which of these will happen. All I know is whichever one happens I'll get 10 days at home with you first. Then you and I can decide what we want to do. Does that sound OK? Please don't be thinking there's anything wrong. I know my letters are short and that I don't write lots of times the way I used to. Blame it on O.C.S. Darling, I just don't have time to write long letters and I'm usually thinking about 1000 other things I have to do when I'm writing. I hope you understand Sweetheart. Please try to.

Well Baby lights go out in about 3 minutes so I have to stop. I love you my Darling, I always will.

All my love Sweetheart,
Your Paul

S.W.A.K.
RIGHT HERE

October 15th, 1944

Hi Darling,

It's a beautiful day here today. This morning when I called you though it was cold as heck. We talked for 14 minutes but it only cost me $4. The operator said she wasn't sure when we stopped talking, she said she thought it was 14 minutes and that's what it really was, but I said I didn't think it was any more than six or 7 minutes so she only charged me for 7 minutes. Not bad huh?

I thought you would have had my letter about Mike. Every time I think of it, it makes me sick. He was one of the nicest guys I've ever known. Well that's war, maybe someday people will realize what fools they really are.

It was swell talking to you this morning Honey. You sounded awfully sleepy. When I came back I showered and shaved and started working on my buddy sheets. I don't know if I told you about them or not. The 5th week and the 12th week each man has to rate the other men in his platoon on their ability as combat leaders. It's a heck of a job. I just finished it about 15 minutes ago.

This Wednesday we have our last physical achievement test. It's supposed to be awfully tough so wish me luck, I'll need it. Thursday comes our first test in tactics. That's going to be tough too. The 12th week board meets either this week or next week. We'll probably know who's going before it by the end of this week. That's what I want you to cross all the fingers you have for. I will definitely need good wishes, crossed fingers, and everything else.

If I graduate it will be Nov. 29th. We'll probably leave the same day we graduate or at the most a few days later. I haven't told my father anything about coming down. I really don't want him to. It's too early to talk about it yet anyway. If I'm still here 4 or 5 weeks from now that will be time enough. Do you really want to come to New York to meet me?

Well I guess that covers all the news. I went to church this morning. We have a new chaplain, he's not as good as the other one.

Don't think you're going to win any bets from me. You just can't do it, I bet you didn't even win today's bet about church. Were you late, tell the truth now.

Don't forget to send me those pictures that I put the dot on. That one of you and Millie is really swell.

We're going to the service club late, we usually eat supper there on Sunday nights.

Well Baby I'm going to have to stop. I'll write you again tonight. Boy what a day this would be to go for a ride with you. We'd go to Indian Ladder and neck all day. I feel just like it. How about you? You'd probably come back with at least 10 red spots on you. Remember how I used to get heck for that? I think you liked it though.

By for now Honey, be a good girl and remember you belong to me. I love you Darling.

All my love for always,
Your Paul

S.W.A.K.
RIGHT HERE

October 24, 1944

My Darling,

Another week over, 5 more to go. This week and next week will be the hardest of all I guess. The Board meets this Tuesday and then again, the 14th week. The board that meets this Tuesday is what they call a screening board. They select about 50 or 60 men from the company to interview first to see what kind of men are in the company. Yesterday they told us who they picked and I was on the list. There were about 65 to 70 of us all together. It's not a washout board so don't get too scared yet. However, if when they interview you they don't like you they call you up for the 14th week board and then wash you out. Cross your fingers, toes and everything else for me this Tuesday. Here's hoping they like me. If I get by this board and the 14th week one, then everything should be all set. There is still another board the 16th week though so they really keep a guy guessing right up to the bitter end. You can imagine how I feel, it's just like sitting on a keg of dynamite wondering if it's going to go off. Wish me luck my Darling, I'll certainly need it the next 5 weeks.

I got the pictures. Thanks for sending them so soon. You're really a knockout in that one, (the one with you and Millie together), you've got a very pretty face Miss Getter and that ain't all.

There's nothing else new to write about except that next Saturday we go on a bivouac again for four days. That doesn't make me happy either.

I know my letters aren't very interesting Sweetheart, and I know lots of times they're awfully short but please forgive me. I just can't seem to concentrate on writing. I promise I'll make up for it when I get home. Those nights we're going to spend alone at home will be a good chance for me to make it up to you, O.K.?

I've got a lot to do Baby so I'm going to stop now. I'll try to try to write again tonight. Take good care of yourself my Precious, I love you an awful awful lot.

All of my love my Darling,
Your Paul

S.W.A.K.
RIGHT HERE

October 26, 1944

Hi Darling,

I got a letter from you and a card from Gerald, thank him for the card for me will you.

The 14th week board meets next Thursday. We get back from the bivouac next Wednesday. Next week is going to be an important one, after next week there is only one more board to go that's the 16th week.

There are only 5 men in our hut now. We lost one man on this last board. We started with 13 men in the hut and at the end of the 13th week we'll have 5 men left. After next week there probably won't be 5 men left. We started with 52 men in our platoon, now there are 32 left. Now you can see why I keep saying to keep your fingers crossed.

I'll try to write while I'm on bivouac but don't worry if you don't hear from me, you'll know I just couldn't make it.

I can't seem to write nice letters anymore. It seems as if there's always a million things to do and no time to do them in. You'll just have to forgive me Baby, I'll make up for it when I get home.

Take good care of yourself my Darling. Remember you belong to me for always. I love you Funny Face.

All my love for always,
Your Paul

S.W.A.K.
RIGHT HERE

Original letter from Thursday, October 26, 1944

UNITED STATES ARMY
FORT BENNING, GEORGIA

Oct. 26
THURSDAY
9:30 P.M.

Hi Darling,

I got a letter from you today and a card from Gerald, thank him for the card for me will you.

The 14th. week board meets next Thursday. We get back from the bivouac next Wednesday. Next week is going to be an important one, after next week there's only one more board to go, that's the 16th week.

There are only 5 men in our hut now. We lost one man on the last board. We started with 13 men in the hut and at the end of the 13th. week we'll have 5 men left. After next week there probably won't be 5 men left. We started with 52 men in our platoon, now there are 32 left. Now you can see why I keep saying to keep your fingers crossed.

I'll try to write while I'm on bivouac, but don't worry if you don't hear from me, you'll know I just couldn't make it.

I can't seem to write nice letters anymore. It seems as if there's always a million things to do and no time to do them in. You'll just have to forgive me baby, I'll make up for it when I get home.

Take good care of yourself my darling. Remember you belong to me for always. I love you, funny face.

All my love for always,
Your Paul.

(S.W.A.K.
RIGHT HERE)

Engagement photo

Engaged to Army Officer

MISS BERNICE LAURA GETTER
—(Stanley Costa)

Mr. and Mrs. Irving J. Getter of Esperance have announced the engagement of their daughter, Miss Bernice Laura Getter, to Lt. Paul E. Roberts, son of Paul S. Roberts of this city.

Miss Getter was graduated from Schoharie High school, where she was a member of the National Honor society and is also a graduate of the Mildred Elley Business school, Albany. She is employed at the Citizens Trust Co.

Lieutenant Roberts was graduated from Delanson High school and attended Union college before enlisting in the army. He is a member of Phi Delta Theta fraternity.

Paul Stanley Roberts

Fort Benning - daily schedule 1944

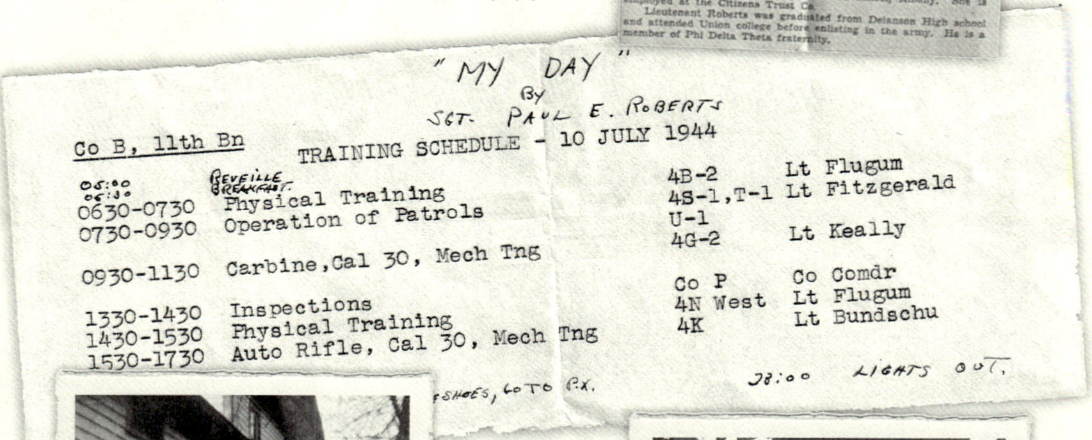

"MY DAY"
By
SGT. PAUL E. ROBERTS

Co B, 11th Bn   TRAINING SCHEDULE - 10 JULY 1944

05:00 REVEILLE
05:30 BREAKFAST
0630-0730 Physical Training
0730-0930 Operation of Patrols
0930-1130 Carbine, Cal 30, Mech Tng

1330-1430 Inspections
1430-1530 Physical Training
1530-1730 Auto Rifle, Cal 30, Mech Tng

4B-2   Lt Flugum
4S-1,T-1   Lt Fitzgerald
U-1
4G-2   Lt Keally

Co P   Co Comdr
4N West   Lt Flugum
4K   Lt Bundschu

SHOES, GO TO PX.   18:00 LIGHTS OUT.

Bernie and Aunt Phil

Parents of Paul Roberts

October 30, 1944

Hi Darling,

Pretty fancy writing paper isn't it. From the looks of the paper you can tell I'm bivouac again. We marched out here yesterday morning, took about 5 hours to get here. We have most of today off, I just finished taking a shower, shaving and cleaning my rifle. Can you imagine taking a shower in the middle of the woods in November. It's still nice and warm here during the day but at night it gets cold as heck. We go back to camp this Wednesday, the 14th week board meets this Thursday. This 14th week board is the most important one yet so cross your fingers baby and wish me luck more than ever. After this week there will be only one more board, the sixteenth one, but that one isn't supposed to be as hard as the one this week. Everyone has ordered their uniforms now. We don't pay for them until the day we graduate. If we don't graduate we don't have to pay anything. The government gives us 250 dollars apiece for uniforms, we get that in cash the day we graduate. A blouse alone costs around 50 dollars so there won't be much of the 250 left. There's only about 120 men in the company now. We started with 205. There probably won't be 100 graduating.

Well honey that's all the news. Four more weeks to go. I sure do hope they go fast. I'm getting awfully anxious to see a certain someone. Guess who?

I hope your all having a swell time. I know you must be. It's been a long while since I've seen Gerald, from your letters I guess he hasn't changed any. I'm glad of that.

We're going to eat in a few minutes so I'm going to stop now. Take good care of yourself my darling. If everything works out I'll be seeing you in one more month. I love you my darling, I always will. You belong to me baby for always.

All my love my sweetheart,
Your Paul

S.W.A.K
(RIGHT HERE)

Chapter 3
Preparing to be deployed
Fort Meade, Maryland
December 12, 1944 to January 7, 1945

On December 12, 1944, Paul arrives at Fort Meade, Maryland, after graduating from Officer Candidate School.

December 16, 1944

My Darling,

This seems like anything but an army camp. I guess I can't get used to being an officer. Boy they really treat us swell. This is the first time I've eaten in an officer's menu and boy the food is good. Not only that but we have table cloths and everything. Today for dinner we had steak, French fried potatoes, mushroom sauce, coffee, apple and mince pie.

They give us a lot of free time. Last night Robinson, Rety and I went to Washington. It's only 18 miles from here. We had supper there, and then went to a nightclub & saw the floor show. We didn't have girls and we didn't drink so don't get angry. It really was a lot of fun. We're going to Washington again tonight for supper and we'll probably go to a movie.

So far, we haven't heard anything about shipping out. If we're still here around Christmas I'm sure I'll be able to get home. It's about a 50/50 chance I guess. Meade is about 3 ½ to 4 hours from New York City so it wouldn't take too long to get home.

The 3 of us bought combat boots today, we've been issued steel helmets and gas masks and a bedroll already.

I won't ever forget those 14 days with you Darling. You were wonderful, you'll always be the only one for me. I love you an awful, awful lot Baby and I always will.

I'm going to try to call you tomorrow afternoon and I'll probably have my address by then, so I'll be able to tell it to you.

Take good care of yourself my Darling. Remember you belong to me and no one else ever. I love you Bernie with all my heart.

Good night my Precious.

All my love for always,
Your Paul

S.W.A.K.
RIGHT HERE

December 19, 1944

Hi Baby,

There's much news to write about Darling. We're almost positive of leaving here this Thursday. I may get a chance to get home from the next camp. If I can't make it home I'm almost sure I'll be able to meet you in New York for a few hours at least. I'll probably get my company tomorrow or Thursday.

Robinson and I are going to Baltimore tonight, we went to Washington last night. It's awfully hard to even sit still when you know you're going overseas. You want to see all the bright lights while you can.

6:30 PM

Guess where I am now. I'm writing this in a restaurant in Baltimore. Robinson and I just got here, fellow came by and offered us a ride so I didn't get a chance to finish the letter at camp.

We'll probably go to the movies in a few minutes, and then go back to camp. I'm going to try to call you tomorrow night. I miss you more than I ever did before my Darling. I know I love you more, I'll never forget those 14 days with you, they were wonderful.

If I don't call tomorrow night don't worry, you'll know I couldn't make it, and I'll call you from the next camp. I think I'll be able to get the call through though.

Be a good girl now and please be happy. I'll never let you down my Darling, I promise I'll be back for you. Take good care of yourself and always remember you belong to me and no one else ever. I love you Sweetheart for always.

All my love my Precious,
Your Paul

S.W.A.K.
RIGHT HERE

Paul gets his orders for being shipped overseas to Europe. Paul and Bernie became engaged to be married during his last furlough home.

December 26, 1944

My Very Own Darling,

Our orders came down today. We'll be leaving here Thursday for Camp Dix or *(illegible)* or someplace like that. I don't know how long we'll be there, I hope long enough so that I can get home to see you or maybe meet you in New York. I not only have a platoon to take care of but going over on the boat I've been assigned as company commander. That means I have 200 men under me and that means an awful lot of work and responsibility. Why they picked me I don't know but I guess I'll just have to make the best of it. Robinson and Rety went on Thursday's shipment, they'll probably be on the one going Friday. I wish we could have stayed together going over, however we may meet again at the next camp. There's not much use of writing to me here because I'll only be here 2 more days. As soon as I get my A.P.O. then you can start writing.

Don't give up hope of my getting home, there's still a good chance. If I don't make it through please don't feel too bad and remember that when I finally do make it, it will be for good and we'll have the rest of our lives to spend with each other. I love you so very much Darling, it hurts an awful lot every time I think how tough all this is on you. You've been wonderful though Sweetheart, so always keep your chin up and wait for me. I'll be back for you, I know I will.

I'm very glad I gave you the ring. I've wanted to for a long time. Every time you look at it remember that all my love and devotion go with it. You're the only girl I've ever loved and that I ever will love, don't ever doubt that.

Take care of yourself my Darling. Keep well and be as happy as you can, please try to have fun.

I changed that allotment from $50 to $100 a month today. It's still going to be at your bank though so please tell them that $100 will be coming each month. I'll tell my father about it when I write to him.

I'm going to try to call you tomorrow or the next night. I might not be able to tell you over the phone all I've said in this letter but you should get the letter soon, because I'm going to send it by airmail.

Be a good girl now. Remember you belong to me for always. As soon as I step off that boat coming back we're going to be married, and I don't think it's going to be so awfully long away.

Good bye for now my Sweetheart.

All my love for always,
Your Paul

S.W.A.K.
RIGHT HERE

From December 29, 1944 to January 7, 1945, Paul was in New York City, waiting to be deployed to Europe.

December 29, 1944

My Darling Bernie,

It's really hard to find time to write. They're really keeping me busy around here, but I really don't mind. When I'm busy I have less time to sit around thinking. I miss you Darling an awful lot, more than I'll ever be able to tell you. I'm in love with the sweetest girl in all the world or did you know that.

Please don't forget all the orders I gave you. And please don't give any more blood, not even next summer. I don't want you to do it Darling, so be a good girl and do as I ask.

I'm anxious to get the picture of you in the paper. Whenever you look at that ring remember that all my love and devotion goes with it. The minute I get back from overseas we're going to be married, so while I'm away you plan on that and look forward to it. That's what I'll be doing every minute. I love you more now than I ever have before Bernie, you've become part of my life and without you I'd feel lost.

Please don't worry about me, I'm feeling fine and I know everything will turn out O.K. Deep down in my heart I know I'll get back to you, our love is too strong for even a war to keep us apart for long.

I'm not afraid or worried about going overseas. I've thought it all out many times. I've really got something to fight for, a wonderful country and an even more wonderful girl. I'm very willing to fight for those things, or even to die for them because without them living would be much worse than death. As I said before I have confidence in myself and faith in God, and if it's His will I know I'll be back for you. So, you see my Darling there's no need for your worrying. I'd much rather you kept on smiling and being as happy as you possibly can be.

I'll write you every chance I get Sweetheart, don't worry though if you don't hear from me for some time.

I wrote a letter to Gerald yesterday, I guess it was about time. I hope you've heard from him by now. Try your best to prevent your mother and dad from worrying about him too much, he'll be alright.

Take good care of yourself Baby and don't ever forget what you mean to me. Always belong to just me, no one else ever.

Tell your mother and dad I was asking for them and that I think the Getters (even the girl with the new wristwatch) are really one swell family.

Good bye for now my Darling. I love you with all my heart and always will. There'll never be anyone but you in my life, don't ever doubt that. Take good care of yourself Baby. I love you.

All my love forever and ever,
Your Paul

Paul tells Bernie that his traditional SWAK (Sealed With A Kiss) closing of his letters is no longer allowed due to censorship requirements.

December 30, 1944

My Darling Bernie,

Another day and we're all busy as usual. My one man that was AWOL returned last night so now all the company is present again. I don't know what we're going to do with him yet. I have another man whose wife just had twins, she's quite sick so he asked for a furlough but it was disapproved at regiment. I went up to regiment last night and talked to the commander and I'm almost positive the fellow will get a 10 day furlough today, so I feel pretty good about that.

I know I asked you about Gerald in yesterday's letter, but I'm still anxious to know if you heard from him. After today I guarantee I won't ask you about him again, for quite a while anyway.

There's nothing else new to write about Sweetheart. I'm feeling fine and everything seems to be going along O.K.

If you should ever need anything Darling or if you're ever worried about something always tell me about it. Don't ever be afraid of worrying me. I always want to know anything that's ever bothering you because I want your troubles to be mine too, and then if there is anything I can possibly do to help, you know I will. The main thing is for you to take good care of yourself. I can't tell you how much that means to me Darling. When I come back I want you well and healthy and looking just like you do now. Take real good care of yourself for me, dress warm, get lots of sleep, and eat good. Be a good girl now and do all those things for me.

I love you so very much my Darling, I'll never be able to tell you how much you mean to me. I think you know though, I hope you do. The happiest day will be the day you become my wife. I've dreamed of that day for a long, long while and I know you have too. Just stick it out a little longer my Precious, our day will come and when it does, we'll have years and years of happiness together.

Once more now take good care of yourself, don't worry, and always keep on loving me, if you ever stop I wouldn't care about living.

Don't ever forget that you belong to me, no other man ever. I never want anyone else to even touch you. You were made for me and no one else. I know that's the way you want it to be too.

I love you my Darling, I'll never stop loving you, because to me you're the sweetest, most adorable girl in all the world.

By for now Baby. Be a good girl and please try to be happy. You know that's the way I want you to be always.

I can't say sealed with a kiss anymore, we're supposed to censor anything like that, so it won't be on my letters anymore but I'll always kiss them just below my name, how is that.

I love you Bernie, from the very bottom of my heart.

All my love and devotion for always,
Your Paul

Bernie is writing to Paul from New York City.

January 7, 1945
New York City

Hello Honey,

Another Sunday but I don't enjoy them without you. I got 3 hours extra sleep anyway.

We had church this morning as usual. It was Communion Sunday. I miss you more than ever in church when we have Communion.

We've had a hard snow storm and there were only a few people to church this morning. We aren't having any church tonight because of the bad weather and roads.

Snow plows will be going over the roads so it will be O.K. by tomorrow morning and I suppose I'll be going into work as usual.

Today is our anniversary, Darling. We've been engaged one month. What a change there can be in just one month! December 7 you were home and we were happy together.

I'm going to write a letter to you, Gerald, Marie and Irene this afternoon so I'll be back to you later in a long letter.

I love you, Darling. All my love always.

Yours, Bernie

Part Two

Chapter 4
ON THE QUEEN MARY HEADING TO SCOTLAND
January 9, 1945 to January 13, 1945

Paul is on the Queen Mary bound for Scotland. Paul is believed to have written these letters in the second week of January 1945. Censorship does not allow him to disclose the exact date and other sensitive information.

I can't put the date on the letter, how long we've been at sea, where we're going, so you'll have to guess all that.

My Darling Bernie,

I can't say much in this letter because of censorship. I can tell you though that I'm writing this on board a ship. I can't tell you the name of it or where we're going but if you remember the things I told you when I was home you'll know most of the story. The food is very good but I've been seasick and so has everyone else on board I think. I feel better now though. When we go on our honeymoon I've definitely decided it will be in a hotel, never on a ship being seasick is definitely no fun. I'll have a lot to tell you about this trip when I see you again Baby. I bet I've looked at your picture a hundred times, gee but I love you. Wait for me Darling, and always belong to just me, I'll never love anyone but you or want anyone but you, I mean that from the bottom of my heart.

I know I'll be back Sweetheart. Something inside of me just tells me that I'll get back to you. You always believe that too and with both of us thinking it,

I know we'll be together again. The main thing is for you to never forget how much I love you. I'll always love you Bernie forever and ever.

I'm not feeling so hot again, we're beginning to bounce around again. The only way to feel good is to lie flat on your back so that's what I'm going to go now.

I'll write all I can Baby, don't worry when you don't hear from me. Take care of yourself for my sake please Darling.

All my love forever and ever,
Your Paul

My Darling Sweetheart,

I'm still on the ocean, but I feel much better than I did when I wrote the last letter to you. We're still rocking a lot but I guess I'm getting to be a better sailor. I still have charge of my company a lot of the boys are from Texas and boy have they been seasick, in fact a lot of them still are. I've been awfully busy as usual but I don't mind that. The worst thing a guy can do is sit down and start thinking hour after hour. That really does get you.

I'd like to tell you all about the ship but of course I can't. Someday I will though, I'll certainly have a lot to tell you about.

I told you before I couldn't just sealed with a kiss in my letters, or the date (that is while I'm on the ship) or can I put the stamp on upside down. I'll kiss the letters underneath my name and you make believe I put the stamp on upside down, how's that.

I miss you Darling more than you'll ever know. You're so awfully sweet and I love you so very very much. We've had wonderful times, together haven't we? I'll never forget even one of them. The longer I've known you the more I've loved you. You've become clearer to me than any other person in all the world and without you, life is a very empty thing. You've grown to be part of me Darling, whatever I do I think of you and how we would be doing those things together. I'm the luckiest fellow in all the world to have such a wonderful girl and every night of my life I thank God for giving you to me.

When I come back the very first thing we'll do is get married and then we'll work out the rest of the things, like building our own home, my finishing college and so on. But I want more than anything to get married first, with you as my wife I'll be able to do anything because I'll have the sweetest most adorable wife in all the world.

Please don't worry about me Baby. I'll be alright. Just you remember to keep yourself well, eat good, and get plenty of sleep and dress warm. I'll be back for you, I know I will so you just keep that chin up and try your best to be happy. You're much more beautiful when you're smiling. That new picture is beautiful Sweetheart. I've looked at it so much I'm afraid I'll wear it out.

I almost forgot to tell you, Robinson is on this boat. His stateroom is just two doors down from mine. Retz isn't here but I certainly was surprised to see Robinson. Right now, he's seasick, and I'm beginning to feel a little funny again myself.

I haven't written you every day because I was too sick at first. It wasn't too long though and I'll be a regular old salt. I think some of the fellows will be sick till we get there.

Tell your mother and dad and Phil I was asking for them and try not to let them worry about Gerald. And don't you worry either. He'll be O.K., and before you know it all the old gang will be back together again, just the way it used to be only you and I will have to start catching up on Gerald and Millie and Effie and George. I'd rather we didn't catch up for a few years though. The first three or 4 years we're married I want it to be just you and I together all by ourselves. After that we'll start having those twins, O.K.? Gee Darling it's going to be wonderful. Don't ever forget you belong to me and don't ever forget how much I love you.

I guess I'd better stop now Funny Face. Once again please take good care of yourself and don't worry. Someday soon I'll be back with you and then we'll have a whole lifetime ahead of us. I love you my Darling.

Good night "Itchy"

All my love forever and ever,
Your Paul

Paul is still on the Queen Mary.

Hi Darling,

Same old thing, we're still on the ocean. I've written to you almost everyday since we've left, but I miss one or two. I've got an awful lot to do each day so that's my excuse. Am I forgiven? I'll always try to write every day though, be sure you do, your letters mean a lot to me Darling, they're the next best thing to being with you.

There's nothing new to write about Sweetheart. Everything that does happen I can't write about.

The food is very good, we get a lot of roast beef and you know I like that. We only have breakfast and supper though, they only serve two meals a day but that is really plenty. We don't do enough exercising to make us hungry.

Some day you and I will go for an ocean voyage. It really must be swell in civilian times. Do you think you'd get seasick? I was only sick one day, since then I've felt fine. I still want our honeymoon to be in a hotel though. If you got seasick on our honeymoon that would be awful. We won't take any chances, we'll go to the Taft. Just thinking about it makes me feel happy, when it actually happens I'll probably be so happy I'll be walking in the clouds. You know something Funny Face, I love you an awful, awful lot.

I've only written one letter home since I've been on the ship. It's hard to write home because there's so little I can say to them in the way of news. You let my grandmother know when you hear from me O.K.?

Well Baby I've got a lot to do so I'm going to stop now. Take good care of yourself, be a good girl and don't ever forget you belong to me and me alone for always. I love you my Darling, I always will.

All my love my Precious
Your Paul

My Darling Sweetheart,

Time to write again. I'm still onboard ship and I'm happy to say that I'm now all over my seasickness. The first night was the worst. After that I didn't mind it very much and now I feel as good as if I were on land.

I wish I could tell you about the trip so far but of course I can't. Lots of the men tried to use tricks in their letters to let their families know the name of the ship and where they're going, but we just cut it out of the letters. Mean aren't we. I don't really blame them though, because I feel like doing the same thing.

There's really not much I can write about, that is about the journey. Robinson and I sat in the officer's lounge last night and talked for about two hours. I told you he was engaged again to the old girlfriend so we both have a lot in common, except of course that my girl is much more wonderful that his ever could hope to be. We both said that the minute we get back we're going to first of all get married (I don't mean he and I are going to marry each other of course) and then we're going to stay in one place the rest of our lives. My most wonderful dreams Darling are of you and I in our own home. Just the two of us with no one to bother us ever. Don't ever doubt my love for you Sweetheart. I love you more, if that's possible, every time I see you. If my father acts the way he usually does, please don't ever let it bother you. I realize that most of the time he acts as if he were above everyone else but don't you pay any attention to it. In order words my Darling I don't want anyone to ever hurt you in any way. To me you're the dearest person in all the world and I wouldn't give your little fingers for anyone or anything. Just you always remember that you belong to me and that I love you with all my heart. To me you're everything I want, you're beautiful, sweet, honest and clean and although I hate to admit it, lots more intelligent than I am. Seriously though Sweetheart I think you're wonderful and I always will think that, even after we've been married 50 years you'll still be my sweetheart.

When we're married Honey, I'm going to do everything I can to make you happy and make up for all the time we're been away from each other. When I think of you having to get up early in the morning to go to work I feel awful. Please take good care of yourself Baby, and don't work too hard, when we're married you're not going to work a bit except in our home, and as soon as we can we'll have a maid to do that. I know you're probably saying to yourself he's still dreaming, but you just wait and see. I've got lots of plans and as long as I have you with me I know I'll be able to make them come true.

It's awfully hard to say in a letter all the things I feel. I think you know how I feel though, I hope you do. Always love me Darling, don't ever stop. It's your love that makes this world beautiful for me, without it life wouldn't be worth living.

Take good care of yourself my Darling. You belong to me Funny Face for always and always, we'll always be together at least for the time we have to be apart we'll be in each other's hearts and that's what really counts. I love you Bernie, I'll always want you, belong to me for always, good night my Precious.

All my love,
Your Paul

Chapter 5
AT THE FRONT LINES IN EUROPE
January 15, 1945 to March 27, 1945

From January 12 to March 28, 1945 Paul was with the 320th Regiment in General Patton's Third Army. They relieved the 101st Airborne at Bastogne, Belgium during the Battle of the Bulge. By the beginning of February 1945 they had reached the German border. The Battle of the Bulge was from December 16, 1944 to January 25, 1945.

January 15, 1945
Somewhere in France

My Darling Bernie,

Well Sweetheart I guess my letters have been few and far between. It's because we have been moving around so much. I can tell you I'm now in France and that I'm in the 3rd Army under General Patton. I've been through Scotland and England. I can't tell you exactly where I am now though and where I am now but I can say one place we passed through was the city of Sedan.

I'm feeling fine Sweetheart and everything is going along O.K. Please don't worry about me my Darling, and don't worry if you don't hear from me regularly. I'll write all I can, but till I get settled someplace I won't be able to write too much.

I miss you Sweetheart an awful lot. Please take good care of yourself, and don't ever forget that you belong to me and to me alone for always.

I love you Bernie more than ever if that's possible. When I get home, we'll make up for all this time away from each other, so you be sure to keep that chin up.

Good night my Darling, I love you .

All my love for always,
Your Paul

January 16, 1945
Somewhere in France

My very own Darling,

I wrote you a V-mail last night so today I'm writing you by airmail, one of them should get to you. I think the airmail will probably be the fastest.

I can't tell you where I am in France, it really doesn't matter much because I won't be here much longer anyway.

I still can't tell you the name of the boat I came over on, but I think you have a good idea of what one it was.

In the V-mail letter I told you I was in the 3rd Army under General Patton. You'll be able to tell approximately where I am by reading the newspapers about Patton and the 3rd Army.

The civilians here in France are in terrible condition. They don't have anything. I thank God that this war is over here and not in the States.

I've been through England and Scotland but I didn't see much of either one.

That's about all the news I can tell you Sweetheart. I'm feeling fine, so don't be worrying about me. For a while you probably won't hear from me regularly but don't worry. I'll write every chance I get, you know that.

I miss you an awful lot Darling. I love you so darn much it hurts. I've dreamed a million times of how things will be when I'm home again. First of all, we'll get married just as soon as we can get the license, then whatever we do after that we'll be doing it together. I know I'll be back Sweetheart, you just keep that chin up and be as happy as you can. That's the way I want you to be.

I told you Robinson was on the boat coming over with me. The last time I saw him was at LeHavre, France. I imagine he's somewhere near me now although I'm not sure.

I know some of the people around Esperance are interested in how the Red Cross is over here. So far, they've been darn good. In our travels we've met them quite a few times and they've had lots of coffee and donuts for the men, also cigarettes and candy. They really are doing a good job.

Well Baby I can't think of much more to write about right now. Please take good care of yourself my Darling. And always remember we've got a long life ahead of us, years and years and Darling I promise I'll make you happy.

By for now Sweetheart, I love you.

Take care of yourself "Itchy."

All my love,
Your Paul

January 19, 1945
Somewhere in Belgium

My Darling Bernie,

I'm with a division now so now I'll have a definite address. This is what it will be from now on.
   Lt. Paul E. Roberts, 01328186
   CO. L. 320 INF.A.P.O.35
   % Postmaster, New York, New York

I've really done a lot of traveling since I left the States and I guess it looks like I'll be traveling until we hit Berlin. That's O.K. by me though. I want to get all my traveling done now and then when I do get home you and I are going to get married and settle down to a quiet life, just the two of us together. That is unless you want to travel someplace. Whatever you want to do we'll do it.

I wish I could tell you just exactly where I am but it really doesn't matter much, just as long you know I'm O.K. and that everything is going along alright.

Here's some Belgium money. This bill is worth about 20 cents in American money. The French franc and the Belgium franc are worth about 2 cents American money. Over here we get paid in the money of whatever country we're in. I did have some English and French money but I don't have any right now to send you. As soon as I can I want to send you some money to get yourself something with it, if I ever get to a place where I can make out a money order I will.

I haven't received any mail from you or from home since I left Kilmer in the U. S. but I know it will probably be sometime before I do because of the way I've been moving around.

When you get this letter Darling, give my address to my grandmother. I'm going to try to write to her today also, and if my letter to her arrives before this one gets to you she can tell you my address. I sent you both a V-mail with my change of address the other day. All the letters you wrote to me would be old A.P.O. will get to me O.K. so don't worry about that. I don't have time to write much more Sweetheart. I love you my Darling more than ever. Always belong to just me Baby, no one else ever. You're the sweetest most adorable girl in all the world and I'll always love you with all my heart for always.

Please take good care of yourself my Precious. Be happy and keep that chin up. I'll be back with you and, when I do come, you and I will be together from then on for always.

Don't work too hard, go to bed early, dress warm and be a good girl. Tell your Mom and Dad and Phil I was asking for them and try to keep them and yourself from worrying too much about Gerald. Before you know it we'll all be back together again.

I love you Bernice. I want you to be my wife more than anything else in the world. I'll never want or love anyone but you.

Good night my Darling, take care of yourself.

All my love for always,
Your Paul

Paul is at a rest camp in France.

January 21, 1945

My Darling,

Well I'm back in France again. I can't tell you just where but I can say I've been in the Bastogne, that's in Belgium, also Luxembourg in France (Luxembourg is actually a separate country). That will give you some sort of an idea of where I am now.

Right now, we're in a rest camp so life is pretty good. Some of the things I've been doing lately don't even seem real to me. It's more like a movie. Right now, I'm writing this letter by candlelight, I'm awfully dirty, I have a pistol belt on with a big 45 caliber pistol hanging on my hip and a rifle standing near me in the corner. If I don't look like a character in some western picture then I must look like one in a horror picture.

If you get to look at a map or read the news you'll read about Bastogne in Belgium. The weather here is really rough, lots of snow and boy it is cold.

Today is Sunday and believe it or not I went to church this morning, can you imagine going to church with a pistol and a rifle slung on your shoulder. The service was very good and I sure did enjoy it.

About three days ago before I was up at the front I went to a movie in a little village in France. After the show we were all surprised when they announced that Mickey Rooney was there in person. You know he's in the Army now. He and two other G.I.'s go around in a jeep and put on shows along the western front. It certainly seemed funny seeing him over here.

The news was good today, the Russians are doing a good job and I sure do hope they keep it up. We have the Belgium Bulge licked now so things are looking fairly good. Well I guess that's all the news Sweetheart. I'm feeling fine so don't be worrying about me.

Here's another funny thing that happened. The first sergeant of L Company lives in Stanford, Conn. That's where Mike O'Connor used to live and he knew Mike very well. In fact, his wife and Mike's wife used to pal around together. I met a Lt. in our Battalion who went to Albany Teachers College. It's really a funny old world.

When you see my grandmother tell her all the news because I don't get a chance to write home as often as I do to you.

My letters probably sound kind of funny because I jump from one thing to another. I write whatever I happen to think of, I hope you can make sense of it.

I'd ask you to send me things if there was anything I really needed, but so far, I have plenty of everything. As soon as I need something I'll be sure to let you know. I haven't received any mail yet and I probably won't for a while, when it does catch up to me I'll probably get about 10 letters all at once.

I never did get around to get a G.I. haircut. My hair is about long enough to braid I guess, and I haven't shaved for a week either. I think tomorrow I'll get a chance to clean up a little, I sure do hope so.

This is a lot different from the Sunday nights we used to spend together. It's 9 o'clock here now. That means it's about 4 o'clock in the afternoon at home. I like to sit and think about what you're doing, I miss you an awful lot my Darling, more than I'll ever be able to tell you. I guess you know that. I've never loved you more than now. When I was home on my leave and at Christmas it was like Heaven being with you. I've loved you for a long time Bernie, but now you've become my whole life. Without you I wouldn't care about living, I really mean that. Every plan I make and everything I think about you're always in it with me. I love you Sweetheart with all my heart and soul and I'll never love any other woman but you. I'll be back with you Darling and when we're together again I'll never leave you. Please take good care of yourself, and always remember you belong to me and me alone. You're my woman, no one else ever.

Keep your chin up Baby and be happy. It won't be long and we'll be together again.

Good night my Precious, all my love for always,
Your Paul

Here's a French 5 franc note. It's worth about 10 cents in American money.

January 22, 1945
France

My Very Own Darling,

Another day over, there is nothing much in the way of news to write about. We're still in France and we're still in a rest camp. I hope we stay here for a while. I got a chance to take a bath and wash my hair. It's standing straight up right now, not like the old Roberts huh? My day will come again though.

I'm writing by the light of a lantern tonight, last night I only had a candle, who knows maybe tomorrow I'll have electricity. Things seem to be improving. I don't know how long we'll be here, it may be for some time, then again, we may leave at any minute. You never know.

That's all the news Sweetheart. Whenever you don't get letters from me regularly please don't worry. Sometimes it's awfully hard to write, that is to find time to write, so please don't worry I'll be alright.

Please don't ever forget how much I love you Darling. I just can't tell you how much I do love you, but I want you to know that it's with all my heart and soul. I'll never love anyone but you as long as I live. You're everything I want in the world and you always will be.

Please take the best care of yourself my Precious. Don't worry and try your best to be as happy as you can. I'll be back with you again soon and once we're together again we'll stay that way for always. I love you so very much my Darling. More than ever before.

Be a good girl now, take good care of yourself and don't ever forget how much I love and want you. You belong to me and me alone for always.

Good night my Darling,

All my love for always,
Your Paul

The 320th went to Alsace, France on January 23, 1945 to help the Seventh Army's sector.

On January 30, the 320th started the 300-mile journey with the Ninth Army to Holland, then Germany.

Paul writes on February 1 that he is somewhere in France. He has been in Scotland, England, France (Dancy, Thionville, Metz and Verdun), Belgium, Luxembourg, Germany, and Holland.

February 1, 1945
Somewhere in France

My Darling Bernie,

It's been over a week since I've written you but it just couldn't be helped. We've been up at the front and the past 7 days and nights we've been right in foxholes so there was no chance to write. In fact, although we're not at the front right now, we're on the move again so I doubt if this letter gets mailed for a few days.

I'm feeling fine, so please don't be worrying about me. Remember I told you that if sometimes you don't hear from me don't worry, you'll know that I just haven't had a chance to write.

I've been all over France, or at least that's the way it seems. I told you before we were in Bastogne in Belgium, also I've been in the cities of Dancy, Thionville and Metz, and Verdun here in France, also many small villages. I've slept in French houses, barns, chicken coops, foxholes, ditches, hay mows, etc. The

Original letter from February 1, 1945 (page 1)

FEB. 1ST. 1945
SOMEWHERE IN FRANCE.

My Darling Bernie,

It's been over a week since I've written you but it just couldn't be helped. We've been up at the front - and the front 7 days + nights we've been right in fox hole so there was no chance to write. In fact although we're not at the front right now, we're on the move again so I doubt if this letter gets mailed for a few days.

I'm feeling fine, so please don't be worrying about me remember I told you that if sometimes you don't hear from me don't worry, you'll know that I just haven't had a chance to write.

I've been all over France, or at least that's the way it seems. I told you before we were in Bastogne in Belgium, also I've been in the cities of Nancy, Thionville, Metz, + Verdun here in France, also many small villages. I've slept in French houses, barns, chicken coops, fox holes, ditches, hay mows etc. The guy who said, war is hell, wasn't fooling. The only worthwhile things in my life now are my dreams of you and when I can be back with you. I'll be back don't you worry baby, and the first thing we're going to do is get married, as soon as I get off the boat.

Original letter from February 1, 1945 (page 2)

SOMEWHERE IN HOLLAND
FEB. 3RD. 1945

I told you this letter probably wouldn't be mailed for awhile, well it wasn't.

I'm in Holland now, that's all I can say. I've been in Scotland, England, France, Belgium, a little way in Germany, and now Holland. Quite a world traveler huh? Oh to be back in good old Esperance though. This stuff might sound nifty and interesting, but I know that every man here would give anything in the world to be home with the people he loves.

I don't have much time to write sweetheart. Don't worry if you don't hear from me regularly. Don't ever forget that I love you with all my heart and that I always will. You mean more to me than anyone or anything in all this world and you always will. Please take the best of care of yourself, keep that chin up and be happy.

We just got a report that the Russians are only 35 miles from Berlin, that certainly sounds good. Here's hoping.

I haven't received any mail yet but I know that's because we've been moving around so much.

(PAGE 3)

I just hope yours getting [through] alright. I'll write as often as I can. Don't ever forget that you belong to me funny face and me alone. I miss you darling so very very much, and I love you more than ever, if that's possible.

Good night my precious, I love you.

all my love forever & ever
your Paul.

guy who said, "War is Hell," wasn't fooling. The only worthwhile things in my life now are my dreams of you and when I can be back with you. I'll be back don't you worry Baby, and the first thing we're going to do is get married, as soon as I get off the boat.

February 3, 1945
Somewhere in Holland

I told you this letter probably wouldn't be mailed for a while, well it wasn't.

I'm in Holland now, that's all I can say. I've been in Scotland, England, France, Belgium, a little way in Germany and now Holland. Quite a world traveler huh? Oh, to be back in good old Esperance though. This stuff might sound exciting and interesting but I know that every man here would give anything in the world to be home with the people he loves.

I don't have much time to write Sweetheart. Please don't worry if you don't hear from me regularly. Don't ever forget that I love you with all my heart and that I always will. You mean more to me than anyone or anything in all this world and you always will. Please take the best of care of yourself, keep that chin up and be happy.

We just got a report that the Russians are only 35 miles from Berlin, that certainly sounds good. Here's hoping.

I haven't received any mail yet but I know that's because we've been moving around so much. I just hope you're getting more alright.

I'll write as often as I can. Don't ever forget that you belong to me Funny Face and me alone. I miss you Darling so very very much, and I love you more than ever, if that's possible.

Goodnight my Precious. I love you.

All my love forever and ever,
Your Paul

The 320th relieved a British unit in Holland, west of the Roer River.

February 4, 1945
Holland

My very own Darling,

Another day passed and everything is going along O.K. I'm feeling fine as usual, my hair is almost long enough to braid it now. When I get back to the States I'm going to lie in a bathtub for about a week. It will take that long to get all the dirt off.

I still haven't received any mail but I understand that. I really am looking forward to them though.

Please don't worry when you don't hear from me. Sometimes it's just impossible to write. I'll write every chance I get, you know that.

I think about you all the time Sweetheart. To be back with you would be more like Heaven than anything I can imagine. If God is willing and I come back to you I'll be grateful and happy for the rest of my life. There's nothing I want more than to be with you for always. That's the way it will be too Darling, I know it will. Just you keep that chin up and be happy. I'll be back with you and when we're married we're going to be the two happiest people in all the world. I'll have to stop now Darling. Please take good care of yourself for me. You're more precious to me than anyone or anything in this world, I guess you know that. Be a good girl and dress warm, eat good, and go to bed early. And always remember Sweetheart you belong to me and me alone for always. I'll make up for all these days and weeks and months we've been away from each other, I promise. The first thing we're going to be married, from then on whatever we do we'll do together.

I love you Darling. I always will. There will never be any other woman in my life but you. Wait for me my Precious, I'll be back, and in the meantime make plans as I am, of all the wonderful things we're going to do together.

Good night my Precious, take good care of yourself and remember don't worry when you don't hear from me regularly.

I love you "Itchy" forever and ever.

All my love,
Your Paul

Paul is somewhere in Germany. His unit relieved the 155th British Brigade in Germany along the Roer River. They have travelled from Annendall to Kraudort, Germany.

February 6th, 1945

My Darling,

As you can see my address has changed again. I am now in the land of Supermen but I can truly say that they are really not so super as they are made out to be. I can't tell you just where I am, but I am at the front and have been for some time. Even here it's possible to write letters once in a while because most of our fighting is in villages and towns so we get a chance to get inside to write.

I still haven't received any mail but I'm not complaining because I understand that it hasn't caught up to me on account of my moving around so much. I hope your getting my letters ok. I've sent them all airmail, except for a couple of V-mails, but I don't like to write V-mail.

I read that it's been very cold in the states and that you've had a lot of snow. I hope your taking good care of yourself, please do, for my sake. When I come back, I want you to be just the way you were when I left you. Every time I close my eyes I can see you, I love you so very much my darling, more than I'll every be able to tell you. My main thought in life is to be able to come home to you and to be with you for always. If god allows me to do that I'll be grateful for the rest of my life.

There's not much more I can write about. I'm feeling fine as always, please don't be worrying about me, I'll be ok. The war news looks very good, here's hoping it will be over soon. If the American people could only realize how lucky they are that this war isn't in America. There's hardly a house standing over here. Everything is in ruins, cows, sheep, goats, wander the street of the little villages, starving to death or blowing themselves up by stepping on mines and booby traps. You can walk in a house and see clothing lying around, children, dolls and toys, broken furniture and dead bodies. If each American could just take one look at what might have happened to our own homes, we wouldn't have to have bond drives and things like that. Every night I thank god that you're in a safe place and that nothing can hurt you. That's one reason why I want you to be careful and take good care of yourself, you mean more to me than anything else in my life, someday I'll be able to show you how much I do love you. I hope and pray that that day comes real soon.

Well funnyface, I have to stop now. Remember, don't worry if you don't hear from me regularly. I'll write all I can but it might be a long time before writing.

We will make up for all the months apart, darling. Just keep that chin up and be happy. I'll be back with you, I promise, don't you ever doubt it for a minute.

Take good care of yourself my darling. I love you with all my heart. You belong to me darling and no one else ever, always remember that.

Good night, sweetheart, I love you.

All my love,
Paul

Paul is at the front in Germany. The 320th is preparing to cross the Roer River in Operation Grenade.

February 11, 1945

My Darling,

Sunday morning in Germany. It's not at all like the Sundays at home. There is no Sunday School, no church, no popcorn in the afternoon, no Young People's Meeting, no church at night, and worst of all, no you. Life is really an existence now, nothing more. Without you that's all it ever will be for me, the one thing that makes it livable is the thought of being back with you. That's what keeps me going and Darling I know I'll be back with you, I'm sure of it so you be sure of it too.

There's nothing much new that's happened. We're still in Germany and are up at the front. It would be pretty hard to describe it to anyone so I'm not going to even try it. Sometimes I feel as if I'm acting a part in a movie, it doesn't seem possible that what's happening is real. This morning one of our planes crashed just in between our lines and the German's. The crew bailed out and so far, we got 4 out of the 6 of them back behind our lines. The other two have been captured, I'm afraid, by the Germans. I'll have a lot of stories to tell you when I get home. You know I like to talk so you'd better be prepared to listen to me.

I still haven't received any mail. I think though I should be getting some soon. I sure do hope so. Most of all I'm hoping that you're getting my letters alright. I don't have time to write much more Sweetheart. I know I say it in every letter but here it is again, don't worry when you don't hear from me, you'll know it's just that I didn't get a chance to write. I promise I'll write every chance I get.

It's about 7AM at home now. 12 noon here. You're probably still asleep, I hope so anyway. I bet you're late to church this morning, as usual, gosh what a bunch you Getters are for being on time. When we're married, we're going to be on time for everything, I'm giving you fair warning.

Take good care of yourself my Darling. I love you very, very much. As soon as I get home we'll be married Darling, there's nothing I want more than all the world. I think you're the sweetest, most adorable girl in all the world, as well as the prettiest and I'll always love you and only you. There will never be any other woman in my life but you Bernie, I mean that with all my heart.

Be a good girl now, keep that chin up, have fun, be happy and take good care of yourself. Before you know it, I'll be back home with you. I love you my precious more than anything or anyone in all the world.

By for now my Darling,

I love you,
Your Paul

February 12, 1945
Germany

My Darling Bernie,

Today was a wonderful day for me. I got a letter from you. It was a V-mail written January 7th. That was just about 5 weeks ago. I can't tell you how much that letter means to me Sweetheart. I wouldn't trade it for $1000. Jan.7 was our 1 month anniversary as you said, a lot can happen one month's time alright, it hardly seems possible. I'll never forget the night we went for the ring. That afternoon I was excited as heck just thinking about getting it, and when we did get it I was happier than I've ever been before in my whole life. I'm so proud of you Darling, everything about you is just perfect. I never thought that I'd love anyone the way I love you. I only wish I could put into words the way I feel, someday I'll be able to show you how much I love you, and I pray to God every night that that day will come very soon.

There's not much in the way of news. I'm sitting in the cellar of a German house writing this. I've got an old wine bottle full of gasoline burning for a light, I've had the same shirt and pants on now for 6 weeks without changing them. My hair hasn't been cut since I left the states and I get to shave about once every week. I sleep with my pistol belt on, with my hand on the butt of my automatic. It really is just like something you'd see in the movies. Sometimes I can hardly believe it's happening. When you think of what misery and suffering men bring upon themselves, it's enough to make you wonder if we're civilized at all.

I think you've probably guessed the name of the boat I came over on. I don't think it would matter if I told you now, it was the Queen Mary. It really is a beautiful ship.

I should be getting the money order from the mail cpl. any day now. I got three money orders, two $25 dollar ones and one $23 dollar one. As soon as I get them I'm going to send them to you, I want you to give one $25 one to my grandmother and keep the other $25 one and the $23 one for yourself. Be sure and buy yourself what you need with it. I want you to spend it on yourself, as I said, I should be able to send them to you in a couple of days, later on I'm going to send you some more to help you pay for your coat. Gee! You were beautiful in that coat, I'm awfully glad you got it Sweetheart. When we're married, I'm going to get you all kinds of nice clothes, I want you to have everything you want. It's going to be lots of fun buying you things, especially those black lace things. I'm going to expect you to model them for me, OK? It had better be. Every night of my life Darling I thank God for giving you to me. I'm the luckiest fellow in the world to have such a wonderful girl. You're the most adorable, sweetest, prettiest girl in all the world, and you'll always be the one and only girl in my life. I love you with all my heart and I'll never love anyone else but you.

Take good care of yourself my Precious, be happy and keep that chin up. I'll be back with you, don't ever doubt it for a minute.

By the way Sweetheart if you can, send me candy or cookies or cake. I think fruitcake would be the best because that keeps pretty good. I know you have to have a request for a package before you can send one, so this is the request. If you can't get it don't worry about it, I know it's hard to get cake and candy and things like that.

Well I have to stop now. I'll write again as soon as I get a chance. Be a good girl now. Tell your Mother and Dad and Phil I was asking for them, also Millie and Dawne and tell Gerald I was asking for him when you write to him.

Good night my Precious. I love you with all my heart and always will.

All my love for always Sweetheart,
Your Paul

February 16, 1945
Germany

My Darling Bernie,

I got another letter from you today postmarked Feb. 7th. That's only 9 days ago. I also received one from my grandmother today also dated Feb. 7th. So far now I've got 4 letters from you and one V-mail, one letter from my father and two from my grandmother. I can't tell you how much your letters mean to me Darling, they're the nicest thing that happens to me now.

I'm glad you sent me Gerald's address. The first chance I get I'll write to him. Whenever you write him tell him I was asking for him. Ward is darn lucky if he's still in England. That's almost as safe as being back in the States. I hope he's able to stay there. When I got off the boat in Scotland, I got right on a train and almost before I knew it I'd gone through Scotland and England and was on an L.C.T. *(landing craft, tank, a military transport boat)* on my way to France. It didn't take me long to get from France to where I am now, and at the present time all I have to do is strain my eyes a little to see Hitler's "so called" supermen. They look very little like the "master race" with an M-1 round through their stupid skulls.

I'm glad my check is coming to the back O.K. I need very little money over here, so I'll be sending you some probably every pay day. I want you to buy things for yourself with it, I'd like to help you pay for your coat too. Every time I think of how beautiful you look in that coat I feel good all over. To me you're beautiful in anything Darling and you always will be.

There's not much I can write about in the way of news. I've got a good bunch of boys in my platoon, they're from all walks of life and they're all ages, from 18 years old up into the thirties.

My platoon Sgt. reminds me an awful lot of Mike O'Connor. He's just as big as Mike was and he even looks a lot like Mike only he has red hair and Mike was blonde. I like him a lot and he really is a fine soldier.

There's not much else to do in our spare time over here but think. Darling, every spare moment I have I think of you. I love you more than ever Bernie, with all my heart and soul.

Don't worry about me Honey, I'm feeling fine and everything is going along O.K. I'll be coming back to you soon don't you ever doubt it, not even for a minute. I want you to take the best care of yourself all the time, please do that for my sake, as long as you keep well and try to be happy then I'll be well and happy too.

I have to stop now my Precious. Be a good girl now and don't ever forget that you belong to me and me alone for always.

All my love my "Itchy"

The 320th began crossing the Roer River. Paul began burning Bernie's letters due to censorship. One of his duties involved reading and censoring other soldiers' letters.

February 23, 1945
Germany

My Darling Bernie,

I've got 4 letters from you to answer. I haven't had a chance to write for the past few days. First, I'll answer a V-mail from you had written Feb. 2. I got it yesterday. Airmail is faster than V-mail it seems. You said you had just received my first letter from Belgium. I hope my letters start coming in O.K. now. At the present time I can't keep your letters with me. As soon as we read our mail we have orders to burn it, so that our outfit could not be identified by the address on the envelope or mention of the outfit in the letter itself.

The next letter I'm going to answer is the one you wrote me February 8th. I got it about 3 days ago, but haven't had a chance to answer it yet. It doesn't matter if you put 2nd Lt. or just Lt. on my letters, I'll get them either way. You said Bing Crosby was singing "Good Night Sweet Dreams Sweetheart" and "Saturday night is the loneliest night in the week." They sure are appropriate songs. Are they on the hit parade now?

You should wear your fur coat all the time. When that one wears out we'll get you another one. I want you to be good and warm darling, so please wear it. I'm going to send you some money to help pay for it as soon as I get some more.

Now to answer your letter written Feb. 13th. I received it yesterday the 22nd. Darling I'm so sorry my mail hasn't been coming regularly. I'm writing all I can but remember I told you there would be some big gaps between letters. Please don't worry. It's just that sometimes it's impossible to write. Every chance I get I'll write you, you know that.

You said your mother was home and feeling good. I'm awfully glad about that. I didn't even know she was sick until I received my grandmothers letter saying she was going to the hospital. This was the first letter I got from you saying anything about her being sick. Be sure and tell her I was asking for her, and tell her to hurry up and get well, before the rest of your family all have to go to the hospital from Phil and your cooking. Now don't get angry, that was only was supposed to be a joke, I really think you're a wonderful cook sweetheart, in fact everything about you and everything you do is wonderful to me.

Keep on having those nice dreams honey. They'll be coming through one day soon and when they do you and I will be the two happiest people in the world.

Any wedding announcement that you like I know I'll like, gee funny face how I'm looking forward to that day, when you become my wife I'll be the proudest and happiest man in the whole world.

I'm glad you get mail from Gerald so fast. Don't let your mother worry about him too much, it won't do him or her any good. If he gets one day a week off and is able to go to church on Sundays he must be living in a fairly decent place.

I haven't got your valentine yet.

Now to answer the next letter, the one Feb. 14th. I got it yesterday too. It was postmarked the 15th and I got it the 22nd, that's only 7 days to get here. That really is fast. I hope mine get to you that fast.

I wish I could have sent you a valentine honey, but the Germans don't seem to be selling them this year.

I don't have time to write much more right now honey. Don't worry about me, I'm feeling fine and everything's is going alone O.K. I miss you so much it actually hurts, but I know I'll be back with you someday, soon I hope, and I know you'll be there waiting for me, and that means more to me than I'll be ever able to tell you. I love you my darling with every bit of love that's in me, I wouldn't trade your little finger for all the rest of the women in the world. You were made for me baby and me alone, your mine and no else's ever.

Please take care of yourself sweetheart. Keep that chin up, and try to be happy. Don't ever forget how much you mean to me, I'll love you with all my heart for always.

Goodbye for now my "itchy"

I love you.
Your Paul

February 24, 1945
Somewhere in Germany.

My Very Own Darling,

I received 3 letters and a V-mail from you today, so naturally I'm feeling very good. Your letters are really what keeps me going over here, I just can't tell you how much they mean to me. Two of the letters and the V-mail were to my saltwater address, the other letters were to my regular address. I'll answer the first one, you wrote it Jan. 9.

I'm very angry, a fine thing calling a Jap "Itchy." I think I'll write a nasty letter to that paper. My pet name for you is "Itchy" so naturally I'd be mad when someone calls a Jap that. I never will forget that night Darling. You were so very cute when you said that. I'll never forget it, if I live to be 100 years old.

I got the announcement of our engagement, the one that was in the Schoharie County News. I still haven't received the one that was in the Gazette, or your picture that was in the paper either. I should be getting it soon. I'm keeping the little announcement you sent me in my wallet, I bet I've read it at least 10 times today. I wish I could tell you how proud I feel when I read it. I'm the luckiest fellow in the world to have such a wonderful girl as you and don't think I don't know it.

You said in this letter Judy was better tonight. I haven't received any letter saying she was sick, but anyway I'm glad she's better.

Don't worry about my changing Darling. Some things about me may change a little but I promise that my love for you will never change, you'll always be the most wonderful person in the world to me, and I'll always love you with all my heart.

Now to answer the next letter. This one was written Jan. 10. In this letter you said you had received your first letter from Gerald. In your other letter that I've already got you've said you have been hearing from him regularly and I really am glad about that. I know you all must worry about him a lot, but try not to worry too much, before you know it he'll be driving the Ford up in front of the house again, and if you look close you'll probably see an old beat up 2nd Lt. riding with him, namely me.

When you pick out that Bridal gown, I want it to be the prettiest and the best one you can get. The sweetest, and most beautiful girl in the world should certainly have the best Bridal gown that was ever made.

You mentioned that you've been reading the book "A Tree Grows in Brooklyn." I've got a Sgt. in my platoon from Flatbush, Brooklyn. I bet he's probably seen that tree. (That wasn't a very good joke I admit.)

You said you slept with your ring on every night. I'm glad you do Sweetheart, the ring itself isn't much, but every time you look at it I want you to know that all my love and devotion goes with it. I think the night I gave you that ring was the happiest night of my life. I'll never forget how you looked, oh gee! Bernie, I love you so very much.

The next letter to answer is the V-mail. It was written Jan.14. In it you said you'd be expecting a cable gram from me. I never did get a chance to send that cable gram Darling. I went through Scotland and England so fast I hardly saw them. I went through London about 8 o'clock one morning, so I didn't have much more than a glimpse of it. I'll undoubtedly get a much better look at Berlin, if there's anything left to look at, and I doubt if there will be.

Now to answer the last letter. This one was written Feb. 15., postmarked the 16th. Today is the 24th. That means it only took 8 days to get here, that's really fast.

You said in the letter you had received the letter from me written Jan. 21. I'm awfully glad my mail is getting there O.K., even if it does take quite a while. I haven't written many V-mails to you because I think airmail is faster and because I know you'd rather get a letter than a V-mail.

We usually can't name places that we're near because it would give away our location. Sometimes they let us name cities and so forth and every time they do I'll let you know.

It seems like a long time ago that I saw Mickey Rooney, he looks just the same as he does in the movies. He doesn't actually come within 10 miles of the front lines, naturally he couldn't very well put on a show up here anyway.

I got my pistol when I joined my company. I carry it plus a carbine, plus a knife. Just like a bad man in a movie but where we are, all of those things come in very handy.

I've only had a chance to go to church a couple of times since I've been over here, that was when we were back in reserve. I haven't seen a chaplain at the front yet, but actually you can't blame them for that, you can't hold church services up here. Usually the chaplains stay back by Battalion Headquarters and the Battalion aid station which is about 3 to 5 miles behind us most of the time.

You said you still owed $150 on your fur coat. I'd like to pay the rest of that for you and I think maybe I will be able to when we get paid the next time.

I'm very glad your mother is feeling better. Be sure and tell her I was asking for her. Also, your Dad and Phil.

Well I guess that answers all the letters Honey. There's not much I can write about in the way of news around here. Please don't worry about me Darling, I'm feeling fine.

I think this is Saturday night. It's kind of hard to keep track of what day it is over here. What a difference between this Saturday night and the way Saturday nights used to be. They'll be that way again though Baby, just you keep that chin up and keep smiling. We'll make up for the Saturday nights and all the other nights we've been apart, and Darling I promise I'll do my best to make you the happiest girl in all the world.

I have to stop now Funny Face. Take good care of yourself, don't worry and be a good girl. Always remember that you belong to me and me alone for always. I love you my Precious forever and ever.

All my love my Darling,
Your Paul

While Paul was in Germany, some of his fellow soldiers were selling German pistols to the Air Corps, artillery soldiers and the clerks in the rear of the front lines. Paul was issued a Bulova watch from the army. He explains how he was able to get two of his soldiers transferred off the front lines.

February 25, 1945
Germany

My Darling Bernie,

How do you like this writing paper? Some class isn't it. I picked it up in a bombed German house. I don't know if the sensor will let this through or not but I really don't see why they shouldn't. Let me know if it comes through O.K.?

I saw a set of silverware today that would cost at least $100 in our money. It was all wrapped up in tissue paper and then in a beautiful velvet box. It was lying in a basement of a bombed German house, I think perhaps it might have been a store at one time. We're not allowed to send anything classified as loot to the States. If they did allow it, the guys would be sending everything from women's girdles to grandfather clocks.

I haven't received any mail yet today. I answered the four letters I got yesterday last night, so I have no letters to answer right now.

The Army issued me a watch the other day. It's a Bulova, it really is a very good watch. I've also been issued a $90 pair of binoculars, a compass and my 45 automatic. We really do have good equipment. I still have the watch I had when I came over, but I think I'll sell it. It only cost me 21.90 and already I've been offered $50 for it. Money doesn't mean anything over here. Some of my boys have sold German pistols that they took off dead Germans for as much as $125 to the artillery and rear echelon boys who aren't actually up at the front. Most of the air core, artillery and clerks and so on get their souvenirs that way, from the poor sad sack infantry riflemen who had to kill someone to get it, and then finds he can't carry it along with him so he sells it to the boys who don't have to live in cellars and foxholes.

By the way I'm sitting in a cellar writing this, and really, it's a pretty good cellar. The German who built it did a good job. I bet he never thought an American would be sitting here writing on German paper to his girl back home. It's a funny old world isn't it.

I got two transfers for two of the men in my platoon today. One man is 39 years old and has been with this outfit for a long time, he's married and has two children. He'll be back in the rear somewhere now so at least he'll be safe. The other boy had a bad case of nerves so I got him back too. The war is over for those two fellows, and for that I'm glad.

It's now it's 3:30 Sunday afternoon here. That means it's about 10:30 AM at home. You should be in church now. Unless you're later than usual of course. I'd give anything in the world to be with you Darling. I love you such an awful lot and I miss you so very, very much. The only thing I'm living for is the day that I can come back to you. That's really going to be a wonderful day Sweetheart. We're going to be married just as soon as possible after I get back. We'll wait just as long as it takes to get a license and for you to get ready. I'll be ready the minute I step off that boat.

Don't ever forget how much I love you Funny Face. You belong to me for always. You're my woman Darling and mine alone. We were made for each other my Precious and I promise you that there will never be any other woman in my life but you. You're the only woman I'll ever want and you're the only woman I'll ever love. I mean that from the bottom of my heart.

Take good care of yourself Bernie, dress good and warm, be careful crossing streets, and please don't work too hard. I wish with all my heart that I was there to take care of you but until I do get there you be a good girl and take good care of yourself. Do that for me please.

Don't worry about me now. I'm feeling fine and everything is going along O.K. I'll write every chance I get but don't worry if there are gaps between letters. Sometimes it's just impossible to write. Tell your mother and dad and Phil I was asking for them.

Keep that chin up Baby, be happy and before you know it I'll be back with you again. I love you my "Itchy" for always.

All my love my Darling forever and ever.
Your Paul

On February 26 and 27, the 320th was fighting within the Siegfried Line, a heavily-fortified German defensive line. The division captured twenty-three towns.

February 26, 1945
Germany

My Darling Sweetheart,

I really am doing good. This is the third letter to you today. The second one really wasn't a letter. It was a small envelope with a small handkerchief in it. I hope it gets through alright, let me know if you get it. I picked that handkerchief up in a German house, just like I picked this writing paper up. I actually think the place must have been some sort of a store because there was box after box of writing paper, silverware, handkerchiefs etc. I don't know if it's a good handkerchief or not but it looked pretty so I sent it to you. I also sent one to my grandmother. If you don't get it don't worry, it wasn't big enough to blow your nose on.

In our present situation I've been lucky as far as writing is concerned. I was able to write a letter last night, one this morning, send the handkerchief this afternoon, and write again tonight. One of my boys found me a candle, so I'm now sitting in a German cellar writing this by this by the light of the candle. My platoon Sgt and runner are sitting here with me. We've got a little stove, that throws off heat once in a while, but most of the time it just smokes. We have to be pretty careful about lights because the Germans aren't very far away from us. In fact, it's just a matter of a few hundred yards. Our own artillery fires over us all the while, after the first few days you don't even notice that though. The nights are very black and dismal, shutter, creak and groan in the wind, cows and horses wander about the streets of the ghost towns, you hear cats crying and once in a while a dog will howl. It's hard to believe that this is actually me sitting in a cellar writing to you. I always seem to have the feeling that I'm acting in some kind of play or movie. Well anyway I hope the last act will be coming soon, I'm ready to go home any time now.

That cartoon "The Sad Sack" that you sent me is really good. That and "Up Front with Madeline" are really true to life, I think the guy that writes "Up Front with Madeline" must be in the infantry himself.

I'd like to tell you some things about the company I'm in, but I can't say very much. It's a rifle company and I command a rifle platoon. A rifle company consists of approximately 6 officers and 200 men. When I found this company in Bastogne it consisted of one officer and 42 men. Since that time, we've been built up again.

Well I guess I've talked enough about the war for a while. It definitely isn't my favorite topic anyway. I think you know what is, it's you.

I'm sending back the first letter I got from you. I've been carrying it around with me and I'm really not supposed to, so I'm sending it to you for you to keep. It was the first letter I got, and Darling I'll never be able to tell you how much that little piece of paper meant to me. I read it so many times I almost memorized it. You keep it and when I get back we'll read it together.

My candle is getting pretty short, so I have to hurry up and finish this. Tell my grandmother about the handkerchief I sent her because I won't be able to write to her tonight.

I miss you an awful lot Darling. I can't put into words the way I feel. I'll never be happy until I'm with you again. You're just as much a part of me as you could possibly be.

Life without you is just an existence, nothing more. I love you with all my heart and soul Bernie, I don't think any man ever loved a woman more than

I love you. Keep yourself for me and me alone my Precious, I'll make up for these months apart, I promise. We're going to have a home of our own, and you're going to have whatever you want, and we're not going to wait to do all these things either. You're going to become Mrs. Roberts just as soon after I get off that boat as possible. We'll be married first and then whatever we do after that we'll do together.

Take care of yourself Sweetheart. You belong to me "Itchy" for always. I love you Darling.

Goodnight Sweetheart,
Your Paul

Paul mentions singer Frank Sinatra going for another military physical. Sinatra was ultimately classified as 4F (not acceptable for service in the Armed Forces) by his local draft board.

February 26, 1945
Germany

Hi "Itchy,"

Two letters and a V-mail from you today. Boy I'm a lucky guy to have such a wonderful gal as you are. I wish I could tell you how much your letters mean to me Darling. Anyway, I think you know.

First, I'll answer the V-mail. It was written Feb. the 8th. So, Frank Sinatra is going for another physical. Here's hoping he passes, I could use a good singer in my platoon, I'm sure the boys would enjoy having him around. V-mails don't take very long to answer, so I'll answer your two letters. The first one was written Jan. 12th, you were still writing to my saltwater A.P.O. then. I'm glad I had the picture taken with Dawnne on my lap. You know I like to hold young ladies anyway. Especially one young lady, she's really very wonderful and I love her more and more every day. In fact, my main ambition in life is to hold her close to me and kiss her and tell her that I love her with every bit of love that's in me. Maybe you've met the gal, you'd know her in a minute, she has beautiful hair, very nice eyes, the nicest lips in all the world and a darn cute figure, as a matter of fact she's really a knockout and to tell you the truth I'm crazy about her. If you meet her let me know, she answers to the name of Bernie, Funny Face or "Itchy." Don't call her by those last two names though they're reserved especially for me.

You probably think after reading that last paragraph that I'm getting a little shell shocked, but seriously though Darling I mean every word of it.

You told me what Gerald said about our engagement. He certainly was right when he said it was about time. I guess I'm just awfully slow.

He must have it fairly nice if he's living in tents. I'm glad he's in the Air Corp. Although you might not think so that really is a break for a fellow. At least you live like a human being most of the time and not like an animal. I could start acting the part of a caveman anytime now. I'm beginning to think I've lived under the ground almost as long as I lived on top of it.

I still haven't received the Valentine or the announcement for our engagement. I did get the little announcement in the Cobleskill paper but not the one from the Gazette.

Please don't worry about me Baby. I really am feeling fine and don't you worry about my back. I'll be back with you before you know it. And don't you think for a minute that I won't be able to win that bet. It's going to be wonderful proving it to you Darling.

I haven't heard a radio in weeks so of course I haven't heard "Goodnight Sweet Dreams Sweetheart." It sounds like a swell song.

Now to answer letter number two. It was written Feb.11th. In this letter you told me about your mother being sick. Sometimes it's good getting your mail mixed up, I heard about her getting better before I even knew she was sick. Be sure and tell her I was asking for her and tell her I said to get well quick.

How do you like this paper? It's some more German paper that I picked up in a wrecked house. Might nice of these Germans to supply me with writing paper isn't it.

Well Baby, I'm going to stop now so I can send this letter back to be mailed. If I get a chance I'll write again tonight.

I also received a V-mail from my grandmother today, but she didn't put any date on it so I don't know when it was sent. Airmail is much faster than V-mail though, that I'm sure of.

Once again Funny Face, please don't worry. Take good care of yourself and don't ever forget that you belong to me and me alone my Precious forever and ever. I love Bernie more than anyone or anything in the world. I'll never want any other woman but you and I'll never love any other woman but you. I thank God every night for giving you to me and I ask Him to bring me back to you soon. I know our prayers will be answered Darling, just you keep that chin up and keep smiling, I promise we'll make up for these months apart. I love you my Precious for always.

All my love forever and ever,
Your Paul

On February 28, Task Force Byrne was formed as a motorized force to breach the Siegfried Line in the Roer Valley. The 320th was part of the force.

There were no letters from Paul from February 28 until March 5.

The Thirty-fifth Division (the 320th was part of it) took the Trier region in Germany. They cleared the Moselle River which was a tributary of the Rhine River. The 320th joined the Seventh Army and swept through the Saar region of southwestern Germany and Palatinate, which was the southernmost quarter of the German area, which became Rhineland and Palatinate after the war.

Letters to Bernie started up again. Paul wrote that in Germany, "things are happening fast," and that a lot of Germans are waving "white flags."

March 5, 1945
Germany

My Darling Sweetheart,

I haven't had much of a chance to write for the past few days. I think the last letter I wrote was Feb. 27th.

A couple of days ago I got almost 20 letters most of them from you. Most of them were written to my saltwater A.P.O. Last night I got 15 more letters from you and home. I think I have just about all my back mail now. It was lots of fun reading all those letters.

I'll number my letters starting with this one. I'll probably forget the numbers though, so if I do don't think anything of it.

It's hard to remember all the things you ask me in your letters Sweetheart. One thing though I definitely don't want you to smoke nor do I want you to join anything like the waves, the wacs, spars or anything else. You're doing plenty to win the war right where you are. Let me do the fighting for the family, you stay on the good old home front.

I don't have much time to write this letter Honey. Things are happening pretty fast over here. Germany the land of the supermen is rapidly filling up with hundreds of white flags. I'm writing this letter in a German house, the whole German family is still in the house, we've been pushing so fast and hard that they haven't even had time to evacuate the civilians. We don't stay in any one place very long, we're on our way through Germany and it really is a fast trip.

I'll try to write more soon Darling. Don't worry about me, I'm feeling fine and getting plenty to eat. German chicken tastes just like ours.

Oh gee! I almost forgot. In one of the letters was your picture, the big one about our engagement. I showed it to all the other officers and my company commander and all of them in fact said what the heck does a beautiful girl like that see in you. I told them that I wasn't always this dirty and my hair wasn't always this long, so that probably explained it. The picture of you was swell Darling, I got it in my wallet.

I have to stop now Baby. Take good care of yourself my Precious.

All my love forever and ever Itchy.
Your Paul

Paul was finally able to mention the division he was in again. He was with the Thirty-fifth Division (also known as the Santa Fe Division) with different armies.

March 6, 1945
Germany

Hi Itchy,

This isn't very good paper but it's the best I could dig up. I got another letter from you last night, it was postmarked Feb.27th. That means it only took 6 days to get here. That really is fast. It was letter number 12. I've received letters one, two, nine, and twelve in the last three days or so.

We are allowed to mention our division again. You should know it by now but if you don't it's the 35 division. Don't be surprised if you read about the 35th with a different army than the one I told you I was with before. Sometimes they assign us to a different army entirely. Remember what you've been reading in the paper for the past week or so, our division has been in that news mailing.

I'm writing this letter in the same German house that I wrote my last letter from. It's very hard for these Germans to believe that Americans are in their homes and they're living out in the barns. They're learning what it's like to be the oppressed instead of the oppressors. We don't stay in any town very long, it's usually just a matter of a few hours then we push on.

I guess that's enough of the war news for today. We haven't been paid for February yet, as soon as we are I'm going to send you some more money, I want to pay for the rest of your coat if I can.

I hope you're taking good care of yourself Darling. When I come home I want you to be just the way you were when I left you. The same sweet, beautiful girl.

I love you so very much my Precious, more than I'll ever be able to tell you.

I don't want you to smoke ever. You just stay the way you've always been, don't ever change, even a little bit.

Well Baby I have to stop now. Be a good girl and don't ever forget how much I love you.

All my love my Precious for always,
Your Paul

P.S. Here I am back again, I've still got a few minutes to write so I guess I will while I have a chance. Those two articles were in the Army paper The Stars and Stripes. It will give you a little news about the 35th Div. You can see by reading these articles what I said earlier about our not always being in the Army you thought I was in. In fact, the division has been in three different armies since I've been with it.

March 7, 1945
Germany

My Darling "Itchy,"

You've been getting letters from me on about every kind of paper there is I guess. I usually can find paper in envelopes though, we use the Germans. I would like you to send me some airmail stamps though. Just one or two booklets that will be plenty.

I got a letter from you yesterday. It was number 10. I also got a swell letter from Gerald. His was written Feb. 23rd. I'm going to write him the first chance I get.

In your letter you ask me about giving more blood. I definitely do not want you to give more blood. I thought we had that all settled. Please Darling be good and do as I ask you.

I'm sending you another article that was in today's "Stars and Stripes" that's the Army frontline newspaper. It will give you a little more information about the 35th Division, also what Army we are now in.

There's nothing much new to write about Sweetheart. I'm feeling fine, my hair is awfully long again but outside of that I guess I don't look much different than I did three months ago today. This is our third anniversary isn't it? Boy what a happy guy I was that night. If I was that happy then I wonder how I'm going to feel the day we get married. Gee Baby I love you so very much.

Don't ever forget for even a second that you belong to me and me alone forever and ever. You're my woman and no one else's.

Please take good care of yourself Honey, keep that chin up and before you know it I'll be home with you again and this time it will be for good. I love you my Darling for always.

All my love my Precious,
Your Paul

Paul is writing from a German farmhouse.

March 8, 1945

My Darling Sweetheart,

Well it's 4 o'clock Thursday afternoon at home, 9 o'clock Thursday night here. I was just thinking of the Schoharie free movies, there were on Thursday nights, weren't they? I think my fraternity meeting was on Thursday night also. It certainly is a funny old world isn't it. There isn't a free movie for miles around here nor a fraternity meeting, in fact social life at the present time seems to be nonexistent.

I'm writing this in another German house. It's a farm house, there are lots of cows out in the barn, also chickens and pigs. I just finished eating supper which consisted of a piece of cheese and some crackers and coffee. If we're still here tomorrow there will be a few less chickens running around. The German family who owns this house are still here, they're down in the cellar, there are three women and two men. It must be a shock to them when they see Americans coming in their homes. I wonder what they think of their "Fuhrer" now. Here's a stamp I found on a letter, I guess Hitler is on every German stamp there is.

I wrote you a V-mail a little earlier today. I'll write one every once in a while. In my last two or three letters I forgot to tell you I received the Valentine you sent me. I got it 4 or 5 days ago. It was swell Sweetheart, thanks a lot. You're good at picking out cards.

I've had this Holland bill in my wallet for quite a long while and I've been meaning to send it to you. It's our invasion money for use in Holland. One "guilder," that's what this is, is worth about 37 ½ cents in American money.

I wrote Gerald a letter yesterday. I received a letter from him about two days ago. I guess that's all the news Honey, now let's talk about us.

Gee Sweetheart how I miss you. I'd give anything in the world to be sitting with you tonight, to hold you close to me and kiss you. It seems like months and months since I've done that. I love you so very much Bernie, more than I'll ever be able to tell you. Always belong to just me Darling, no one else ever. They'll never be any other woman in my life but you. I'll never want anyone else. I'll be back with you again soon my Precious and when I do get back you and I will make up for the months apart, I promise.

I suppose everyone at home thinks the war with Germany is just about over. We're all hoping the same thing here. Every little town we take even the size of Esperance means that more men are killed or wounded, both German and American. Not that I'm sorry to see dead Germans, they brought it on themselves and they deserve everything they're getting.

I don't know why I keep thinking about the war, I don't mean to but it's kind of hard to forget when it's only a few hundred yards away from you.

How's your mother feeling? Tell her I was asking about her, also your Dad and Phil. I know you probably get tired of me telling you to take good care of yourself but I just can't help it Darling. Please be careful and be a good girl and obey all these orders I gave you. I know you worry about me, I'd feel bad if you didn't, but don't worry too much, I really am feeling fine and don't you ever doubt for a minute about my coming back. I'll be there just as quick as they'll let me and just as soon as I do get back, you're going to become Mrs. Roberts, then we'll have years and years of happiness ahead of us. Until then, keep that chin up and keep smiling, it won't be long now. Be good Itchy, I love you with every bit of love that's in me.

All my love my Darling for always,
Your Paul

Paul is still in Germany. He tells Bernie that the clippings from the Stars and Stripes will give an idea where they are. He is now in the Ninth Army. Task Force Byrne took the town of Drupt, Germany.

March 9, 1945

My Darling Bernie,

I wrote you a V-mail and an airmail yesterday, and here I am again so I'm doing pretty good. I try to write all I can while I have the time.

These clippings I'm enclosing will give you a good idea of just where I am. They're out of yesterday's, "Stars and Stripes" the Army paper. I underlined the things that pertain to my outfit. As you can see by the clippings we're now in the 9th army. By the time you get this letter we may be back with the 3rd again. The best way for you to follow the news is to follow both armies and whenever you see the 35th Div. mentioned that means me. I can write all this now because they've lifted the secret ban from us at least for the time being. Things are certainly looking good, we've all got our fingers crossed over here. Show my grandmother these clippings, it will give her an idea of what's going on.

We haven't received any mail yet today. Sometimes we get mail delivered to us almost every day, sometimes it's 5 to 6 days before it catches up to us.

Today is Friday, I think, it's awfully hard to remember what day it is around here. They all seem to run in together. I haven't had a chance to go to church for 6 or 7 weeks now, the last time I went we were back in Metg. I've finished about two months of combat duty now. Sometimes it seems like two years other times it seems as if it's gone very fast.

I'm feeling fine, dirty as usual but I'm getting used to that. My hair is so long I can feel it down to my chin, I must look like a broken down orchestra conductor.

All I can think of Baby is what you and I are going to do when I get home. The first thing will be to get married, from that time on we'll do everything together. Gosh! That's going to be wonderful. We're going to have a home of our own, just you and I together with no one to bother us. We're going to have an open fire place, a beautiful kitchen and bathroom, and a swell bedroom with the biggest softest bed we can find for us, no twin beds. Of course, there will be other rooms in the house too, but those are the ones I think about the most. What a wonderful day that's going to be. I don't think we'll have to wait too much longer either, you just keep that chin up and before you know it we'll be together again.

Three of my sergeants are married, one of them has a little girl. My platoon Sgt. isn't married not engaged either so at least I'm better off than he is. Well anyway Baby you and I will make up for these months apart. We've got years and years ahead of us and I'm going to do everything I can to make them happier than you ever thought they could be.

I have to stop now Funny Face. If I get mail from you today I'll try to write again later on. Let me know if you get the clippings O.K.?

Take good care of yourself my Darling, don't ever forget how much I love you. By for now "Itchy."

All my love,
Your Paul

Paul is now in a forty-eight-hour rest camp in Holland. The Thirty-fifth has reached the Rhine River.

March 10, 1945

Hi Darling,

I know you're probably wondering about my being back in Holland. Well I got a 48 hour pass to a rest camp back here. Our division sends so many enlisted men and officers who are on the front lines back to this place in Holland for a two day rest and then we go back up to the front. I've been at the front for almost two months straight without a break so it was my turn to come back for a couple of days. I got here about 12 noon today and I'll be back in Germany at the front again sometime Monday afternoon.

This is a swell place. It's a great big building with little individual rooms. Two officers sleep in a room, we even have electric lights. At noon today, I had a swell chicken dinner and I took a hot shower. The showers are in a coal mine right near here. This afternoon I went to a U.S.O. show that they held here, it was really good. There was a boy in it from Amsterdam, New York. I talked with him afterwards and he told me he had some relatives in Sloansville. Can you imagine that. There are two Red Cross girls here and they have hot coffee and donuts any time you want them. I was standing eating a donut and drinking coffee when a 2nd Lt. walked up to me and said "How you doing Roberts?" It was a boy I graduated from Benning with. He's back here for a 2 day rest also. It was really good to see him. He's also in the 35th Division.

Tonight, they had a movie. It was "A Tree Grows in Brooklyn." It was very good although it was sad. I know you read the book and said you liked it. I just got out of the show a few minutes ago. It's 11:15 now so I'm going to bed soon.

Tomorrow morning (Sunday) I'm going to eat breakfast, go down to the coal mine and take another shower and then go to church. It will be the first time in about 7 weeks that I've had time to go to church. Tomorrow afternoon they have another U.S.O. show so I'll probably see that, or I may just sleep all afternoon. I'm really awfully tired. I want to try to get my hair cut tomorrow too. We leave to go back to the front Monday morning. I never thought two days could mean so much to a guy.

They have Dutch girls from the town that this place is in wait on the tables. Imagine from foxholes to waitresses in just one day travel. It's really a crazy war.

I'm going to write you a long letter tomorrow afternoon. Right now, I think I'll go to bed.

I wouldn't have accepted the pass here but my company is in Battalion reserve for the next few days so my platoon won't be fighting. If they were fighting now I wouldn't have left them. As it is they're all getting a couple of days rest too. They certainly deserve it, they're a darn good bunch of boys, for the past 3 weeks or so they've been right up there all the time, but we've been darn lucky, I've only lost a very few men.

Just before I left for this place I got about 10 letters, all old ones from you and my grandmother. I think I must have all my back mail by now. I can't tell you how much your letters mean to me Darling, they're the thing that keeps me going. You're wonderful to write so often, don't ever do it though, if you're tired. Please be sure and take good care of yourself.

I'm going to stop now. I'll write a long letter tomorrow. I love you my Precious forever and ever.

All my love my Darling,
Your Paul

Paul is still in Holland. He writes that he has been at the front for almost two months with the Thirty-fifth Division. One of the soldiers in his platoon has received a life sentence from a court martial for deserting the unit while under fire.

From March 12 to March 26, the 320th was able to be billeted near Venlo, Holland. With one-day passes, they visited Brussels, Belgium.

March 11, 1945
Holland

My Darling Sweetheart,

I wrote you a letter last night telling you all about my being back here in a rest camp at Holland. You might get this letter before the one I wrote yesterday so I'll repeat some of what I said in that letter.

I'm back here for a 48 hour rest in the 35th Div. rest camp here in Holland. I've been at the front for about 2 months so it was my turn to come back for a rest.

This is really a swell place. I saw a U.S.O. show yesterday and a movie last night. Also had a shower yesterday. This morning I had my first chance to go to church in almost 7 weeks. I really did enjoy it. I also got my hair cut this morning. This afternoon there's another movie on so I'll see that. Tomorrow sometime after breakfast we go back to the front and dear old Germany again.

It seems wonderful to be clean again and to eat out of plates and sit at a real dining table. They have two Red Cross girls here passing out donuts and coffee. The Dutch girls from the town near here wait on the tables. Most of them can speak pretty good English.

I just finished eating dinner. We even had an orchestra playing while we ate. They call this place the Santa Fe slate. I'm enclosing the little paper they give you when you get here.

The place is mainly for enlisted men. They take so many E.M. from each company and send them here. They only take one officer from a battalion, so you can see I was very lucky to have been picked to come. Probably a 48 hour rest doesn't sound like very much but after two months of combat, two days of rest seem like Heaven.

I wouldn't have left my platoon to come on this pass if we had been fighting. For the next 3 or 4 days anyway, I know they're going to be in Battalion reserve so they'll be getting a rest too. They're a darn good bunch of boys, except for one or two lemons of course. Once in a while you find a guy that will ream out on you when you need him the most. One man from my platoon was sentenced to life in prison by a court martial the other day. He left us when we were attacking, it was the second time he had done it. I really don't feel sorry for him, he really deserved everything he got.

This Red Cross stationery is the only kind I could get to write on around here. I don't like it very much, it looks too much like a hospital, I hope it doesn't scare you when you get it.

I told you in last night's letter about the fellow I saw in the U.S.O. show yesterday who lives in Amsterdam, New York. He knows where Esperance is of course, even has relatives in Sloansville.

The war news certainly does look good. I don't think they can hold out much longer. Most of the prisoners we've taken look as if they're dead on their feet. The German civilians act different than I thought they would. First of all, they're very much afraid of us, they're very polite. I thought they'd be sullen and angry but instead some of them seem to be almost glad to see us come into their villages and cities.

If you try to follow the 35 inf.Div. in the news don't just watch one army, we've been shifted around quite a lot. Since I've been with the outfit I've fought with three different armies. For the past few weeks we've been with the 9th army. I can tell you all this because in the Stars and Stripes newspaper they came out and said we were with the 9th Army so it can't be a secret any longer. How long we'll stay with the 9th I don't know. The 35 is one of Patten's favorite Divisions so he might want us back.

Well I guess that's all the latest news. The movie starts at 2:30, it's now 1 o'clock so I think I'll go take a shower again. I'll write again tonight after supper. My pen just ran out of ink so I borrowed this one from another officer.

He's going over to take a shower with me so I'd better stop for now.

Don't worry about me Darling, I'm really feeling fine. Just you be sure and take good care of yourself. I love you such an awful lot Funny Face. Don't ever forget that you belong to me for always. No one else ever.

Be a good girl now. Keep that chin up and before you know it I'll be back with you again.

All my love forever and ever "Itchy"
Your Paul

March 11, 1945
Holland

Darling "Itchy,"

The second letter to you today. I really am doing good now. I wrote you once this morning, one last night and now one tonight. I also wrote one home tonight.

I went to church this morning, it was very good. After that came dinner, then a movie this afternoon and tonight after I finish writing this I'm going to listen to the radio for a while or read and then go to bed early.

In the letter I wrote last night and the one I wrote this morning I told you all about the rest camp I'm at. I'll be going back to the front tomorrow morning sometime. It really has been swell here. It was one 48 hour period I won't forget for a long time. I won't tell you any more about it in this letter because I've already told you in the two letters I wrote before this one. You're probably get this one first and the other two after and be wondering what it's all about. Maybe you'll get the other two letters first, I hope so.

There's nothing much new to write about Honey. I gave you all the news in this morning's letter.

I still haven't been paid for February. We've been moving so fast they haven't been able to pay us. As soon as we are paid though I'm going to send you some more money. I want to pay for the rest of your coat if I can. Did you ever get the other money orders I sent you? There were two, one for 25 and one for 23 dollars.

Please take good care of yourself my Darling. I love you so very much more than I'll ever be able to tell you. You'll always be the only one for me, for always and always. Be a good girl now, keep that chin up and before you know it I'll be back with you again.

Good night my "Itchy"

All my love for always,
Your Paul

Paul is back in Germany and beginning to speak a little German.

March 13, 1945

My Darling Sweetheart,

Well I'm back in dear old Germany again. Those two days back at the rest camp were really very nice. I'm sitting in some German house again writing this letter.

I got the picture of you in the paper. I have two of them now, but I'd like to keep them both unless you want me to send one back. Don't forget to send me some airmail stamps, I don't have many left. One or two books of them will be plenty for now. We do get airmail envelopes every once in a while.

I'm getting so I can speak a few words in German now. I really wish I could speak it well, it would come in darn handy. I have my whole platoon in this house with me along with the Germans who own the place. The German civilians asked me if they could stay in the cellar so I told them O.K. It sounds hard hearted making people live in the cellar of their own home, but after you've seen a few dead American soldiers you lose all sympathy for these people. They brought this all on themselves, now they're reaping the harvest.

I got the 4 letters from you last night also some from my father and grandmother. We were paid yesterday, so as soon as I can get a chance to make out a money order I'm going to send you some more money. The army issued me a Bulova wristwatch so I sold mine. It only cost me $21.90 at McClellan and I got $40 for it, so I didn't do bad. I want to send you $75 and my grandmother $25 as soon as I can make out the money orders. It might be quite a few days before I get the chance. Let me know if the $100 a month comes to the bank regularly.

I got your letter saying what you were going to buy with the other money I sent you. I wish you'd spend it all on yourself instead of buying bonds. When I send you this $75 please buy things you need and would like to have. I want you to have a good time with the money, that black lace must be expensive, so you'd better start getting some of that.

Don't worry about me Darling. I'm feeling fine and right now things are pretty quiet.

I'm going to have to stop for now. Be a good girl and take good care of yourself. Don't ever forget how much I love you "Itchy," it's with all my heart for always. You belong to me Darling, no one else ever.

All my love my Precious,
Your Paul

March 14, 1945
Germany

My Very Own Darling,

I got two letters from you today, number 14 and one written Jan 11. My father's was written on Jan. 4th. I'm sure all my back letters should have caught up with me by now. Your mother's letter was written Jan. 4th, the other one she sent me was written to Gerald. That sounds funny I know but she must have made a mistake and written a letter to Gerald and put my address on it. It was letter number 7 written Tues. Feb. 27th. I read the letter, I hope she doesn't mind. I guess I'd better send it back, maybe she wants to send it on to Gerald. I'll enclose it with this letter. You tell her I censored it and it's O.K. to send it on (that's supposed to be a joke.)

You're definitely not the best bowler in the world but that really isn't a bad score. I never made 200. I think 190 something was the best I ever did. In your letter you mentioned that your mother wrote me a letter that night. She probably sent my letter to Gerald and his to me. She must be in love or something, think that's it? You'd better not send me any letters written to some other guy, I won't return them to you. That package you're sending really sounds swell. I should be getting it soon. I'll be looking forward to it. I'll make this a request for another package although I really don't think I should keep asking for them. I really don't need much. The flashlight would be a good idea, I could use one.

"The" sad sack you send me in every letter is really good. You're swell to bother about little things like that. You're really wonderful Darling, and besides that I love you like the very dickens, heaps and heaps.

In that next package please send me some Vaseline hair tonic. No, I'm not trying to woo these German gals, but I would like to comb my hair like I did back in the good old days just once or twice. I still have the lighter I had when I came over, it's pretty well beat up though now.

I'm feeling fine, in fact I believe I've gained some weight. Maybe it's just the added dirt that makes me feel heavier.

I don't have time to write much more tonight Sweetheart. Please take good care of yourself my Precious. I love you an awful lot. You mean more to me than anyone in this whole world and you always will.

Be a good girl now. Before you know it, I'll be home with you again.

I love you "Itchy" forever and ever,
Your Paul

On March 15, Paul sent a copy of the Stars and Stripes "Santa Fe Express" edition, Volume 2, Number 9. The headline was "Rhine reached by the 35th" (in seventeen days). They crossed the Roer River, and took hundreds of thousands of prisoners during the Ninth Army's drive to the Rhine. They crossed the Siegfried Line to Wesel, Germany. The 320th's Third Battalion liberated Venlo, Holland, conquered Straelen, and did a night assault on another town. The Nazis showered them with propaganda saying the Roer Valley was impregnable. They took Drupt, Germany and were relieved by the 134th Infantry. The Thirty-fifth division was one of eight divisions in the Army National Guard. The Thirty-fifth Division Santa Fe patch was a wagon wheel because the unit trained in the vicinity of the Santa Fe Trail.

A photo of the patch appears on page 184.

Paul is in Holland, being treated like family by Dutch people who are grateful for being liberated.

March 16, 1945

My Darling Sweetheart,

Well I'm back in Holland again and darn glad of it. The whole division is back here this time. We don't know what is coming off yet but whatever it is it's better than being at the front, we're all in agreement on that point.

I got those letters from you today. They were all old ones written to my saltwater A.P.O. It seems as if I should have received all the old letters by now. Neither old or new, they're the nicest thing that happened to me over here, I can't tell you how much they mean to me.

These people here in Holland treat us as if we were one of the family. We liberated quite a few of these towns not so long ago, one city we liberated had been under German rule for 5 years. Those people were really happy when we moved in and drove the Germans out. There was quite a difference when we came in the town in Holland and when we went in German towns. Quite a different reception.

There is not much news Darling. I'm feeling fine as usual. Please don't be worrying about me. Just you be sure to take good care of yourself.

I have to make this a short letter tonight. There's an awful lot of things I have to do.

Be a good girl now. Don't ever forget how much I love you. You belong to me for always.

All my love my Precious forever and ever,
Your Paul

March 19, 1945
Holland

My Darling Sweetheart,

Well I'm back in Holland again. I can't tell you just what we're doing but I can say it's safe so you don't have to worry the least bit as long as I'm back here.

I've got a lot of letters of yours to answer so here goes. I'll answer 3 of the latest ones.

First the one you wrote Jan. 28. No wait a minute, that definitely isn't a late one. I'll answer letter number 19. It was written March 5th.

The handkerchief I sent was from Germany. By the way I'm sending you another one today. This one is a souvenir of Brussels. I had a pass to Brussels just for one day. It's the capital of Belgium you know and it really is quite a city. That handkerchief was about all I could find to buy for you though.

Next comes the answer to letter number 24. It was written March 11 and I got it the 18th. It only took 6 days to get here.

I'm sorry to hear that your dad was sick. You'd better get that Ma and Pa of yours on the ball and quit scaring people. Be sure and tell both of them and Phil that I was asking for them. Also, Gerald when you write to him.

I got the paper that Dr. Larrabee sent the other day. In it was a notice that Walt Warner had been killed in Germany. Remember him? He was a fraternity brother of mine, lived in Albany. I was really sorry to hear about him, he was in the infantry. We took basic together at McClellan. He went to A.S.T.P. *(Army Specialized Training Program)* for a while and when they closed that he went back into the infantry as a private.

I'm glad my $100 a month is getting to the bank O.K. After that is taken out and 6.50 for insurance and $21 for meals I actually receive about $60 a month, which isn't bad at all. I'm going to send you a money order for $75 and one for $25 for my grandmother. It (both of them) will probably be in my next letter. I want you to spend the money on yourself and have a good time with it. Don't be buying bonds, spend it on clothes and things like that. Get things you wouldn't get otherwise. I like white chiffon, pink chiffon, black chiffon, black lace, white lace, pink lace, green lace, in fact anything as long as you're in it. Buy a whole bunch of it.

I was surprised to hear that you heard from Robinson. I'm going to write to him as soon as I get a chance. Did you put perfume on the letter you sent him? If you did I'm mad, I still don't get it on mine. He must be in the 78th Div. according to his address. I don't know what army that puts him in.

Well Baby I'm going to have to stop for now. I'll try to write again tonight. I've been awfully busy the last few days.

I'm feeling fine, and as I said before while I'm back here in Holland there's not a thing for you to worry about.

Take good care of yourself my Precious. I love you with every bit of love that's in me. You belong to me for always.

By for now "Itchy"

I love you.
Your Paul

Paul is in Holland, not fighting, resting up after a twenty-mile hike to the rear.

March 20, 1945

Hi "Itchy,"

Another day over. It's beginning to feel like Spring over here now. It can't come too soon to suit me.

I'm sending two money orders in this letter. One to you for $75 and one for my grandmother for $25. Please spend the money on whatever you want now. Have some fun with it. Tell my grandmother to do the same thing. Of course, she had better not buy any black lace with it.

I got a letter from you tonight, also one from my grandmother and also the program of the firemen's party in Esperance, sent to me by Jim Gage. I just finished a letter to him thanking him for sending it to me. It really must have been pretty nice.

As you probably have guessed while we're back here in Holland we aren't doing any fighting, that doesn't mean however that we sit just sit around and rest. Believe it or not we had a 20 mile hike today, the reason, to keep in good fighting condition. Oh, how I love this wonderful army. It really isn't so bad though, anyway I guess it could be worse. I don't think there's a man here who wouldn't rather take a 20 mile hike in preference to 20 minutes at the front.

There's not much news to tell you Sweetheart. I'm feeling fine as usual. Remember now I want you to spend the $75 on yourself. Buy yourself clothes and things you wouldn't get otherwise.

Be a good girl and always remember that you belong to me and no one else ever. I love you Darling and I always will forever and ever.

Keep that chin up and before you know it I'll be home with you.

All my love Funny Face,
Your Paul

> Paul describes the fighting. He leads an infantry rifle platoon. They fire M-1 rifles, use bayonets, throw hand grenades, and fight using hand-to-hand combat. "I've done these things," he explains.

March 22, 1945

My Darling Bernie,

I received three letters and an Easter card from you tonight. The card was swell Darling, thanks a lot. It smelled good too. Your letters were postmarked March 13, 14, and 15, so that's making it in good time. I also received a letter from my father postmarked Feb.2. His letters seem to take an awful long while getting here.

I like the picture of the dress you're getting. Get a few more with the money I sent you the other day. I really like to have you dress nice. You said in your letter it was time to go to bed and that you wished we were going to bed together in our own home. Gee Darling, I wish the same thing, if you only knew how hard and how often I've wished that. For the past few nights we've been sleeping in a bombed Catholic convent, but it seemed like Heaven because it's dry and quite warm. Sleeping on a stone floor with one blanket under you and one on top is really wonderful after sleeping 10 or 14 days straight in some foxhole in the woods. Another Lt. and I sleep together or at least we have been for the past few nights, he commands the third Plt., I think I told you before I have the second platoon. If anyone ever asks you what I do in the army you can tell them I lead an infantry rifle platoon and when you tell them you can be proud of it. I know I am and I can honestly say that there's not a Tougher job in the army. The men in an infantry rifle platoon are the ones who fire M1 rifles and use bayonets and hand grenades and often fight hand to hand with the enemy. I know it's true because I've done those things with them and when I say I'm a rifle platoon leader I'm darned proud of it.

I'm sending you a little paper put out by our division. I'm in the third Battalion of the 320 inf, so it will give you an idea of what we've been doing. We were told the other day we could send the paper home so I'm not violating any rules by sending it.

That was some dream you had. It's funny but I haven't dreamt once I don't think since I've been over here.

By the way, this other Lt. I mentioned before who leads the third Platoon graduated from Benning the day after I did. He was in class 367.

Well Sweetheart that's about all I have time to write tonight. Be a good girl now. Always remember that you belong to me and me alone. Take good care of yourself my Darling. I love you my Precious with all my heart for always.

Good night "itchy." I love you,
Your Paul

Paul is still in Holland. He sent Bernie the Santa Fe Thirty-fifth Division patch.

March 22, 1945

Hi "Itchy,"

I've been so darned busy the last couple of days I've had very little chance to write.

I'm feeling fine and as you can see still in Holland. Things are much nicer here than in Germany and that's no fooling.

I'm sending you my division patch. It's supposed to represent a wagon wheel. The 35 div. is called the Santa Fe division. It originated around the Santa Fe trail. The patch is worn on the left shoulder just the way I used to wear the I.R.T.C. patch.

PART TWO - CHAPTER 5   **184**

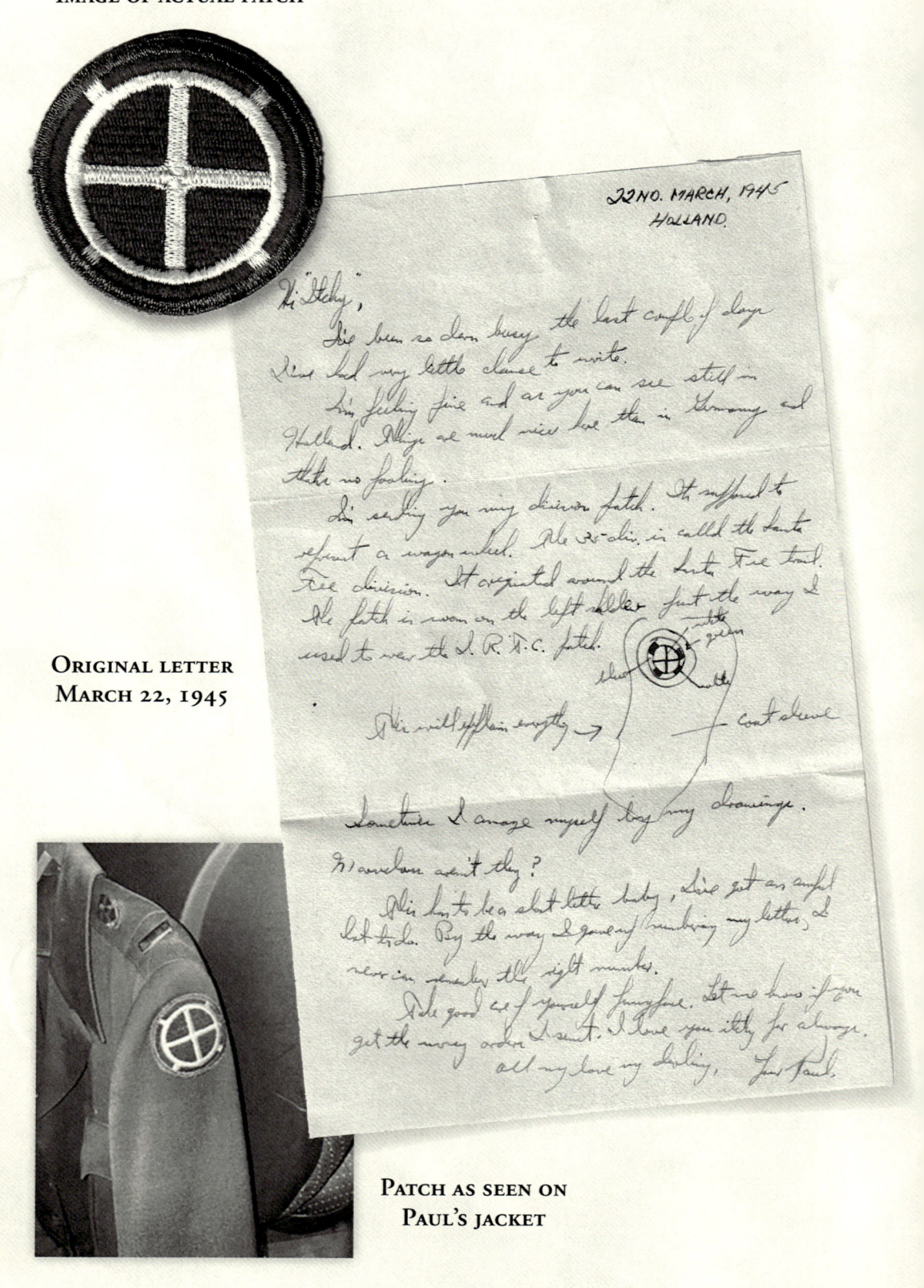

IMAGE OF ACTUAL PATCH

**ORIGINAL LETTER
MARCH 22, 1945**

**PATCH AS SEEN ON
PAUL'S JACKET**

(See drawing on the original letter of the patch to the left.)

Sometimes I amaze myself by my drawings. Marvelous, aren't they?

This has to be a short letter baby, I've got an awful lot to do. By the way I gave up numbering my letters, I never can remember the right number.

Take good care of yourself Funny Face. Let me know if you get the money order I sent. I love you itchy for always.

All my love Darling
Your Paul

Paul is still in Holland. He has spent some time in Brussels.

March 24, 1945

My Darling Sweetheart,

You're probably die laughing when you see these pictures. I couldn't help looking like that, the guy said watch the birdie and that's just what I was doing. I got these taken in Brussels, Belgium while I was there on a one day pass. While we've been back here they brought our duffle bags up to us so consequently I was able to put on my combat blouse and a necktie to go to Brussels in. They've taken the bags back now so I probably won't see my good clothes for quite a while again. We never carry anything like that with us, they always hold it back at supply points then when we get back for a rest they bring our things to us. It was the first time I've had my good things on since I've been over here. Brussels is a big city and they gave so many men each day a pass to go there. Most of the people can speak a little English there. Things are very high priced, a cup of coffee costs about 60 American cents. Those other officers from the Battalion went the day I did. We had dinner together and it cost each of us about 300 francs. The Belgium franc is worth more than the French franc so it cost us actually about $7 a piece for what would cost about 75 cents in the States.

Of course, there are a lot of soldiers in the town both American and English. I honestly think that about 90 percent of the women in the city are prostitutes.

It's almost unbelievable that the morale of a place could be so low. They come up to you on the streets and in a very businesslike way tell you how much they want to sleep with you. It makes no difference whether you're white or black. I guess I never told you about that situation over here, did I. The women in England and France, Holland and Belgium like colored soldiers just as well if not better than the white ones. It's not unusual in England or France to see a white woman pushing a baby carriage with a colored baby in it. The Germans are different. I've seen German women beg white soldiers not to let colored soldiers into their homes. In fact, it happened to me once, a German girl actually got down on her knees and in broken English begged me not to let any more colored troops into her house.

Well to get back to the pictures, I had three made in a little place something like a 5 and 10 cent store back home. The man told me to keep watching a little duck (by the way he had lived in New York City for three years.) I guess by the look of the picture I was really intent on watching the duck. They're really awful pictures but they're better than nothing. That's the 35 Div. patch on my sleeve, and the combat infantry badge over my left pocket. We get that after being in combat for one month. Both Enlisted men and officers get it. I'm really quite proud of it, you have to be in the infantry to get it and you have to have actually been in combat for at least a month. The pictures only cost 50 francs. That's $1.14 in our money. That is darn cheap for Brussels.

I also had my picture taken in another place but the fellow couldn't give them to me the same day so he said he would mail them to me. I should get them tomorrow (if we're still here and don't move back to Germany on a minute's notice) so as soon as I get them I'll send them to you. I hope they're better than these. Give one of them to my grandmother and you keep the other two or give her two and you keep one, which ever you want to do. Explain to her why I look so funny. I don't go around looking like that all the time, I hope. I made a mistake I have 4 of the pictures so you keep two and keep my grandmother two. Well I guess that's enough talk about my picture. If I get the others tomorrow I'll send them to you right away. Tell my grandmother not to worry, when she sees me without glasses she'll think I broke them. I didn't. I just didn't put them on for the picture. Let me know how you think I look. I don't think I've changed any, have I?

I got a letter from you tonight with the book of stamps. Thanks Darling. I also got a letter from my grandmother with about 6 airmail stamps, so now I have plenty of them. Your letter was number 28 written March 15th. That package you're sending sure sounds swell. I'll make this a request for another one but I really don't need anything more. Please make the next one just a small one.

Those dreams you're having really sound swell Baby. You keep on dreaming, I promise to make all the nice dreams come true, real soon.

By the way while I was at Brussels (one day) I spent all my time walking around and at the Officer's club. Don't ever worry about me doing anything wrong. I belong to you just the way you belong to me, I don't believe in being faithful just on one person's heart. You'll always be the only one Baby, no one else ever.

Well Darling I have to stop now. Don't worry about me, as I said before as long as I'm in Holland you shouldn't worry about me even a little bit.

Take good care of yourself my Precious and don't ever forget how much I love you.

All my love Itchy forever and ever.
Your Paul

Paul remains in Holland. His regiment, the 320th, spent time patrolling in the vicinity of Rheinberg. The Thirty-fifth Division is crossing the Rhine River at Wesel, Germany.

March 25, 1945

My Darling Bernie,

I just came from church. Today is Palm Sunday, I didn't even know it till I got to church. I really enjoyed going this morning, I've only had a chance to go two or three times since I've been over here. They sing the same songs you sing in church at home. All I have to do is close my eyes and it seems as if I'm right back there. Gosh Darling how I wish I were back there. I miss you such an awful lot. We're going to make up for these months apart Sweetheart, I've promised myself that at least a thousand times. You just keep that chin up for a little while longer Darling, we'll have years and years ahead of us and every minute of those years will happy ones. Just you be sure to take good care of yourself Funny Face till I get back, then I'll take care of you from then on.

We haven't received mail yet today so I'm going to make this a short letter and then write again later on in the day.

I love you "itchy" with all my heart for always. You belong to me and me alone Darling, don't ever forget that for a minute.

By for now Sweetheart. I love you.

All my love, Paul

Paul has learned that several of his college classmates have been killed in action.

March 25, 1945
Holland

My Darling Sweetheart,

The second letter to you today, that's pretty good. I received a V-mail from you tonight, also a paper from Dr. Larrabee. I'm sending the paper to you, I think they're really pretty good, maybe you'd enjoy reading it. I underlined the part about Donny Ford. Remember him, he lived in Albany and was a fraternity brother of mine. Also, Dick Lent. I think I told you about Lent. Mr. Jessen told me when I was home that Lent had lost both legs. Both Ford and Warner have been killed, also Paul Santee, and one other boy from the fraternity house. I underlined all the fellows' names that I knew well while I was at Union.

Your V-mail tonight was number 25, written March 12th. I get one letter from you every day now. I can't tell you how much they mean to me Darling, they're the nicest thing that happens to me over here.

As usual I have an awful lot of things to do so I can't write too much. Be a good girl and take good care of yourself. I love Bernie, with all my heart for always.

All my love my "itchy"
Your Paul

On March 26 there was no letter. The 320th and 137th Regiments crossed the Rhine on the "Doughfoot Bridge." They were east of Rheinberg, Germany. With the 320th in reserve, the 134th and 137th pushed into the Ruhr region. The Thirty-fifth was crossing the Rhine River.

Paul writes that the war against Germany shouldn't last much longer.

March 27, 1945

My Darling Bernie,

Back again in Germany, way in this time. Things are going pretty good so far, we all have our fingers crossed that it won't last much longer. It doesn't seem possible for them to stand this pounding much longer, when they'd all rather be dead than give up.

There's not much that I can tell you about just where I am or what we're doing, I think you can tell pretty well though by reading the papers.

I'm feeling fine so don't worry about me Sweetheart. We had a pretty nice rest while we were back in Holland.

I don't have very much time to write this Baby, but even a little letter is better than none at all.

Please take good care of yourself my Precious. Keep that chin up. I'll be back with you soon.

I love you Bernie, more and more every day.

All my love my "itchy,"
Your Paul

March 27, 1945
Germany

Darling Bernie,

This is the second letter to you today. After I wrote the first one I received a letter from you and one from my grandmother and also two little packages from you. One had the candles, the other gum and candy. Thanks a lot Sweetheart, I really appreciate them. I'm using one of the candles now. Your letter was written Sunday the 18th. It was number 30. I was sorry to hear about your aunt's death, I know she was a very fine woman and that you'll all miss her very much, but as you said maybe it's for the best.

There's nothing new to write about. I'm feeling fine and everything is going along O.K. so far. It doesn't look as if they can hold on much longer, at least we all hope they can't.

I'd give anything in the world to be home with you Darling. I'm getting so I hate the dark. You'll probably never be able to get me out of the house at night. Nights over here are horrible things, sometimes I don't think Hell could be any worse. If you don't mind we'll just sit before a big old fireplace and listen to the radio and maybe neck a little or better yet it's neck a lot.

I have to stop now Baby. Be a good girl and take real good care of yourself. Don't ever forget how much I love you "itchy."

All my love for always,
Your Paul

Original letter from March 27, 1945

27 MARCH 1945
9 P.M.
GERMANY.

Darling Bernie,

This is the second letter to you today. After I wrote the first one I received a letter from you & one from my grandmother and also two little packages from you. One had the candies, the other the gum & candy. Thanks a lot sweetheart, I really appreciate them. I'm using one of the candles now. Your letter was written Sunday the 18th. It was number 30. I was sorry to hear about your aunt's death, I know she was a very fine woman and that you'll all miss her very much, but as you said maybe it's for the best.

There's nothing new to write about. I'm feeling fine and everything is going along O.K. so far. It doesn't look as if they can hold on much longer, at least we all hope they can't.

I'd give anything in the world to be home with you darling. I'm getting so I hate the dark. You'll probably never be able to get me out of the house at night. Nights over here are horrible things, sometimes I don't think hell could be any worse. If you don't mind we'll just sit before a big open fire place and listen to the radio and maybe read a little or better yet let's neck a lot.

I have to stop now baby. Be a good girl and take real good care of yourself. Don't ever forget how much I love you "itty".

All my love for always, Your Paul.

Paul was hit in the right arm by shrapnel from a German eighty-eight-millimeter artillery shell at eleven a.m. on March 28. He explains this in detail in his April 4 letter from England.

The 320th joined in the attack over the Rhine that day and met heavy fire as it fought through woods to reach the Autobahn highway. By six p.m., leading elements of the regiment captured part of the Autobahn. The 137th and 320th made progress against heavy resistance and managed to advance one-and-a-half miles on March 29.

The "German 88" was a versatile eighty-eight-millimeter (3.46-inch) multi-role artillery piece. It was used extensively by the Germans in World War II as a field artillery piece and as an anti-aircraft and anti-tank cannon. It was the most effective anti-tank gun used by any side in that conflict.

By April 1, the regiments held and improved their positions along the Herne Canal.

Chapter 6

HOSPITALIZED IN ENGLAND
April 2, 1945 to June 11, 1945

Paul is in a hospital in England. He starts writing letters left-handed due to his wounded right arm. He is in the 4176 hospital plant at Malvern Wells, Worcestershire, England, about one hundred miles from London. He eventually spends his last days in England at the 4175 hospital plant.

April 2, 1945

Hi Darling,

I'm writing this with my left hand so you can understand why it looks the way it does.

I'm feeling pretty good and receiving the very best of care please don't worry about me, I was really very lucky. My right arm and shoulder were where I was wounded. The doctor tells me that it is going to be ok, it will be more a matter of time. At least I am all in one piece yet and that's what counts.

I'll probably be able to tell you more of the details later on. This address is where I am now. It will probably change though with my next letter. I think they are going to move me to another hospital in England.

I won't be able to write much at first so don't worry if you don't hear from me every day. I'll write as often as I can. Let my grandmother and father read this letter.

Take care of yourself darling.

I love you,
Your Paul

Paul describes his wound in detail in this letter.

April 4, 1945
England

My Darling,

Here I go again with another left-handed letter. Maybe it is easier to read than some of my right-handed ones have been in the past.

As I told you in my letter the other day I was wounded in my right shoulder and arm. My arm was broken and also the nerves in my arm have been cut by the shrapnel that went thru my shoulder. I was very lucky in not losing my arm, so there's something a lot to be thankful for.

I'm in a special nerve hospital now where'll they'll probably be able to fix me up as good as new. We're getting excellent care so please don't worry about me.

The address on the envelope will be my new address for the next few weeks so start writing to me at that address. Give to the folks too so my grandmother and father can start writing. Take care of yourself and don't worry.

All my love darling,
love your Paul

Original letter from April 2, 1945

My Darling,

*April 2nd
England*

I'm writing this with my left hand, so you can understand why it looks the way it does.

I'm feeling pretty good and am receiving the very best of care. Please don't worry about me, I was really very lucky.

My right arm and shoulder were where I was wounded. The doctors tell me it's going to be O.K., it will be more or less a matter of time. At least I'm all in one piece yet and that's what counts.

I'll probably be able to tell you a few more of the details later on. The address is where I am now. It will probably change though with my next letter. I think they're going to move me to another hospital here in England.

I won't be able to write much at first so don't worry if you don't hear from me every day. I'll write as often as I can. Let my grandmother & father read this letter.

*Take care of yourself darling. I long love you,
Your Paul*

On April 6, the 320th was attached to the Seventy-fifth Division, aiming at Dortmund, Germany, as the war in Europe draws to a close.

Paul tells Bernie about how and when he was wounded after they crossed the Rhine River, and that his arm and hand are paralyzed.

April 9, 1945
England

My Darling Bernie,

Here I go again, I know these letters look awful but there better than nothing I guess.

I'm feeling pretty good. They've operated on my arm twice so far. The wound + the broken bones are coming along O.K. They won't be able to work on the nerves in my arm for quite some time though. My right arm + hand is paralyzed because the nerves have been cut. I was hit by a German 88 shell, we had crossed the Rhine. Happened the 28th of March about 11 o'clock in the morning. I was flown from an evacuation hospital in Germany here to the hospital in England. The doctors here say I'm coming along fine + that the nerves in my arm will be alright again after some more operations + of course with lots of time to let the arm heal.

There's a good chance that in 2 or 3 months, I'll be sent back to the states to some hospital.

I'm not sure about this yet but that's the way it looks now, so keep your fingers crossed for me.

ORIGINAL LETTER FROM APRIL 9, 1945

9 April, England

My Darling Bernie,

Here I go again, I know these letter look awful but there better than nothing, I guess.

I'm feeling pretty good. They've operated on my arm twice so far. The wound & the broken bones are coming along O.K. They won't be able to work on the nerves in my arm for quite some time though. My right arm & hand is paralyzed because the nerves have been cut. I was hit by a German 88 shell, we had crossed the Rhine. It happened the 28th of March about 11 o'clock in the morning. I was flown from an evacuation hospital in Germany here to this hospital in England. The doctors here say I'm coming along fine & that the nerves in my arm will be alright again after some more operations & of coarse with lots of time to let the arm heal.

There's a good chance that in 2 or 3 months I'll be sent back to the states to some hospital. [They're] not sure about this yet but that's the looks now, so keep your fingers [crossed] for me.

[I was] very lucky in not loosing my arm. [They] told me if the shell fragement had [gone] 1/8 of an inch one way or another it would have cut the main artery & [they'd] have had to take my arm off. [I have] a lot to thank God for.

[Don't] worry about me, I'm getting the best of care. Please read this letter to my grandmother & father. In a couple of more weeks I'll be able to write more. Its pretty tiresome right now. Be sure & write to me, use my address on the envelope.

Take good care of yourself funnyface. I love you very much. With luck I'll be back with you soon.

All my love for always
Your Paul

I was very lucky in not losing my arm. The doctors told me if the shell fragment had entered my arm 1/8th of an inch one way or another than it did, it would have cut the main artery and he would have had to take my arm off. I really have a lot to thank God for.

Don't worry about me, I'm getting the best of care. Please read this letter to my grandmother + my father. In a couple of more weeks I'll be able to write more. It's pretty tiresome right now. Be sure + write to me, use my address on the envelope.

Take good care of yourself Funny Face. I love you very much. With luck I'll be back with you soon.

All my love for always,
Your Paul

Paul provides a progress report about his recovery and his reaction to President Roosevelt's death.

April 13, 1945
England

My Darling Bernie,

Here I go again Funny Face, these left-handed letters are really a job.

I'm feeling O.K., the wounds in my arm are starting to heal, they have the bone set so it will start knitting now too. As yet they haven't done any work on the injured nerves in my arm but that will come later.

We heard here this morning of President Roosevelt's death. It was really a sad thing to have happened to our country at this time. It was a shock to everyone over here.

As I said in my other letter with luck in about 2 or 3 months I'll be out back to the States to a hospital there. Keep your fingers crossed. It will take a long time for me to have complete use of my arm again.

Be sure and write often Sweetheart. The days are awfully long now, + they seem to go by very slowly.

They've got my arm stuck up in the air with weights + pulleys + all sorts of things on it, that's to keep the bone in place. The wound is quite large, it goes from just below my shoulder almost down to my elbow so it will take quite a while to heal. I hate lying flat on my back all the time but there's not much I can do about it I guess.

Don't worry about me Honey, I'm going to be O.K. Take good care of yourself, + remember I may be seeing you in a couple of months. So that's something for us both to look forward to.

By for now Darling, I love "Itchy" for always.
Your Paul

April 15, 1945
England

Hi Darling,

Sunday in England, it's just like every other day here in the hospital. I just finished eating supper. They put the tray on my chest + I manage to eat pretty well with just my left hand.

Remember Rodgers? He was one of the four of us at O.C.S. Well, he's here with me. He was wounded in the left arm + right foot. He's in better shape than I am though, because his wounds were both small. That leaves Retz and Robinson still up at the front as far as I know.

I'm feeling pretty good, so please don't worry about me. Be sure and take good care of yourself my Darling. I love you with all my heart for always.

All my love "itchy"
Your Paul

April 16, 1945
England

My Darling,

I got a letter today from your mother, Laura Montagne, Fred, my grandmother, my father and Dorothy Edwards, all written on the 10th. No letter from you though, that's a fine way to treat a guy. Maybe yours will come tomorrow. I'm glad my letters got there the same time as the telegram.

I'm feeling pretty good, we just heard Pres. Truman's speech over the radio. He sounded very good to me. We're six hours ahead of you at home. Six o'clock here is noon time at home.

It's awfully hard to write Darling. I have to stay flat on my back. I hold the writing board between my knees and it gets awfully tiresome.

Take good care of yourself Baby, don't worry about me. I love you more than ever if that's possible.

All my love my Precious,
Your Paul

Paul explains his daily routine at the hospital as he continues to recover.

April 19, 1945
England

Hi Darling,

Another day almost over. Some of them go awfully slow. I'll try to describe "my day" to you.

They wake us up at 6AM to take our temperature. At 6:30 they bring in breakfast. I hate to eat with the tray on my chest, because I have to lie flat on my back. After breakfast we clean our teeth, try it lying in bed sometime, after that the nurses wash us as if we were a bunch of two year old babies. Then I do my best to shave + comb my hair (which by the way will undoubtedly be down to my shoulders in another couple of weeks.) The doctor comes in to look at our wounds sometime during the morning. At 11:30 we have lunch, then another temperature reading, also vitamin pills 3 times a day. In the afternoon I try to read or listen to the radio (we get a break because the officer's ward is the only one with a radio.) About 4 o'clock we get our mail. By the way, I got two letters from you today, one from my father and one from Helen Montagne. Supper is at 5 o'clock. I do my letter writing around 6 or 7 o'clock. At 10 o'clock the lights go out. So far, I haven't been able to go to sleep much before one or two o'clock. My arm always seems to hurt more at night.

Well that's a brief outline of my days as I'm spending them now. Not an awful lot of fun but still far better than some days in the not so long past.

If you could send me some candy or cookies I'd like it. Don't send too much though.

I'm hoping that I'll get my duffle bag with my clothes in it. The hospital has sent for it, but I'm afraid the chances of my getting it are slim. By now it's probably lying in some mud hole in Germany. Better the clothes than me though, huh?

Remember the little package with three candles in it that you sent me? I got that the night before I was hit. I used one of the candles that night in a German house with a dead woman lying in the same room that I had for my Command Post. Down in the cellar were two Germans that both had wooden legs and another one that was a raving maniac from shell shock. You can see how welcome just the light from a little candle was in those surroundings.

Bing Crosby just came on the radio. He's singing "Don't Fence Me In" It sure does sound good. He's still far better than Frank Sinatra in my opinion.

I wish my picture hadn't been in the paper. I really don't like things like that. You certainly can feel as if you're helping me to get well Sweetheart. They gave me two pints of blood just a few hours after I'd been hit. So, you see you gave me two pints of blood.

They're singing "One meatball" on the radio now. Boy what will they think of next. That's the first I've heard that one.

Well Darling I guess I'd better stop before they have to put the left arm in traction too.

It's becoming easier to write with my left hand, but it's still pretty tiresome.

Take good care of yourself Darling. I love you Funny Face very, very much.

Good night my Darling,

All my love for always,
Your Paul

The doctors visited and they described the wound.

April 20, 1945
England

My Darling,

Nothing new to write about. I'm still flat on my back. Today three doctors came in the ward inspecting each of us. They discussed me for quite a while, it seems that the bone in my arm is not only broken but that for about a space of about 3 inches it was shattered so bad it's just like powder. They seem quite confident about their being able to fix it up though so I'm not worrying. The nerve will be the toughest job to repair I guess. As soon as the wounds stop draining and heal up good, they'll operate on the nerve and also work on the bone. Sometime after that they'll probably put me in a cast and send me to a hospital in the States for further treatment.

I got Purple Heart the other day. When the Red Cross girl comes around I guess I'll have her send it home for me. It would look kind of funny wearing it on my pajamas, don't you think.

I got a nice letter from Prof. Larrabee today, also the V-mail you wrote the day the telegraph came. V-mail is much slower than airmail.

I was just thinking how can I drive a car and put my arm around you. I could sort of drape my arm around your shoulder. It's a funny thing I can make a fist but I don't have the power to open my hand up.

This traction they have me in is, I think, one of the most horrible inventions of man. Traction is just a nice word for a bunch of not very nice ropes and pulleys that pull and tug at you in a most unsympathetic way.

It's really not as bad as it sounds. I realize I could be a lot more uncomfortable than I am. I thank God I still have both of my arms.

Well Baby, take good care of yourself and remember that I love you like everything.

All my love my Darling, Your Paul

April 24, 1945
England

My Darling,

I got nine letters tonight. Three from my grandmother, 3 from my father, one from my grandmother in New York, and two from you. That was really a haul, wasn't it?

Captain Bacon who is in the bed beside me is being sent home sometime this week. I've asked him to call home when he gets back in the States. Rodgers will be going with him and I've asked him to call you when he gets back, so sometime in the next couple of weeks you'll probably get a call from him. Rodgers' wound wasn't as bad as mine and he hasn't any nerve injury either. He was also wounded before I was, about 18 days before. I think I'll be very lucky if I start for the States a couple of months from now. The wounds are still draining so they can't operate on the nerve or the bone until the actual wounds are completely healed.

My father and grandmother seem to think that I'll be sent to Rhodes General Hospital in Utica. I really hope they're right but I'm not planning on it too much. The army still works in strange and mysterious ways. Of course, it may come true, if it does I'll be very grateful. My father also seems to think that I'll be discharged, I think he's forgotten that the war with Japan is far from over. 2nd Lt's even with beat up right arms will probably be in popular demand down there. Of course, he may be right in that too, I might be discharged, but that's really hard to believe.

I'm glad you're using the foot locker. Don't worry Darling, we'll have that heart to heart talk when I get back. I've got a few ideas about my future too. Right now, I'm wondering if my right arm is going to play a part in that future, or if I'm going to be carrying it around in a sling for the next few years. The doctors sound very encouraging though so I'm pretty sure it's going to be alright.

The weather has been beautiful over here for the past two weeks. The sun has been shining every day. I can lie here and look out of the windows at beautiful green lawns and shrubs. It makes a guy feel awful lying in bed and not being able to get out.

I also got a letter from Effie. She writes nice letters, you thank her for me.

The pictures of you were good Darling, the snapshots I had taken in Brussels were really awful weren't they. I really don't think I look quite that bad.

Well Darling I guess I'd better stop now. Don't worry about me, I'm coming along O.K. In a couple of months if things go as they should we'll be together again.

I love my Darling, with all my heart for always.

All my love Funny Face, Your Paul

April 28, 1945
England

Hi Darling,

Well it was one month ago today that I was hit. Sometimes it seems a lot longer than that.

I got a letter from you today written last Sunday, also the Upper Room and a letter from my father and one from Gerald. I've never received a nicer letter in my life than the one I got from Gerald. He sure is one swell guy and I really mean that. I'm going to try to write to him tonight or tomorrow.

I'm feeling fine, if I could only get out of bed, I'd feel 100% better. The guy that invented traction had an evil mind. You asked about the pulleys and weights, they're on 24 hours a day. The wounds are still draining however they are slowly healing.

I know I'll get heck for this but there's a little rhyme I heard today from Captain Tiegs who's in the bed next to me. His sister sent it to him.

> Here's to Eve the Mother of our race
> She wore a fig leaf in the proper place
> Here's to Adam
> The Father of us all
> Who was Jonny-on-the spot
> When the leaves began to fall.

Now don't say you didn't think that was good because if you do I won't send you any more of my good poetry.

By the way I got a card from Betty Gage, so you see you've got competition.

Well Baby take good care of yourself. With a little luck we ought to be together again in a couple of months.

I love you Darling, just because I don't say much about coming home don't think I'm not thinking about it. It's just hard for me to believe it until I actually get back.

Good night Darling. I love you.

All my love "Itchy,"
Your Paul

May 2, 1945
England

My Darling,

Got three letters from you tonight, the latest one postmarked the 28th. Only 4 days, that's really good. I also got another letter from Gerald. He's certainly been swell writing to me so much. I wish I could write the kind of letters he does, they're really interesting.

In one of your letters you mentioned people who have sons in the army and not giving blood. I agree with you they should be ashamed of themselves, who knows, maybe my father is, (I doubt it too.) As for you giving more blood, I wish you wouldn't. I think you've done more than your share. I'm not going to say any more about it. You know how I feel.

I'm still in the old bed flat on my back. It rained almost all day today. Bob Hope just came on the radio. It's 8PM here. I'm going to take time out to listen. By the way it's 2PM in Esperance now. There's six hours difference in time.

No, the nurses didn't put the stamp upside down. I'm the guilty one. When we first came over they told us not to do that.

By the way the nurses aren't bad. We have two on our ward in the daytime and one on at night. Are you jealous? After all I only can use one arm. I really don't feel much like flirting with nurses though so don't worry. I'm being conceited now?

Did you know a girl was like a nightie, pull one thing and it's all off. Gerald told me that one in his letter.

I was paid for April and May today. I got about 25 pounds, that's around 100 dollars. I feel guilty getting paid for lying in bed. You American taxpayers are getting stuck.

Well Baby I'm going to stop now. Be a good girl. It shouldn't be more than two more months before I'm back in the States. Save up a lot of hugs and kisses. I love you.

All my love "Itchy"
Your Paul

Paul has been moved out of traction to a cast and finally was able to get out of bed and walk for the first time in a month.

May 5, 1945
England

Hi Darling,

Something new to write about tonight. I'm sitting up. The doctor took me out of traction yesterday and now I'm in a cast. Boy what a cast. It goes from my hips up to my neck. The darn thing feels as if it weighs 50 pounds. I got out of bed today and walked around, but not for long. After being in bed for a month my legs are awfully weak. My wounds are still draining. The doctor thought they might stop quicker if he took me out of traction and put me in a cast. So far, I don't know which is the lesser of the two evils, traction or the cast. I hope the wound stops draining now.

Last night I got almost 60 letters. All the mail from the company came. There were lots of letters from you. I got the old letters from Gerald too. I also got the pictures I had taken in Brussels. I'll send them as soon as I find an envelope to put them in. I didn't get any of the packages though. They'll probably come in a few days.

I also got two letters from you written April 3rd. I'm going to stop now Darling, I feel pretty tired.

Take good care of yourself Sweetheart. I love you.

All my love my Darling,
Your Paul

May 6, 1945
England

My Darling Bernie,

I walked around quite a bit today. I'm still quite weak, but my legs are getting stronger. I told you in last night's letter that they took me out of traction and put me in a cast. You see the wounds were still draining quite a lot so the doctors thought that if my arm were put in a cast instead of traction the wounds might heal faster. If within the next week or 10 days the draining stops they'll take the cast off and operate on the nerve and bone. If the draining doesn't stop in that time they'll send me back to the States without operating and it will be done in a hospital back home. I know this probably sounds funny but I hope the draining stops so that they can operate on me here. This hospital specializes in nerve cases so I think they probably do a better job. Of course, if they don't operate on me here, I'll get back to the States probably at least a month sooner than I would if they perform the operation here. Well in a week or 10 days I'll be able to tell you what's going to happen. Which do you think would be the best getting the operation here or back home?

I'm sending you three of those pictures I had taken in Brussels in another envelope. I sent my grandmother two of them. They were taken about one week before I was hit. I also sent the envelope with the address where they were taken. Don't get frightened when you look at them.

I got a letter from you tonight written the first of May. I've been getting letters regularly from Gerald. He certainly writes wonderful letters. I'm going to try to write to him again tomorrow.

I guess I told you about the cast they put me in in last night's letter. It encloses my whole right arm plus my body from my neck to my hips.

You know how a waiter carries a napkin on his arm, that's the position they have my arm in in the cast. When I put my left arm up where my right one is I look just as if I were about to do a Russian dance. My left arm is just about worn out from writing, I wrote a letter home before I started this to you.

I know I don't say much about coming home Darling, but don't think I don't think about it. The thought of seeing you again seems almost like a dream. I guess it's about time some of our dreams started coming true huh?

Take care of yourself Baby. I love you Darling forever and ever.

Good night my "Itchy"

All my love for always,
Your Paul

While in the hospital, Paul listened to the V-E Day announcement with the formal acceptance by the Allies of Germany's unconditional surrender. There were speeches from Churchill and Truman.

May 8, 1945
England

My Darling,

V-E day at last! Everyone has certainly waited a long while for it haven't they. When V-J? day comes we really will have a lot to be grateful for. I hope it isn't going to be as long in coming as I think it's going to be.

I'm sending you the front page from an English newspaper. Keep it for me, 50 years from now we'll show it to our grandchildren.

By the way, does my watch still work O.K.? Remember I told you I sold the one I came over with, and the G.I. watch they issued me was broken the day I was hit, so now I don't have any. When I get back to the States I'll start wearing the old one, that is if it still runs.

I wrote a letter to Gerald today and one to Prof. Larrabee. This makes the third letter so I'm doing pretty good.

We heard Churchill's speech today at 3 o'clock. Pres. Truman was speaking at the same time in the States, that was 9 AM your time.

I guess that's all the news for today. I'm feeling pretty good, the arm is still draining, but not quite as bad as it was so that's something. At least I can walk around now that I'm in a cast, and that helps a lot.

Well Sweetheart it shouldn't be too much longer before we'll be together again. In my opinion it will be anywhere from 4 to 8 weeks before I start back to the States, but I may be wrong. But even if it's 8 weeks that really isn't so awfully long to wait.

Oh, I almost forgot, the box of Fanny Farmer's candy came last night. All the fellows send their thanks and me too. It tasted swell Honey.

I got a letter from you tonight, a card from Romona, a letter from Irene Hunter, and two letters from my grandmother, a V-mail from Larrabee and one from Dr. Waldron at Union, quite a popular guy, huh.

You ought to go to a doctor to find out if you're lacking something in your diet that would make your teeth get cavities like that. I know you probably won't do it, but it is a good suggestion, no fooling.

I guess I'll stop now. Be a good girl, and don't forget you belong to a banged up 2nd Lt by the name of Roberts. I love you Funny Face, lots and lots, for ever and ever.

Good night "Itchy," I love you. Your Paul

Paul reports that his nerve operation will take place in the United States and he expects to be returning in less than a month.

May 14, 1945
England

My Darling Bernie,

Well they looked at the arm today and decided to let the nerve operation go until I get back to the States. That means I'll probably be starting back in about 2 or 3 weeks. My guess is that I'll be back sometime between the 15th and the 30 of June. Of course, that's only a guess. I'm sorry they're not going to do the nerve operation here, but there's nothing I can do about it. I'll be getting back to the States quicker this way so that's something.

I got two letters from you today and two packages of cookies, thanks Darling, they were swell. In one of your letters were the pictures of the snow banks.

In my letter the other day I told you I didn't have a watch. I have one now. A friend of mine had two G.I. watches so I got one. It's exactly the same as the Bulova I had when I was hit.

I hope I go to a hospital in New York State. I'm going to request Rhodes General in Utica, but if that isn't a nerve hospital I won't be able to go there. Well where ever I go I'll be a lot closer to you than I've been for the past 5 months.

I know you've probably been told a thousand time by my "family" just how you and I are going to live, where we're going to live etc. All I can say is don't let it bother you, if you can possibly help it. When we get married let's live at least 100 miles away from relatives. Maybe 200 miles would be better.

If you can find a leather watch strap that doesn't cost too much I'd like you to send it to me. I think you could send it in a regular envelope. The width of the strap should be about the same as that required by my old watch that you have. I don't care what color it is.

Well Baby I guess that's all for tonight, Funny Face. I should be seeing you in 4 to 6 weeks from now.

Good night my Darling,
Your Paul

Paul is awaiting orders for his return to the United States.

May 19, 1945
England

My Darling Bernie,

I haven't written for the past couple of days because I haven't felt too good. It wasn't the arm that was bothering me it was my stomach. I feel better tonight though. I guess I'd better answer your letters first of all.

I bet the pillowcases you made are nice. You're quite a gal, can sew, cook (and good too) and besides all that you've got brains and are beautiful. Of course, I've got brains and I'm handsome but I can't sew or cook very well. So, you see I'm getting the best of the bargain.

I'm glad Capt. Bacon called home. I hope Rodgers calls you. Bacon lives in Detroit and he called from South Carolina. You can see how close he got to home. Of course, they may move him from there. He has a daughter, and I guess a son he's never seen.

I sure do remember when Millie shot the salad into my lap. And Darling I'll never forget the night when you said (and you said as if you could hardly believe it) it itches. Every time I think about it I have to laugh. It was so unexpected. You're cute Baby and I love you very, very much.

I could leave here any day now, I'm just waiting for the orders to come out. I think it will be at least a week though before I leave, maybe even longer. The way I feel now that I know they're not going to do the operation here, the faster I start for the old U.S. the better. Of course, there's a certain gal over there that's making me kind of anxious to get back to.

You said George and Bill both had points enough to get out. That point system doesn't apply to officers you know. They'll only be released if the army decides they're no longer needed when they are. That makes an air corps or infantry officers chance of getting out very slim.

You asked if the cast itched. That is putting it mildly. I always thought long underwear was bad but it hasn't anything on this outfit.

I got a letter from Phil tonight. Who is this "hunk of man" up at Herbie's farm? He sounds as if he's taken Murry Cashers place. Tell her thanks for the letter and your mother too, I got one from her tonight.

Well Baby I guess I better stop. I have to write my grandmother yet, I got a package of candy and cookies from her last night.

I've missed you these last 5 months Sweetheart an awful lot. I can hardly believe that I'll be seeing you again soon. I told you a little old war couldn't keep us apart for long. Of course, I could be coming in a little better shape than I am, but I thank God that it's not lots worse than it is. Before you know it, I'll be able to hug you with that arm as good as I always could. Come to think of it I think I can make you holler Uncle with just one good arm anyway. Think I can?

I'm glad you like the pictures, I guess they were better than the little ones. I think I've shown your picture to every officer in the ward. They all look at the picture and then at me and say what the h – does she see in you. Then I explain to them how much prettier I am without a cast.

Be a good girl now. Take good care of yourself and remember you belong to me for always. I love you "Itchy."

All my love my Darling,
Your Paul

May 23, 1945
England

My Darling Bernie,

Another day gone and I'm still here but there are strong rumors that we may be leaving this Saturday or Sunday. I sure do hope so. I'll have been in this cast three weeks tomorrow, I hope my arm will be knit enough to take me out of it when I get back to the States. The wounds are still draining, I'm beginning to think they'll never stop. Maybe by the time I get back to the States they will have stopped, if they do I'll be ready for the nerve operation. I was talking to the doctor today and he said that if the nerve is completely severed it will take from 8 to 12 months for me to get the use of my arm and hand, that's 8 to 12 months from the time of the nerve operation. Of course, there's a chance that the nerve isn't entirely cut, it may only be out of order because of the scar tissue around it, in that case I get the use of my arm much quicker. They can't tell whether or not it's cut until they operate but 2 to 1 it is cut because of the wound being so big.

I kind of hope they send me to Halloran Hospital in New York City. It's a nerve center and it would be close to you. You see once my arm gets well enough so that I can carry it in a sling instead of in this cast, I'll be able to get sick leave + passes from any hospital that I go to. They can't do too much for me in the hospital, it will be just a matter of waiting for the nerve to grow back.

I just keep hoping that they send me on the East Coast somewhere. The hospitals back there are pretty crowded so we've heard, so that means your chances of going to the hospital you want to are kind of slim.

I got two letters from you tonight and three from my grandmother. By the way I've forgotten whether or not I've told you to tell Effie to congratulate George for me. I'm glad he got his first, the war they're fighting in the South Pacific is a lot tougher than the one we had over here in my opinion.

I ate the olives last night and then dreamt about you all night, it was a good dream too. I'll tell you about it when I see you.

I think I'll probably only be able to write one more letter before I leave here, unless I'm wrong as to when I'm leaving.

Be a good girl, take good care of yourself and don't ever forget that you belong to me and me alone. I love you Baby forever and ever.

All my love "itchy"
Your Paul

Letter from Bernie to Paul in the hospital.

May 24, 1945

My own Darling,

I don't know when I've been as happy as I am tonight. I got three letters from you today and that alone would make me happy but the contents of those letters make me extra especially happy.

In your latest letter of the 19th you said you expected to leave within a week so Honey you may be on your way back home now or at least you're nearly ready to leave.

This is my last letter until I see you. I'll miss writing these letters, Darling, but I'm so happy that you're coming back in the U.S.A. I hope they do send you near home but no place in the U.S.A. is too far for me to come. I'm an experienced traveler you know and I'd go any place to see you. I hope you'll be able to let us know as soon as you land. I think I'll get a hat tomorrow so I'll be ready to leave on a moment's notice.

Your letter of the 14th didn't come until today so I won't send your watch strap. I'll buy it for you and bring it with me because it's too late now to send it.

I'm glad you're coming home for the operation. I think they can do it better here and besides I'll see you much sooner which doesn't make me a bit unhappy.

I'm awfully sorry you were sick, Honey. I hope you're O.K. now. I'm sure the food in the U.S.A. will agree with you.

I'll let Phil tell you all about her "hunk of a man." That sister of mine is quite a character. She only has 3 more weeks of school. She'll be a Sophomore next year.

Paul, I do thank God that you're no worse. In time, you'll be able to use both arms but until that time, I'll be in my glory. I should be able to overpower you with only one arm. You won't be able to squeeze me so hard that it hurts (war has its advantages).

I was thinking tonight that I'm happy for two reasons — one is that I love the Lord and the other is that I love you and God has answered my prayers and is sending you home.

We had a Union service at the Presbyterian Church tonight. They had a colored trio in a family of 5 that played, sang, etc. That colored fellow gave one of the best sermons I've ever heard. It was really swell. There were 2 couples sitting ahead of us holding hands — it reminded me of the good old days.

I may see you before you get this letter. I hope so.

I'm keeping my fingers crossed for next week.

I love you so much, Baby.

Yours for always,
Bernie (S.W.A.K.)

Paul's return to the United States is delayed, and he is transferred to a different hospital in England.

May 28, 1945
England

My Darling,

Well Sweetheart I'm still in merry old England. Two months ago, today I received my souvenir from the Germans.

Yesterday, I think, was the most disappointing day I've ever had. Yesterday morning orders came through saying that I was to leave for the States this morning. I got all ready to go and then the nurse discovered that they had made a mistake on the order and had classified me as an ambulatory patient (in other words a walking wounded patient) rather than a littered patient. (That is a patient who has to be taken on a litter because he has a cast on.) Well the nurse called up the shipping office and told them that they had made a mistake and had classified me as ambulatory instead of litter. Well to make a long story short they had made a mistake and because they had I had to be taken off the order. I'll be put on the next shipping orders, they may be out in a day or two at the most not be out for a couple of weeks. It all depends on how soon boats are available.

If that weren't enough to have happen to a guy in one day, the hospital (4176) is going to close because it's getting ready to go to the S. Pacific, so all of us who had not been shipped out were transferred to another hospital. You've probably noticed the new address on the envelope. This hospital is only 2 miles from the old one though so I didn't have far to go.

Everything else is just the same. They won't do any work on my hand at all actually all I'm doing is sitting here waiting for transportation to the States, and as I said, I could leave tomorrow, or I could sit around waiting for two or three more weeks.

The arm is feeling O.K. (I'm still in the cast of course) but gee I was disappointed when they told me I wasn't going just when I thought I was ready to leave. The Army has played some dirty tricks on me but never one as bad as that.

I suppose I shouldn't tell you all this because it will only make you feel badly. But after all it could be worse, it really only means a couple of weeks delay in getting home and it may not even mean that much.

Well Honey that's the latest news. I don't know what to tell you about writing. I may only be here a couple of days or it may be a couple of weeks. I'll leave it up to you, if you think it's best to write well then do it.

This is a nice hospital so don't worry about me. Right now, I feel as if someone had given me a ticket to Heaven, let me keep it for a very little while, and then taken it away from me. Going home means going home to you, and that's the nearest thing to Heaven that I can think of. Be a good girl, take good care of yourself and remember you belong to me and me alone.

Good night my Precious, all my love for always
Your Paul

May 30, 1945
England

My Darling Bernie,

No shipping orders yet, oh woe is me. If they don't get me on a boat pretty soon I'll be a mental case. With luck I should leave sometime this week, without luck sometime next week. I'm so darned anxious to get home and get this nerve operation over with. And even more anxious to get home to you. All I'm doing here is sitting around waiting for transportation and it's getting awfully tiresome.

I didn't get the last few letters you wrote to me, maybe they'll forward them from the other hospital to this one. (Both hospitals are within two miles of each other.)

I wish I could tell you just when I'll get to the States, but your guess is as good as mine. Just hang on I'll get there sooner or later if I have to swim.

Take good care of yourself Funny Face. I love you more than anyone or anything in all the world. Be a good girl, I'll be seeing you soon. (I hope.)

All my love , "itchy," forever and ever,
Your Paul

Today marks Paul's second anniversary of enlisting in the army.

June 5, 1945
England

My Darling,

Well today is my second anniversary in the army. I think it was June 5, 1943 that I reported to Upton. That's seems like an awfully long time ago. In that time, I had two furloughs, one leave and one 3 day pass. All together that adds up to about 27 days, no more than 30 at the most. One month with you, 23 with Uncle Sam. Not quite balanced is it. You've been wonderful though Darling, writing all the time and I've never one second had to doubt that you'd be there waiting for me. Remind me to tell you that I think you're swell and I love you very, very much.

Still no news about our leaving. We're all sitting here slowing going crazy. Well it shouldn't be too much longer now. Please forgive the short letter Honey. This hanging around waiting is the hardest thing in the world for me to do. I just can't seem to concentrate on writing.

Be a good girl, take good care of yourself. I should be seeing you sometime this month. Keep your fingers crossed. I love you "Itchy" for ever and ever.

Your Paul

This is the last letter from the hospital in England.

June 11, 1945
England

My Darling Bernie,

Well Baby this is the last letter from England. I'm supposed to leave tomorrow for the States. Will go by train from here to Scotland or to South Hampton, I don't know which, then get on the boat for home. I'm almost certain that it isn't a hospital ship, it's a transport of some kind. It will probably dock in New York because the hospital ships are usually the ones that go to South Carolina. It takes quite a while to load these boats so it probably will mean that we won't actually start until around the 15th. The trip can take anywhere from 5 to 20 days it's all according to what boat it is. The Queens can do it easily in 5 days, but some of the transports take anywhere from 2 weeks to 20 days. With luck I should get to the States somewhere around the 25th of the month.

I got some mail yesterday. It was all written in May. There was a card from Nellie Bissel, you know, the gal who agrees with me and says you have pretty legs.

Well Darling it won't be long now. Keep your fingers crossed for me to be sent to a hospital on the East Coast. It's going to be wonderful to see you again Sweetheart, it seems a lot longer than six months since the last time.

Be a good girl and take good care of yourself. I love you "Itchy" forever and ever.

All my love my Darling,
Your Paul

Chapter 7

HALLORAN GENERAL HOSPITAL, STATEN ISLAND, NEW YORK AND ESPERANCE, NEW YORK

June 17, 1945 to January 27, 1946

Letter from Bernie to Paul, who is in Halloran General Hospital on Staten Island in New York City.

June 17, 1945

My darling,

It's been 3 weeks since I've written to you. I expected to see you long before this but as you said, you can't depend on the Army. It can't be too much longer now and we're really lucky when you think how long some couples have been separated.

I sent you a cablegram last Saturday. I hope you left before you got it. You have printed groups of words that you can take and that's all. Because I hadn't written, I thought that would be better than nothing. The letter I got yesterday was written June 7th. Every time I don't hear from you I think you're on the way. If I don't hear from you in a few days, I'll wait again. If I do get more letters, then I'll send you another cablegram and write again. I wish they'd forward your mail from the other hospital.

I'm anxious to hear what you dreamed the night you ate the olives. In fact, for some reason I'm getting darned anxious to see you. I love you so much darling. I lay awake at night thinking how wonderful it will be when you get back to the States. I do hope they send you near home but anyplace in the USA, a well traveled gal like me could get O.K.

I'd also like you to know that my big brother is a "Sargent." Last June you got your Sgt's rating and this June he got his.

Tonight is Children's Day. Our little girls have pieces and I have to play a couple of songs for Phil's class and the little kids.

Last Sunday I went to Dot Vrooman's wedding and next Sunday I'm going to one of the teacher's weddings at Schoharie. She's the one who came up and talked to us at the basketball game when you were home.

I'll save the rest until you get home. For the first couple of months, we'll probably talk continually.

I'm O.K. and very much in love with a Lieutenant that had better be on his way home pretty soon.

I'm so glad your arm has healed up. You should be already for the nerve operation when you get home.

See you soon Darling.

I love you with all of my heart for always,
Your Bernie
(S.W.A.K.)

There were no more letters from Paul until November 26. He was able to return to Esperance on different leaves from the hospital.

Paul is writing from his hometown of Esperance, New York. Bernie is at a school in Providence, Rhode Island. We do not know what the school was or what it was for, but Paul expresses his concern about it changing Bernie and her desire for him to change. This is one of the few times in the letters that there appears to be tension between them.

November 26, 1945
Esperance, New York

My Darling Bernie,

I'm a bit out of practice writing letters, but here goes anyway. I guess I'd better describe without you in dear old Esperance.

My father went back to the city last night so I didn't get up until 9:30 this morning. I went to the city and drove him over to Scotia on a call, then ate lunch and then came home. I tried to get the new muffler put on the car but Milton didn't have time to do it. George asked me if you had left, I said yes, then he told me he didn't think much of the idea, I felt like saying you're not the only one but I didn't. Next, I laid down and slept for an hour, then Nord came in and we talked for a while. After that I ate supper, asked my grandmother if she would like to go to the movies, she didn't feel like going so Bill and I took a ride to the city, looked at the new Buick, then came back and had ice cream at Eastman's and then came home, and so here I am now at the close of my "happy day" writing to you.

I like talking to Bill, maybe because he agrees with me quite often. He thought the guy at church last night was a jerk too, he said he would have walked out, if he hadn't been sitting with the hunters. We talked about you going to school and he didn't think much of the idea either, yes, I like to talk with Bill.

I hope you remember and think about some of the things I said last night Sweetheart. I've tried very hard to be the kind of a person you want me to be but I can only go so far, it has to be a 50/50 proposition. I'm more than willing to give up drinking, I already have done that, and I'd be happy to go to church on Sunday mornings like most good people do, but I'm never going to go any farther than that. I'll never be the kind that shouts Amen and Praise the Lord, I'll never be taken in by people who to me are ignorant and crude in their so called religions and because I think you're very intelligent and because I love you very much, I don't want to see you taken in either. I said I was afraid the school would change you and although you say it won't I'm still afraid it will. It's changed Irene already, Bill said to me tonight he thought she was a little nutty on the subject of religion and I think she is too.

You probably think I'm terrible for saying that, but oh Darling, can't you see what happens to a person in a school like that. You don't have to be one bit more religious than you are right now. You'll go to Heaven and be loved by God just as much if you live a normal healthy life, writing verses on cards, going up before people in church, those things won't make you loved anymore by God, but it will do something to our love, it will push us farther and farther apart until we'll never be able to get together. When the "minister" called you up beside him last night, he called you away from me, we were oceans apart then and can you honestly say you felt nearer to God, don't you think God would have loved you just as much if you have stayed at my side?

Maybe this letter will do nothing more than to make you angry with me, I hope it doesn't do that but I do hope you understand what I'm trying to say. I love you and I want to marry you, but mindfulness and fanaticism in religion will always keep us apart. As I said before Darling I'll meet you half way church on Sundays that is intelligent church going, no holy rollers stuff, and no drinking, and all my love for always. I think that's meeting you half way, don't you?

Well I guess that's all for tonight Baby, it's 11 o'clock now. Time for all good 2nd Lts. to be in bed, that is all 2nd Lts. whose girls have left them.

I'm going to stop up at your house tomorrow to find out how your trip was. If everything goes O.K. I'll be down to get you on the 19th.

I love you my Darling, very much, I always have. I know I've acted pretty awful in the last few months, I'll try to make it up to you if you give me the chance. Please think about what I've said in this letter and what I said last night. It's going to mean a lot to both of us.

Take good care of yourself, don't work too hard and don't ever forget that I love you.

Good night "Itchy."

All my love, Your Paul

November 28, 1945
Esperance

My Darling,

Got your letter tonight and also the phone call a few minutes ago. I guess there's no use trying to persuade you to come back before Christmas. All I can say is we've sure wasted a good part of one leave. When two people are in love with each other it seems to be that they're just a little bit silly to stay away from each other when they could be together. I admit I've been wrong, and I'm the one that caused this whole thing to happen, how long do I have to be punished?

I just came back from your mother's. I told her you called and that I had a letter from you. I also told her I thought you might stay home when you came for Christmas. I told her I wanted you to. I couldn't say any more than that because the two little girls were there and Phil. She said she thought you should stay, but I'm hoping she said that because she didn't know the whole story. I got Gerald's address from her, I'm going to write to him maybe he'll be on my side.

I think the end of this week I'll go back to the hospital. I'm just about fed up with doing absolutely nothing here. I haven't got my check yet so I have to wait for that. As soon as I do get it I'll send you some money. I wish I could have given it to you before you went.

I don't know what to say about Dec. 7. I was hoping I could put the ring back on your finger that night. As you said on the phone tonight though it can wait another week. It will have to I guess. I don't want you coming home alone on the bus that weekend, it would be better to wait until I bring you home at Christmas.

Please Darling make up your mind not to go back after your Christmas vacation. If you love me you used to and the way I think you still do you won't want to go back.

It's going to be a long time until the 19th, but I'll be down to get you then, maybe I'll have to be AWOL to do it, but I'll be there.

Your mother just called and said she called you, she wanted to know if you had told me anything you hadn't told her. I'm going up to see her now.

I'm back. I told your mother I wanted to marry you and that I knew I'd been wrong in the way I acted in the last few months.

I also told her I wanted you to come back home because I could be with you more. I didn't say why I didn't like the school because I was afraid she wouldn't understand. I think your mother's a swell person Bernie but I think you know too that she just couldn't imagine anything wrong with these guys like we heard Sunday night. That way I didn't tell her why I didn't like the school.

Well Sweetheart I hope you decide to come home before Christmas, if not I hope you decide to stay home when you do come home for Christmas.

I love you Darling, I always have and always will. I'll be waiting for your call Friday night.

Good night Darling,

All my love for always,
Your Paul

P.S. Your mother found your camera.

Paul is back at Halloran General Hospital on Staten Island having the nerve operation.

January 22, 1946

My Darling,

I got your letter today and just finished talking to you a few minutes ago.

I don't see why Gerald and Millie can't take you with them when they go bowling. After all the nights they all went out in our car I should think they could do that much, at least until I get home.

The razor certainly got there fast. I'm glad it works O.K. Remember I want you have the $13.

I don't know what to say about the apartment. I really don't like that part of the city very much. Of course, it's hard to get a place anywhere, I realize that too. If I get home this weekend we'll go up and look at it. O.K.?

I'm going to call my grandmother tomorrow night after I call you. After I finish this letter I'm going to write to her and send her $10. I'll call my father Thursday morning, and maybe I'll be able to tell you something about the car when I call you Thursday night.

If they take the stitches out Thursday or Friday I'm pretty sure I'll make it home over the weekend. I certainly hope so Honey, I miss you like heck. You haven't mentioned about coming down with Gerald and Millie, so I don't know if you're still planning on that.

My cold is better I think, in a couple of more days it should be all gone, I hope. My hand + arm doesn't hurt at all now, it's just uncomfortable with this darn cast on.

Lots of mail the last couple of days. I got quite a few cards from different people in Esperance. They've all been very nice to think of me.

The guys were playing poker when I called you tonight. That's what all the noise was about. There not going to operate on Jack until next week. He + Joe just went to the movies, "My Reputation" is playing at the post theatre.

This is the 10th day since the operation, about 20 more days to wear this cast, oh woe is me, time is going awfully slow it seems.

Well Honey I still have to write to my grandmother. Please take good care of yourself and be happy. It won't be much longer now. Be a good girl and always remember that you belong to me and me along forever and ever. I love you my Precious, I always will. When we're married, and that's going to be soon, I'll be able to show you just how much I do love you. Good night my "Itchy," dream nice dreams.

All my love for always,
Your Paul

Paul is recovering from his nerve operation. The doctors took the stitches out and he is looking forward to returning home.

January 26, 1946
Halloran General Hospital
Staten Island, New York

Hi Darling,

I was sitting on my bed this morning reading the morning paper, when the doctor who operated on me came in. He asked me how long it had been since the operation, I said 2 weeks, he said well let's take the stitches out. The ward doctor had said the day before that they wouldn't take them out for 3 weeks. I guess the doctor who did the operation should know though, so anyway the stitches are out and I'm glad they are. My hand hurts quite a bit tonight, but I think it will feel better tomorrow. The cast I have on now stops just below my elbow, the only trouble is they have my fingers spread out, so that I can't get my hand through my shirt sleeve. My hand looks something like this *(Paul drew a picture of his hand)*. I have to be in the cast 2 more weeks. In one more week I start getting P.T. and after the 4th week I just have to wear the cast at night. I'd have liked to have come home today Honey, but I really didn't feel like it. Besides the doctor said it would be best not to for a couple of days. When I call you tomorrow night I'll probably be able to tell you when I can make it home. I'll be calling you at 9 tomorrow night. You won't get this letter till Monday, so I guess there wasn't any use in saying that.

There are strong rumors floating around that they're going to close Halloran by June. I don't know what they'll do with all the guys that are here. I certainly ought to be out of here by then anyway.

This Thursday is payday. This will be the first month in a long while that I haven't owed anyone anything. I only have one dollar left though, so I guess I will owe a little.

I'm anxious to see all the new things you bought, especially that one special item, I know I'll like that.

Please go to the doctor Honey. He probably could give you something to make you feel a lot better, you shouldn't feel tired like that all the time, that's not good. I'll gladly give you the money to go, I want you healthy and strong, you'll have to be that way if you want to win any of those bets we have.

Well Baby they're going to turn the lights out in about 5 minutes so I'll have to stop. We had a movie in the ward tonight, Wallace Berry in "This Man's Navy," that's why I didn't start writing till 9.

Be a good girl now, take good care of yourself, always remember that you belong to me and me alone, and that I love you with all my heart forever and ever. I'll be with you soon.

Good night "Itchy"

All my love for always,
Your Paul

The last letter.

January 27, 1946
Halloran General Hospital
Staten Island, New York

My Darling,

I thought I'd be able to come home the first part of this week but I guess I'm not going to make it. The doctor was around today and he decided he wanted an X-ray of my arm, he made the appointment for Tuesday. I told him I'd rather have it on Monday so that I could go home on a pass, but he said he couldn't get me in before Tuesday and besides he didn't want me to travel that far until the end of the week anyway, so I guess I'm stuck till Thursday or Friday anyway. I'll do my best to get 2 passes from Thursday till Monday. The X-ray is just to check up on my arm, I haven't had one for 3 months now. I'm anxious to see it myself, the bone should be a lot stronger by now, I hope. My hand feels a little better tonight, another day or two and it should feel fine.

I'm going to call you at 9 tonight, I look forward an awful lot to those calls Darling, it's the next best thing to being with you. If I get home Friday and I'm sure I will we'll have a swell weekend, I'll be paid Thursday so we'll go to Keelers or wherever you want to go. You be a good girl and go to bed early Monday, Tuesday and Wednesday nights, so that you'll be all ready for me Thursday, Friday, Saturday, and Sunday nights. O.K.?

I tried my shirt on this afternoon and I got it on by just cutting the sleeve a little bit. I didn't try my blouse or overcoat but I'm pretty sure they won't fit over the cast, I'll have to wear them without putting my arm through the sleeve. In 2 more weeks, I'll have the cast off anyway so it won't be so bad.

They don't deliver mail here on Sunday, so no letter from you today. I sure do miss it. Please don't get up extra early in the morning to write to me, I'd rather have you get the sleep. You know if you went to bed at 9 o'clock a few nights you might not feel so tired, how about doing it for me, will you? Please take care of yourself Darling, you worry me like heck when you're not feeling well. Don't be stubborn, go to bed early, eat good and if you don't feel

100 percent, go to a good doctor I'll gladly give you the money for it. Don't be doing everyone else's job at the bank as well as your own, and don't work overtime. I know I'm giving a lot of orders but I'm only doing it because I happen to love you very, very much. As I said in last night's letter, I want a good strong, healthy wife, and if you ever expect to win any of our bets, you're going to have to be in A-1 shape. You probably won't be able to come close to winning them, but I don't want you to have any excuses, when you lose the bets.

I borrowed this writing paper, it looks suspiciously like the air corp but it will have to do. The pen I borrowed from Ike, I just told him I didn't think much of it.

Monday or Tuesday I think I'll call my father and see if he's heard anything more about the car. With luck we should have it soon.

Gee Baby I miss you, I had a nice dream about you last night, by the way, you'd better be dreaming some nice dreams too, I'll do my very best to make them all come true very, very soon. I love you so very much Bernie, let's always try to understand each other so that nothing will ever spoil our love in any way. If we always do that we'll always have each other, and there's nothing more I want in the whole world than you.

I'm going to finish this after I call you. I have to go around the ward now and try to get some change just in case the telephone girl doesn't come in and I have to make the call out in the hall at the pay phone. I'll be back to finish this about 9:15 or so, don't go away.

9:15

Boy! Making a telephone call around here is as hard as pulling teeth. I made the call from the ward last night, tomorrow night I guess I'll make it from the pay booth in the hall.

I tried to explain everything in the 3 minutes, but if it sounded confusing, this letter ought to clear it up. I hope you meant it when you said you were feeling better. If you keep on bowling like that, I won't go with you anymore, you're making my 120 look sick.

Well Baby I'll be seeing you this Thursday or Friday, I'll let you know in a couple of days which day it will be.

Be a good girl now. Remember you belong to me and me alone for always. Good night my Darling, I love you.

All my love "Itchy," forever and ever,
Your Paul

The last letter

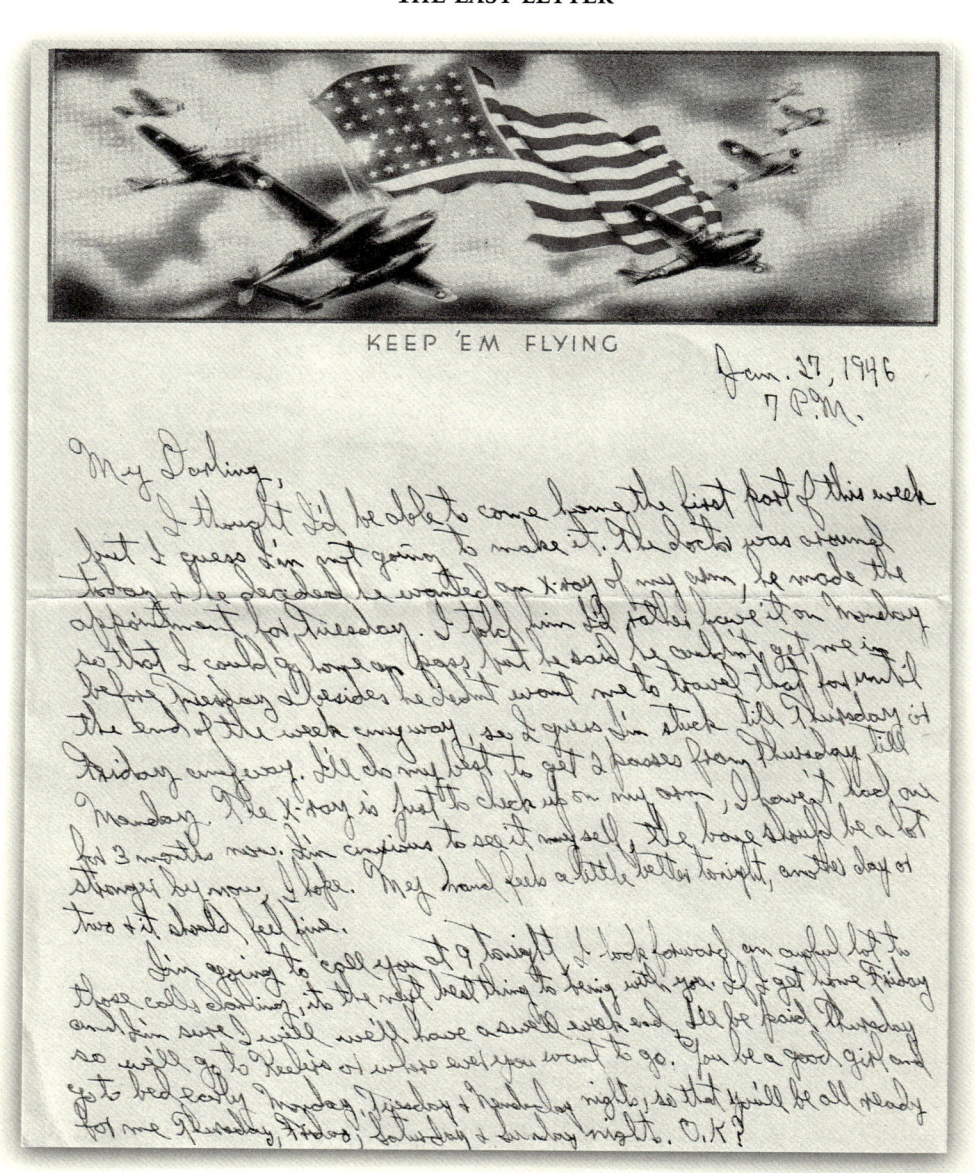

KEEP 'EM FLYING

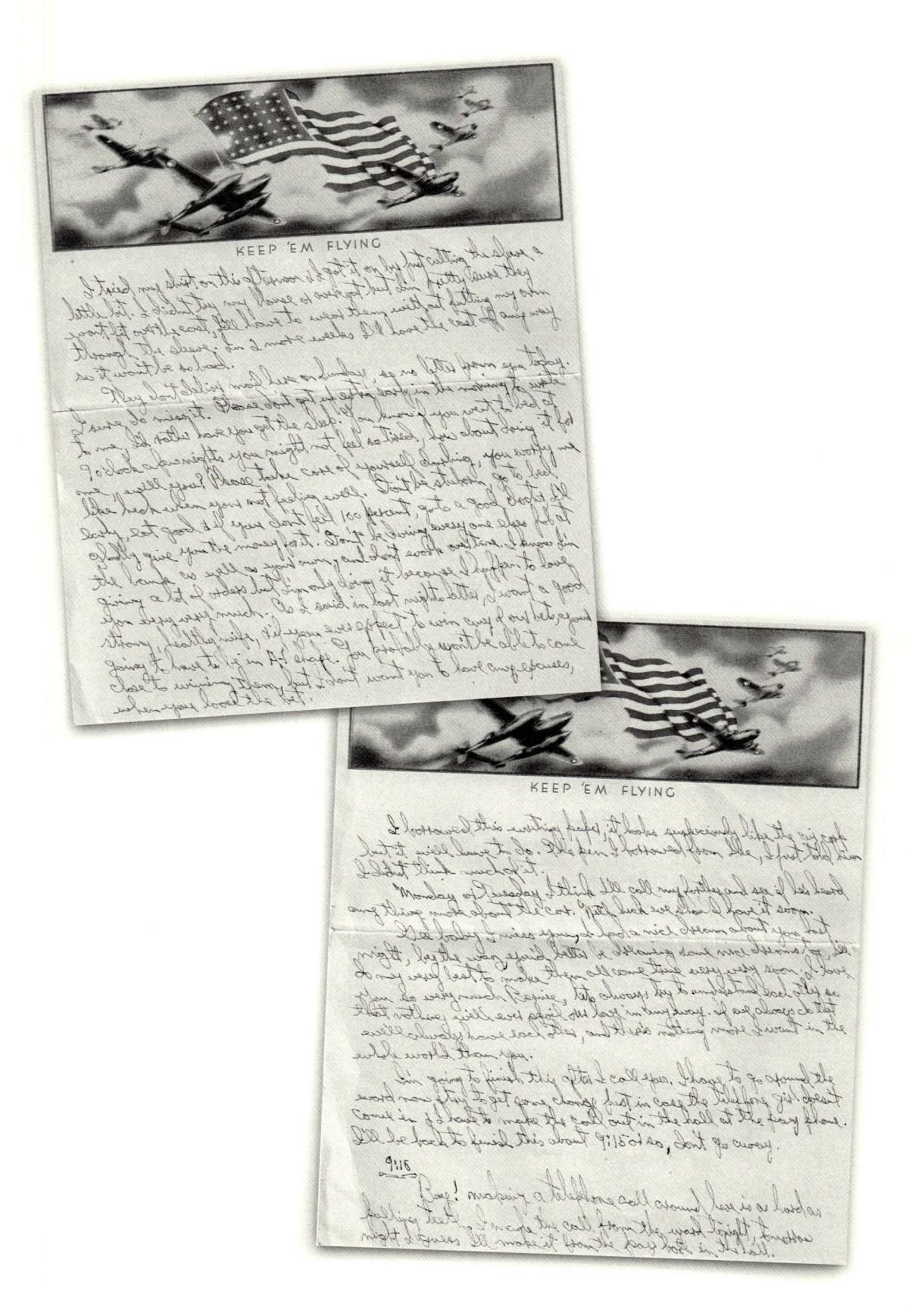

I tried my shirt on this afternoon & got it on by just cutting the sleeve a little bit. I doubt if my pants or coat got but I'm pretty sure they won't fit over my coat. I'll have to wear them without putting my arms through the sleeves. In 2 more weeks I'll have the cast off any way so it won't be so bad.

They don't deliver mail here on Sunday, so no letter from you today. I sure do miss it. Please don't get up so early in the morning to write to me. I'd rather have you get the sleep. You know, if you went to bed at 9 o'clock a few nights you might not feel so tired. How about doing it for me, will you? Please take care of yourself darling, you worry me like heck when you're not feeling well. Don't be stubborn, go to bed early, eat good & if you don't feel 100 percent, get a good doctor. I'll gladly give you the money for it. Don't be doing everyone else's job at the bank as well as your own, and don't work overtime. I know I'm giving a lot of orders but I'm only doing it because I happen to love you very very much. As I said in last night's letter, I want a good strong, healthy wife, & if you ever expect to win any of our bets you're going to have to be in A-1 shape. You probably won't be able to come close to winning them yet & I don't want you to have any excuses when you lose the bet.

KEEP 'EM FLYING

I borrowed this writing paper, it looks suspiciously like the air cot but it will have to do. The pen I borrowed from Ike, & just told him I didn't think much of it.

Monday or Tuesday I think I'll call my father and see if he's heard anything more about the cot. Jiffy luck we'd have I have it soon.

Gee baby I miss you, & had a nice dream about you last night, by the way you'd better be dreaming some nice dreams too. I'll do my very best to make them all come true very very soon, I love you so very much. Regine, let's always try to understand each other, so that nothing will ever spoil our days in any way. If we always do that we'll always have each other, and I wish nothing more I want in the whole world than you.

I'm going to finish this after I call you. I have to go around the ward now & try to get going along just in case the telephone girl doesn't come in & I have to make the call out in the hall at the pay phone. I'll be back to finish this about 9:15 or so, don't go crazy.

9:15

Boy! making a telephone call around here is as hard as pulling teeth. I made my call from the ward tonight, tomorrow night I guess I'll make it from the pay hole in the hall.

KEEP 'EM FLYING

I tried to explain everything in the 3 minutes, but if it sounded confusing, this letter ought to clear it up. I hope you meant it when you said you were feeling better. If you keep on improving like that, I won't go sick. You sure note, you're making my 130 look sick.

Well baby, I'll be seeing you this Thursday or Friday, I'll let you know in a couple of days which day it will be.

Be a good girl now. Remember you belong to me & me alone for always. Goodnight my darling, I love you.

All my love "Itchy" for ever & ever,

Yours,
Paul.

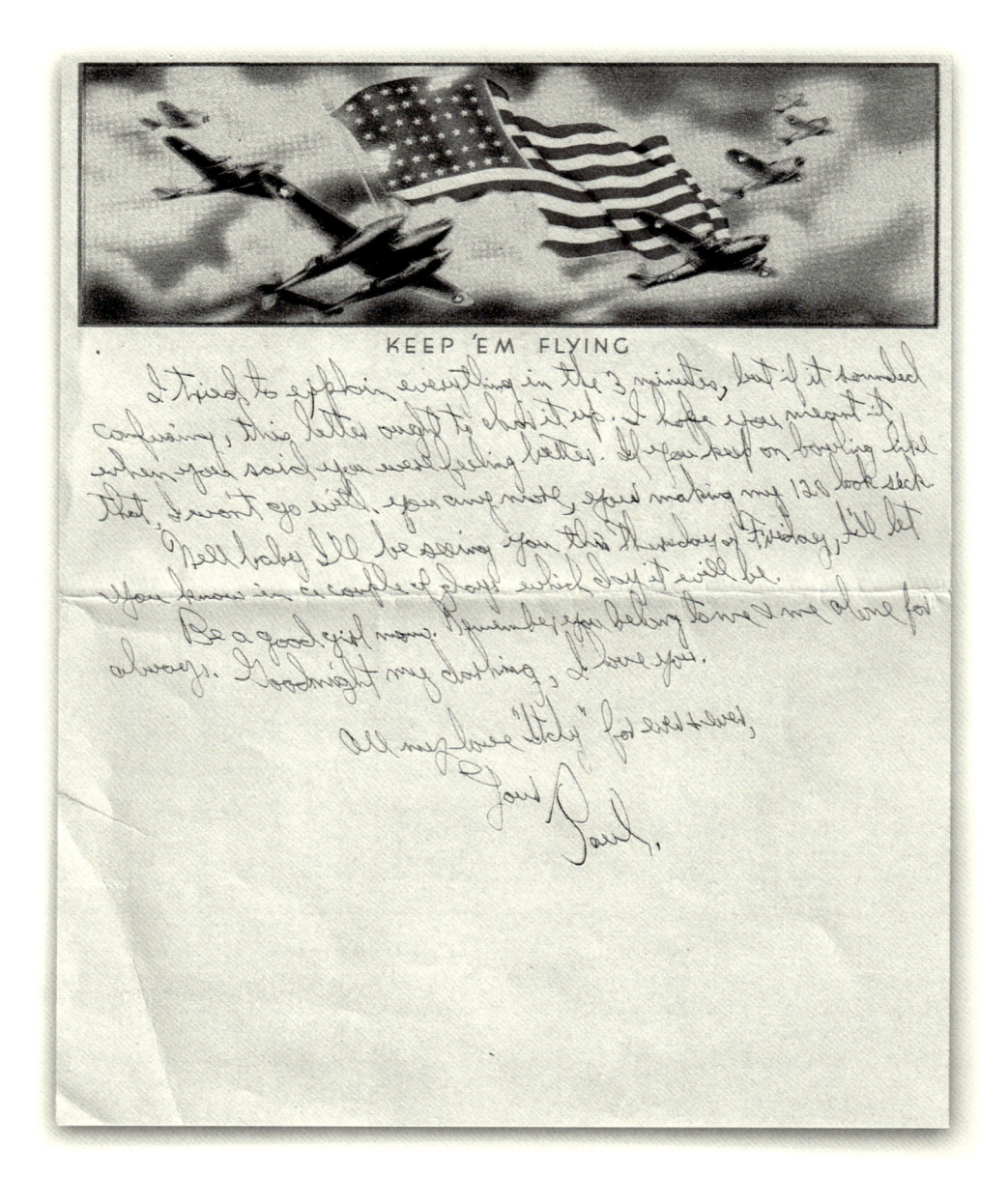

Epilogue

After the war was over, Paul finished his degree at Union College and was a member of the Phi Beta Kappa honor society. He wanted to be a history teacher but ended up in Schenectady with his father in the piano and organ business. They sold Baldwin pianos and organs, Magnavox Stereophonic High Fidelity record players, and Magnavox television sets. My father's store was open every day except Sunday, though he also went in to work on Sundays, and the store was also open on Thursday evenings as well.

Bernice and Paul were married on May 4, 1946 and had two children, a girl and a boy, myself and my brother Michael. After my parents were married, they lived for the rest of their lives in Scotia, New York.

My father suffered from losing his mother at age sixteen and living without any siblings. He didn't talk about the war, although he and my mother took my brother and me to Europe to visit the place where he was wounded when we were teenagers.

In his early forties, my father was diagnosed with Parkinson's disease. My mother found a neurologist in New York City and they took wonderful care of him.

In the late 1970s and 1980s, downtown Schenectady's effort at urban renewal failed due to suburban competition. This, in addition to the worsening of my father's

PAUL, BERNIE, PAULA AND MICHAEL

Parkinson's disease, forced him to retire from owning and running the Roberts Piano and Organ Company in Schenectady. My father sold the building and didn't work again.

After my father's retirement, my mother and father bought a condo in Lake Worth, Florida in the Lucerne Lakes retirement community. The condo was situated on a golf course, which they played often, and my mother and father spent the winters there. Encouraged by my father's neurologist in New York City, my mother kept my father busy with golf and traveling. They went to Hawaii, Israel and Egypt with their church group, and continued to spend winters in Lake Worth.

They enjoyed their grandchildren very much. Michael and Laurel's children are Bryan and Megan, and Paula's children are Sarah and John.

Parkinson's disease was a very difficult illness for my father to endure. He eventually ended up with a feeding tube, a wheelchair, unable to speak or walk, and died from pneumonia due to Parkinson's. Ironically, my mother's death certificate also gives Parkinson's disease as the cause of her death.

My father died on January 8, 2003 and my mother died on August 20, 2008. They are buried together at the Saratoga National Cemetery in Saratoga, New York.

Internet Sources

history.army.mil/html	World War II Divisional Combat Chronicles
coulthart.com	Path of 134th Regiment across Europe
trumanlibrary.com	Santa Fe Thirty-fifth Infantry Division
armydivs.com	Thirty-fifth Infantry Division
aad.archives.gov	The National Archives
coulthart.com	Presenting the Thirty-fifth Infantry Division during World War II
encyclopedia.ushmm.org	Holocaust Encyclopedia; Jewish Virtual Library
Wikipedia.com	World War II Database; Battle of Remagen
Wikipedia.com	General Patton
Britannica.com	General Patton

Acknowledgments

The first acknowledgment must go to my father, Paul Edward Roberts, who wrote hundreds of letters to my mother, Bernice Getter, before they were married, but deeply in love. I am incredibly appreciative of my father's mostly daily efforts to write to my mother, even after he was wounded to the extent that he nearly lost his right arm, and had to write the letters with his left hand.

I also deeply acknowledge my mother's profound love and commitment to my father. She kept every letter he wrote to her. My dad was unable to keep her letters due to the army's fear that they would reveal where our troops were stationed. But I have no doubt that he read every one and kept it close to his heart.

There were also many letters from my mother's brother Gerald, who was stationed in the Pacific. He and my father kept in touch and were very close and I so appreciate Uncle Gerald's dedication to the relationship he shared with my father.

I want to acknowledge my partner in this project, Stanley Winston, without whom this book would not have been created. Stanley worked countless hours with me, reading and transcribing each letter. Stanley dedicated himself to this project completely and worked tirelessly with Brett, our editor, Rob, our designer, and Lynne, our publisher.

I want to acknowledge my brother Michael Roberts and his wife Laurel for their encouragement and willingness to allow me to create this memoir. My brother questioned whether the emotion might be too personal and private but we decided that this story was not only a love story but truly a remembrance of one of the Greatest Generation and tells a piece of history that all of us should know. In addition, I want to acknowledge that my brother was named after my father's closest friend in the army, Michael O'Connor, who was killed during the war.

My children Sarah and John also encouraged the book's creation so there would be a chronicle of the brave, medal-decorated, seriously wounded, and patriotic soldier who was their grandfather and risked his life for our country.

Acknowledgments

I am deeply grateful and want to acknowledge the Damianos Publishing team of Lynne Damianos, Brett Peruzzi, and Rob Levine. They are extremely talented, deeply understanding of the meaning of this project, and incredibly good at what they do.

My father's was the Greatest Generation. My dad would have turned 100 this past summer. This generation sacrificed their lives for their country and for their loved ones. They lived with the greatest courage and dedication to those they loved. We should never remember them with anything less than the greatest honor and tremendous respect.

About the Author

Paula Roberts grew up in Scotia, New York, and graduated from Skidmore College with a bachelor's degree in elementary education. After graduation she became a teacher working with disabled students. She later moved to Boston to continue her teaching career and earned a master's degree in education from Boston College. She currently lives in Needham, Massachusetts.